Tiger, Ton… …kle

'Tiger, Tom and Tinkle is a must for anyone interested in three Queens of children's literature, Judith Kerr, Philippa Pearce and Kathleen Hale, who all developed a close working relationship with the King of children's drama, David Wood.'

Dame Jacqueline Wilson

'No-one has done more than David Wood to bring the great children's book classics to the stage. The favourite stories and characters of Judith Kerr, Philippa Pearce, and Kathleen Hale, amongst many others, have been adapted by David and played out on stages up and down the country, to hundreds of thousands of children, many of whom have already become parents and teachers themselves and are even now, through David's plays, passing the stories they have loved to the next generation.

Go to London, New York, or any city in this country and abroad, and walk down past the theatres, and you find them putting on popular adaptations of children's books, from Cats to Matilda to Mrs Doubtfire. They fill theatres, stimulate children and families to go to the theatre, to read stories. David Wood was and is the great pioneer of all this. Writers, readers, children, grown-up children, we all owe him a great deal. And it's this wonderful book that gives us some idea of how all this was achieved.'

Sir Michael Morpurgo

'Appealed to the nosy parker in me. An absorbing peek behind the scenes of your adaptations – Judith displaying a real understanding of what works with little children, Philippa being sensitive to historical language and accuracy and the complexities of her time travel plot, and Kathleen taking such care about the angle of a hat and the quality of colour. None of the three embodies what belittling stereotypes might suggest about ladies of their years. Their diligence, warmth and originality endured – a Great Granny Gang of their own.'

Nicolette Jones, Sunday Times children's book critic

Tiger, Tom & Tinkle

Creative collaborations with three much-loved grandes dames of British children's literature

JUDITH KERR (The Tiger Who Came to Tea)
PHILIPPA PEARCE (Tom's Midnight Garden)
KATHLEEN HALE (Orlando the Marmalade Cat)

Notes and Correspondences

DAVID WOOD

Edited by Tamsin Collison

The Book Guild

First published in Great Britain in 2026 by
The Book Guild Ltd
Unit E2 Airfield Business Park,
Harrison Road, Market Harborough,
Leicestershire. LE16 7UL
Tel: 0116 2792299
www.bookguild.co.uk
Email: info@bookguild.co.uk

The manufacturer's authorised representative in the EU
for product safety is Authorised Rep Compliance Ltd,
71 Lower Baggot Street, Dublin D02 P593 Ireland (www.arccompliance.com)

Typeset in 12pt Minion Pro

Printed and bound by CPI Group (UK) Ltd, Croydon, CR0 4YY

ISBN 978 1835743 508

British Library Cataloguing in Publication Data.
A catalogue record for this book is available from the British Library.

MIX
Paper | Supporting
responsible forestry
FSC® C013604
FSC
www.fsc.org

To my darling wife, Jacqui, who shared with me these special associations and friendships. Judith, Philippa and Kathleen all adored you, as the recollections in this book make clear. All my love and thanks to you for more than half a century of happiness, patience and encouragement.

DW

Contents

INTRODUCTION

In this book, I celebrate my working collaborations and much-appreciated friendships with three legendary children's writers. Two of them are also fondly remembered for their brilliant talent for illustration. These three great ladies – Judith Kerr, Philippa Pearce and Kathleen Hale – I came to know when adapting their classic works for the stage or for television.

I was privileged to create the musical play version of Judith's *The Tiger Who Came to Tea*, which was nominated for the Olivier Award for Best Entertainment and Family (2012). At the time of writing, the production, which I also directed, is in its seventeenth year of touring the UK and abroad, and has played eleven West End seasons.

The play I wrote based on Philippa's *Tom's Midnight Garden* was commissioned by Unicorn Theatre, whose production won the Theatre Management Association's Equity Award for Best Show for Children and Young People (2001). The very same award was won by the Manchester Library Theatre production of the play (2003).

And for many years I tried to create a television animation film or series based on Kathleen's *Orlando the Marmalade Cat*. Sadly, this never came to fruition.

Two successful projects and one unfortunately less successful. But three unforgettable experiences, collaborating with three of the UK's most loved and respected giants of children's literature.

Philippa and Kathleen both wrote witty, informative letters; in my correspondence with them about our respective projects, their illuminating comments, notes and reflections sparkle with humour and enthusiasm.

The 21st century had arrived by the time I began communicating with Judith, who, in her eighties, had taken with ease to email. So we rarely used the postal service, except for birthday and Christmas cards. We spoke on the telephone – she rang regularly, and I loved our updates about our other projects as well as about *Tiger* – and she wrote pithy emails, some of which are included in this book.

My ever-loving thanks to Judith, Philippa and Kathleen. I will always remember them with lasting admiration and affection.

David Wood OBE

JUDITH KERR

THE TIGER WHO CAME TO TEA

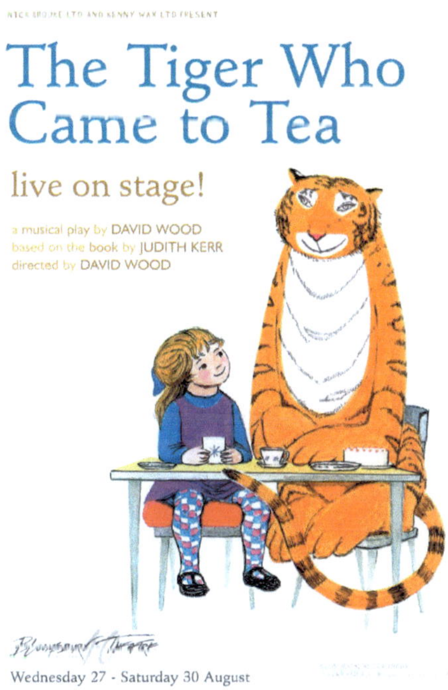

Flyer for the first production of *The Tiger Who Came to Tea* – Bloomsbury Theatre, 2008

JUDITH KERR

Judith Kerr OBE was born on 14th June, 1923, in Berlin, and managed to escape from Hitler's Germany with her parents and older brother in 1933, when she was nine years old. The family passed through Switzerland and France before arriving finally in England in 1936. Judith went to eleven different schools, worked in the Red Cross during the War, and won a scholarship to the Central School of Arts and Crafts in 1945. She later worked as an artist and a BBC television script writer. In 1954 she married the writer Nigel (Tom) Kneale (the creator of *Quatermass*); they lived happily together until his death in 2006. Judith first came up with the ideas for her children's books when she was making up bedtime stories for her own children, Tacy and Matthew. First came *The Tiger Who Came to Tea* (1968), followed by the series of books about Mog, a forgetful, mischievous and clumsy cat, an amalgam of the series of cats owned and much loved by the family. Alongside these picture books, Judith created a trilogy of autobiographical novels, written as fictional, about her early life. *When Hitler Stole Pink Rabbit*, *Bombs on Aunt Dainty* and *A Small Person Far Away* are internationally acclaimed. In 2012, Judith was awarded an OBE for her services to children's literature and Holocaust education. In 2016 she received the Book Trust Lifetime Achievement Award, and in 2019 she was named Illustrator of the Year at the British Book Awards. Her books have sold more than nine million copies, have been translated into twenty-five languages and have been adapted for stage and screen. Judith died in May 2019.

Key Players

Judith Kerr	Author/Illustrator
Nigel Kneale	Author/Playwright, most notably of tv drama such as *Quatermass* – husband of Judith Kerr
David Wood	Adapter (book, music and lyrics)/Director of the *Tiger* play
Jacqui Wood	Actress and Teacher, David Wood's wife
Nick Brooke	Theatre Producer
Matthew Kneale	Author, son of Judith Kerr
Tacy Kneale	Artist, daughter of Judith Kerr
Susie Caulcutt	Set and Costume Designer of the play
Emma Clayton	Assistant (later Associate) Director/ Choreographer of the play
Scott Penrose	Magic Adviser, creator of the magic of the play
Peter Pontzen	Musical Director, Arranger and Incidental Music Composer
Angie Burns	Wardrobe Supervisor
Abbey Norman	Actress – Sophie in the play
Devon Black	Actress – Mummy in the play
Alan Atkins	Actor – Tiger, Daddy, Milkman and Postman in the play
Neil Hillyer	Company Stage Manager for the play
Rachel Baynton	Wardrobe Mistress/understudying Sophie and Mummy
Matthew Dudley	Assistant Stage Manager/understudying Tiger, Daddy, Milkman and Postman
Kenny Wax	Co-Producer
Robert Allsopp	Maker of Tiger costume

How it all began...

'David and I met at Buckingham Palace,' Judith would announce, with pretend grandeur, if we were introduced to someone new. It became a standing joke. And it was true. In 2006 I was asked to host a reception for children's authors and illustrators, to be held at Buckingham Palace in June as part of the Children's Party at the Palace, celebrating Her Majesty the Queen's 80th birthday. Later in the afternoon, I comprèred a programme of readings by a distinguished selection of children's authors, including Michael Morpurgo, JK Rowling, Philip Pullman, Roger McGough, Malorie Blackman, Michael Bond and Eric Hill, who strutted their stuff in a marquee in Buckingham Palace Gardens, before watching, along with two thousand children and one thousand adults, a play called *The Queen's Handbag*, in which I had attempted to create a story featuring all the iconic characters in British children's literature. It was quite a day!

The authors' reception took place in a room in the Palace, overlooking the gardens. As I greeted the arriving guests, I noticed, in the corner, an elderly lady I didn't recognise. Someone kindly told me it was Judith Kerr. She was then eighty-three years old. Excited, I immediately approached her, almost going down on one knee, introducing myself and telling her that *The Tiger Who Came to Tea* had been both my daughters' favourite book. Judith graciously received this news, then completely took the wind out of my sails by saying, 'It's very nice to meet you, and my husband sends you his best regards'. I hadn't a clue who her husband was. Seeing the embarrassed look on my face, Judith put me at ease by explaining that her husband was Nigel Kneale, the legendary television playwright, whose work dominated the small screen in the 1950s and 60s, including the *Quatermass* series, which I remembered, as a child, gripping the nation every Sunday. Some thirty years earlier I had acted in one of his plays called *The Chopper* in the BBC series, *Out of the Unknown*. Mr Kneale came regularly to rehearsals and we chatted quite a lot. I discovered that he had trained as an actor at RADA, and missed the camaraderie of performance, now he led the lonelier life of a writer. So he enjoyed coming to rehearsals and being part of the team. Not only had he remembered our meeting all those years ago, but he had also realised that I had later become better known as a children's playwright than an actor, and had noticed, in the publicity for the Children's Party at the Palace, that I was writing the celebratory play, which was to be broadcast live on BBC1.

Judith told me that Tom (her name for her husband) was unwell, but that she thought he would love to see me again. She suggested I visit for tea, but this plan never came to fruition because Tom sadly died soon after.

A few weeks went by. Jacqui, my wife, and I were invited to attend a charity event at the Savoy Hotel, in which Michael Morpurgo, who had become the hotel's writer-in-residence, would be interviewing Judith. At the end of a delightful afternoon, I plucked up the courage to approach Judith, who graciously said she remembered our meeting at Buckingham Palace. She reiterated her invitation to tea, though sadly her husband would not now be present. Jacqui and I duly went to Judith's home in Barnes. We had a long chat. We went out to a café for tea. Just before saying goodbye, Judith asked if I knew a theatre producer called Nick Brooke. I replied that I didn't. 'He thinks *Tiger* might work on stage,' Judith said, almost laughing at the idea. 'I don't think such a short story could be translated into a theatre play, do you?' she asked. I replied that, if they wanted me to have a go, I was happy to give it a try. I could hopefully come up with a possible treatment or synopsis.

In later years, Judith told this story somewhat differently. She said that she had told Nick Brooke she would only consider the idea of *The Tiger Who Came to Tea* being put on the stage if David Wood did the honours. This was very flattering, but I'm not sure if it was true!

It wasn't long before a rather splendid afternoon tea was organised at Claridge's. Judith brought Stephen Durbridge as her adviser. Together with Nick Brooke, the producer, and Tom Erhardt, my agent, we amicably worked out a way forward. And the rest is history.

Or nearly. My first treatment was pretty hopeless. My instinct had been to try to update this classic story, which was firmly rooted in the 1960s, to make it more accessible to a modern audience. I suggested that Sophie, the little girl in the book, would now be a mother, indeed a working mother, who struggled to spend enough time with her small daughter. In desperation, to stop her daughter being bored, she tells her a story about when she, the mother, was a little girl, and suddenly a tiger arrived at the door…

Judith's response was, quite rightly, negative in the extreme. She questioned the use of a play within a play, and gently but firmly asked me if I really thought that the audience of three-year-olds would understand flashback.

She was right, of course. I started again, and kept the story in the 1960s, even though 21st century political correctness might criticise the idea of Daddy returning from work and expecting his supper to be ready on the table. And I was conscious of the fact that children these days have rarely experienced a milkman delivering to the house. Many of them have surely never even seen a milk bottle? But I can honestly say that no child has ever questioned such anomalies.

I was determined to be faithful to the story, but decided to add a new beginning, in which we see Daddy going to work, the Milkman delivering and the Postman bringing a parcel for Sophie. This gave several excuses for the doorbell to ring, creating a sense of anticipation in our young audience. By the time the Tiger actually arrives, they are really excited.

Judith wasn't sure when I told her I didn't want the Tiger to speak. He does speak in the book. But I explained that I wanted him to mime his hunger and thirst, and for the audience to be the interpreters. I felt such an interactive device would work well. After seeing the reaction of the audience to an early performance, Judith was generous enough to tell me I had been right.

Judith's support for the theatre production over more than a decade was truly heartwarming. She occasionally agreed to come on stage and wave to the audience, and always enjoyed being escorted to the wings by her regal, well-mannered Tiger.

I also like to think that the success of the play helped Judith recover from the grief of losing her much-loved husband. Indeed, it wasn't long before she started writing and illustrating a new story. She was kind enough to say that this might not have happened, had the success of the *Tiger* play not given her an enthusiastic new lease of life. Indeed, she went on to write and illustrate several new books before she sadly died. The legacy of her books, of course, lives on. And the continued success of the play fills me with gratitude and brings back the wonderful memories of when Jacqui and I regularly escorted Judith to Sunday lunch and, I like to think, became her friends. We miss her so much.

DW

THE TIGER WHO CAME TO LIFE...

Collaboration with Judith Kerr

2006 – 2019

When asked why she thought *The Tiger Who Came to Tea* was such a successful story, Judith, in her typically modest way, replied, 'I think it's because it's very short.' It is true that when parents, including Jacqui and myself, read bedtime stories to their children, brevity can selfishly be a virtue. But many other stories are equally brief, though by no means as enduring or endearing. Some years after my stage adaptation had begun successfully touring the UK almost continuously, Judith and I did discuss the ingredients in the story that helped to make it so admired, and indeed loved. We agreed that the domestic situation helped; children recognise the routine of family life. A tiger is the central character – children like animals. Food features strongly – children like food. The idea of a tiger ringing on the doorbell and inviting himself to tea is a fantasy idea that children buy into very willingly; they will happily suspend their disbelief far more naturally than adults. So the story has a magical quality, which I hoped to develop in the play, making the audience gasp with delight as food magically disappears, then reappears.

Another ingredient Judith and I identified was the idea of a young child enthralled at being taken out at nighttime, along a dark high street with shops lit up, and a café waiting to serve her a tasty supper. We realised that this experience was less unusual for today's children than those in the 1960s, before the arrival of McDonald's and regular family meals out. But I knew that we could make the expedition exciting theatrically, hopefully having as much impact as Judith's wonderful illustration of the family walking along the pavement.

When the idea of adapting her book was first discussed, Judith, in her typically self-deprecatory way, said, 'the problem with the book is that nothing happens!' This was certainly not true, but I could understand Judith wondering how her compact story could be turned into an hour-long stage entertainment. Would it need to be expanded, and if so, how?

My first idea was to start the story earlier in the day. Why not, I thought, have 'a day in the life' of the family? Instead of starting at teatime, we could see the family having breakfast. One benefit of this plan was that we could meet Daddy earlier than in the book. Maybe he could be late for work, rushing around the kitchen, forgetting to put his shoes on, mistaking a tea cosy for his hat, trying to put his shoes in the toaster rather than bread, and putting his jacket on wrong. I knew I was pandering to the notion of 'silly Daddy', but felt that a mimed to music section, rather like in a silent film, would be fun, and help the young audience get to know the family, without having to listen to too much dialogue.

I also made the decision to mime the breakfast food, even though later we would see 'real' food. This apparent anomaly didn't seem to confuse children, who, after all, often play games miming activities like eating.

When I chose what breakfast food Mummy and Sophie were eating, I thought Coco Pops might be an enticing choice for Sophie. Many years later I was delighted to see, in an article in *The Times*, a photo of Matthew, Judith's son, as a child, having breakfast, sitting next to a packet of… Coco Pops! This photo, taken in the family kitchen, featured in an article written by Matthew after his mother's death. Seeing the kitchen, which our superb stage designer Susie Caulcutt faithfully reproduced on stage, reminded me of the time Judith cooked Jacqui and me a delicious mushroom omelette. We sat eating in this iconic kitchen, which, happily, was saved for the nation after Judith died, and exhibited at Seven Stories, the National Centre for Children's Books, in Newcastle. I also remember asking Judith if I could help her preparations in the kitchen. She replied, 'No. Tom' (her husband) 'used to say that if I was peeling potatoes, and he came in to ask me something, I would stop peeling!'

The 'day in the life' device gave me the opportunity to introduce four doorbell rings, each of which I knew the audience would think heralded the arrival of the Tiger. This meant that the anticipation would build and build, and increase the excitement when the Tiger was first glimpsed. To achieve this, I first had the idea that the late-departing Daddy would need to breathlessly return, having forgotten his door key. Hence the ring at the door. Then I decided the Milkman could come at 'elevenses' time – I was sure that no child would have ever heard of elevenses, but reckoned that wasn't important! The Milkman doesn't feature in the book, except in an illustration. When the doorbell rings in the book, Mummy realises it cannot be the Milkman, because he has already been. In my play, we meet him. He is a jolly, fun-loving, 'Jack the lad' type, who enjoys entertaining his ladies and their children! I remembered milkmen had, since my childhood, been forced to diversify, selling all sorts of other goods. So I created a rhyming list of items for the Milkman to point out in his wicker basket and on the inside of his coat, plus a chicken in one pocket, a fish in the other and a spider in his hat. Sophie and her mother point out that they only want milk, something the Milkman says he doesn't sell. But, as he turns to leave, we see two bottles of milk on his back. Situation sorted.

The third ring of the doorbell could come, I thought, from the Postman. He is not in the book, but it seemed logical to include him. He turned out to be somewhat politically incorrect – elderly and extremely short-sighted! But delighted to be delivering a parcel for Sophie. When we started rehearsals for the play, which I was directing, I realised we needed an amusing end to the Postman's scene. Actor Alan Atkins, improvising one morning, had the inspirational idea of exiting into a cupboard and reacting confused until Mummy shows him out of the door.

By now I had realised that the actor playing Daddy would also be playing the Milkman and the Postman. Furthermore, he would be playing the Tiger too! None of these characters has to appear on stage at the same time as one of the others, so this 'quadrupling' would work, as long as the actor had enough time to change costume between each appearance.

To give us a little more time for each costume change, I hit upon the idea that Mummy, sometimes helped by Sophie, should introduce each section by narrating to the audience a repeated opening to the story, introducing each new mealtime by counting an appropriate number of clock chimes.

To move from one section to the next, I thought that Mummy, in playful mood, could teach Sophie to say 'Tick, tock, tick, tock', repeated several times, to suggest the passage of time. The audience could be invited to join in the 'tick-tocks'.

Having decided that the Postman would bring a parcel for Sophie, I suddenly thought that it should be a soft toy, perhaps a present from her uncle, whom I called Uncle Matty, as a friendly reference to Judith's son. It then seemed obvious to make the soft toy a cat. I knew, of course, that Judith loved cats. Her series of books about Mog echoed her own succession of treasured family pets. I also realised that some children and, indeed, adults, in the audience, might think, when the package was unwrapped and revealed Kitty, that this was the Tiger who was coming to tea! Maybe they would feel a little let down or hard done by, until the arrival of the real Tiger would hopefully satisfy them. When Judith read the first draft of the play, she approved of the use of Kitty, and loved the fact that in a later sequence the Tiger cradles Kitty affectionately – 'This,' said Judith, 'will make it impossible for anyone to find the Tiger frightening'.

As teatime approached, it was important to prepare for the arrival of the Tiger, by setting out all the food, this time 'real' food, on the table, just like in the book. Sandwiches, buns, biscuits and cake! As Mummy and Sophie display and place on the table each plate, I hoped that there would be a tangible sense of excitement in the audience, who would be realising that the big moment was coming!

I also made the decision that I would ask the designer Susie for the Tiger's costume to look as much like Judith's illustration as possible. Often in children's theatre we let the actor's face be visible, when playing an animal. Sometimes the animal head sits on top of the actor's head. The reasons for this are twofold. First, the actor can use facial expression, which helps the audience understand what he is feeling. Second, it makes it less likely that a very young audience will be frightened by the animal, because it is so lifelike. Another method of diffusing the possible alarm is the use of puppetry. But, in this case, I felt it was essential for the Tiger to look just like the illustrations in the book. Furthermore, I was convinced that the Tiger shouldn't speak. Not only would speech be difficult from behind an animal mask that completely covers the mouth, but without seeing the mouth move, understanding of what the Tiger might say would be more difficult. Furthermore, a non-speaking Tiger would be, in my opinion, more appealing to the audience, because they could help interpret what he is wanting to say to Mummy and Sophie. This gives a feeling of empowerment to the children, who often know something before Sophie and Mummy do.

The Tiger's movement was, I knew, something to be carefully approached. He wouldn't be able to walk on all fours. He would always be on two legs, but he needed to move as much like a feline as possible. Not only that, Judith had told me that Matthew, when describing the Tiger in the book, used the word 'regal'. This, in rehearsal, became incredibly important. Emma Clayton, my brilliant assistant director and choreographer, created for the Tiger a regal, almost aristocratic walk and bearing, which, coupled with his expressive nodding and shaking of the head, led to a dual audience reaction, that of awe at his mere presence, but also humour, particularly as he set about devouring everything edible in the kitchen. The section of Judith's book that everyone remembers is the Tiger eating and drinking his way through not only all the teatime food, but everything else, including the food in the fridge and the cupboard, and famously, 'all the water in the tap'. Judith told me that when the publishers were considering her book for publication, they asked her to change what became its most iconic line! They felt that the idea of the tiger drinking all the water was somewhat farfetched! Judith, in reply, asked if they felt that the arrival of a tiger at teatime was realistic! She got her way.

One of the very first things I did, when working on my synopsis, was to make a list of all the magical things we could include. As a member of The Magic Circle, who has performed magic for children since the age of twelve, I knew that Judith's story provided exciting opportunities for magical surprises. All the food being eaten, including the emptying of the fridge and cupboard, plus disappearing orange juice and milkshake – the only addition I made to Judith's 'list' – plus the idea of a magical toaster from which the toast pops up at exactly the right time, some flowers for the Tiger to present magically to Mummy, and a shopping trolley, shown as empty, which then fills up with supermarket goodies. Other ideas emerged in rehearsal. My first port of call for magical advice was my friend Geoffrey Durham, known to many as the former Great Soprendo. He suggested I contact Scott Penrose, who was not only a magical inventor, but also a clever maker of magical props. I had met Scott once or twice, and was delighted when he agreed to take the job. It wasn't long before he became President of The Magic Circle, which added prestige to our creatives' biographies! Scott managed quite brilliantly to create magical effects for everything on my list. At every performance over the last sixteen years, his skills have been rewarded by countless gasps of wonderment from adults and children alike. Scott's contribution to the success of the play is impossible to overestimate. His magic makes it possible for us to achieve each Tiger action in the book, with humour and a genuine sense of mystery. Having said that, it has always struck me that very young children accept the magic as 'real'. In the story, the Tiger eats and drinks everything. They see him do it! They don't necessarily think it is a magic trick. Slightly older children and, of course, adults are the most impressed when seeing the impossible before their very eyes!

It is important to acknowledge, when working out my synopsis, how important Judith's illustrations were, creating images I wanted to replicate on stage, and also helping me think of how to stage certain moments. For instance, there is a lovely picture of Sophie hugging the Tiger. This comes surprisingly early in the book. But I decided to save it until the moment when the Tiger says goodbye. Hopefully this gives a lump-in-the-throat moment. Mummy very sincerely thanks the Tiger for coming, Sophie gives him a hug, and then the Tiger waves farewell to the audience. It's always a heartwarming moment for me, as hundreds of children wave and call out, 'Bye, Tiger!' The illustration of the Tiger's arrival, peering around the door, is one that we always try to reproduce, first just seeing his head, almost as a teaser, before we reveal the whole Tiger. Also, the way he sits at the table with Mummy and Sophie was something I knew we had to represent faithfully on stage. And I was determined that the Tiger would rest on the kitchen units in order to drink from the tap, and that Sophie would be able to stroke his tail.

Sophie's unique and instantly recognisable checked tights were something I knew the stage Sophie should wear. Being faithful to Judith's artwork seemed more and more not just appropriate, but essential.

She later told me on the phone one day how much she enjoyed drawing animals. She was chatting away while working. She was becoming frustrated. 'I'm drawing a crocodile watching the telly – it's the bloody telly I can't draw!' 'I hate doing cars,' she told me once, and talking about crayoning backgrounds, she complained, 'It's hard work, because I'm doing flamingos and they have such thin necks, it leaves lots of background!' But she rarely had a problem drawing animals. Of course, *Tiger* was her very first book. She once told me, 'I was lucky when I started – people realised picture books helped children learn to read. Picture books done all by oneself mean you can write about things you like to draw! You don't have to draw the things you can't draw – but *Tiger* was different – it started as a bedtime story, so wasn't pre-thought on what was drawable'.

It was true, of course, that the story started off as a bedtime story for Tacy, Judith's daughter. Tacy loved the story so much she insisted on hearing it night after night. 'Talk the tiger,' she would insist. And gradually Judith honed and shaped the words, so that, when it came to writing the text, it was all already in her head. And the illustrations had to fit the story. Incidentally, Judith always dismissed outright the idea that the tiger was symbolic of the Nazis' threat to her family, which led to them escaping to France, Switzerland and finally London in 1932. Michael Rosen, of whom Judith was very fond, suggested that the tiger, perhaps subconsciously in Judith's mind, is a sinister stranger about to disrupt the Jewish household. When asked about this, Judith would always say that the story is simply about a tiger who comes to tea.

My major concern, when working on the synopsis, was how the audience would react, following the departure of the Tiger. After all, he was what they had come to see. One imagines the build-up at home, over the days and weeks before the theatre visit. 'We're going to see the Tiger!' My worry was that once the Tiger left the stage, the audience would lose interest. Luckily, however, Judith's story gave enough variety and added interest to ensure that audience involvement was retained. First, Daddy comes home, and at first quite reasonably doesn't believe that a Tiger has been visiting. The success of this scene on stage is again due to the sense of empowerment we give the young audience. They know more than Daddy knows. They know that a Tiger really has been to tea, and they are eager to tell him!

When Daddy, finally convinced, or at least he appears to be, suggests that the family go to a café, we are able to change the scene, an effective way of keeping the audience's attention. The family put on their coats and set off. I had the idea that it would be fun if they went to the café by car. Judith was very uncertain about this. I think she was thinking of the actual situation on which the scene was based, when she and her family would walk to Barnes High Street. No car was involved! Eventually I convinced her that a mimed car journey might be quite fun. The cast could make the car out of the table and chairs, with Sophie sitting high up on the table, as though in the back of the car. In production, this mimed scene usually gets some laughs. Very rarely does a child shout out, 'It's not a real car!'

The walk to the café, once the car is parked, gave the opportunity for a nice lighting change, with a mirror ball suggesting a starry sky. Something else to keep the audience's attention. Then the café could be created, again using the table and chairs, and adding a tablecloth, just like the one in the book. The family would mime eating sausages and chips, and, once home again, tell the audience how they went shopping, bought food, and filled up the fridge and the cupboard. And Mummy's trolley, thanks to Scott's magic, could be magically filled with supermarket items. Judith was at first concerned that Daddy was involved in the shopping. She said that only Mummy and Sophie went shopping. I pointed out that it would really be helpful if all three could be involved. Sophie could show the filled-up fridge, Daddy could show the filled-up cupboard and Mummy would show the filled-up shopping trolley. This would lead neatly into, just like in the book, Sophie showing the large tin of tiger food, bought just in case the Tiger should come again… Judith kindly agreed.

Another, to me, natural way of 'expanding' Judith's story was to add music. For many years, particularly in shows for younger children, I have felt that appropriate songs that develop the action, plus incidental music, help and tighten the storytelling. Children like music and rhythm. I'm not a trained musician, but I enjoy writing lyrics and composing tunes, which I very happily pass to my extremely accomplished arranger and musical supervisor, Peter Pontzen, who manages to find the harmonies in my head.

I felt there should be an opening song, in which the actors, not yet in character, welcome the audience to the theatre. Aware that many very young children in our audience would be coming to the theatre for the very first time, I thought perhaps we might explain what a play is – a story acted out. The idea would be to then gently lead the children into the story, by having the actors discover the set – Judith's kitchen – as though it was the first time they had seen it.

The aforementioned doorbell rings gave me the opportunity to write a cumulative song, with a repeated verse about wondering who could be at the door, followed by a growing list of the rejected possibilities. Children rather like repetition, and I hoped that they would find fun in this idea, similar to a song like 'Old MacDonald Had a Farm'.

Having decided that the Tiger shouldn't speak, I wondered how I could give him the equivalent of a song. It certainly seemed appropriate for him to lead a musical number. I also wanted to find a place in the show where the children could have a chance to physically enjoy themselves without actually leaving their seats. Something to interrupt an hour of simply sitting still. I suddenly thought of Tigerobics. Perhaps the Tiger could do his exercises, and invite Sophie and Mummy, plus the audience, to join in. Maybe, I thought, in his quest for more food, he could inadvertently tap the knob of a portable radio, thereby turning it on. And, by an amazing coincidence(!), his favourite radio programme is starting – 'Tigerobics'!

Some years after *Tiger*'s regular touring began, Judith was asked, for a programme article, which song in the show was her favourite. She chose 'Different in the Dark'. Her choice pleased me, because I knew, when I decided to include it, that it was perhaps a bit of a risk. By this I mean that it was not a song that young children might easily respond to. It is the kind of song I have often been determined to include – slightly more sophisticated than the other more catchy, rhythmic numbers. Another example is a song from another of my musical plays, *The Gingerbread Man,* called 'Come the Light', in which the characters sing a fervent hope or prayer that all their problems will be resolved during the night. These songs mustn't be sung 'prettily', but with great energy and conviction. 'Different in the Dark' is sung as the family walk excitedly in the dark, towards the café. The lighting change, in which a starry sky with moving stars is created by a mirror ball, dramatically alters the atmosphere, and hopefully conveys the special feeling experienced by a child taken by his or her parents on a nighttime treat.

Once inside the café, it felt fairly obvious to me to give the family a song about the tasty supper they eat. In the book, Judith gives them sausages and chips. As I wrote a song about their yumminess, it struck me that this was the perfect time to invite the audience to join in with the song, rather like the traditional song-sheet number towards the end of a pantomime. This led to the idea of a canon-style song, 'Sausages and Chips', in which three renditions of the song, started individually at different times, can blend harmonically together. Peter Pontzen helped me musically to create the counterpoint. Very small children sometimes unsurprisingly don't join in, but school parties join in with gusto, along with many teachers and other adult audience members. The song provides a sequence combining control with sometimes raucous abandonment! It also provides an excuse for another piece of Scott Penrose magic. I asked him to create a menu, from which the family chose their meal, which would then open out to reveal a child-friendly guide to the song – not the words, but pictures of a sausage, some chips, and the ice cream they have for pudding.

The final song was relatively straightforward, a title song to remind us that,

> 'It doesn't happen every day,
> That a tiger comes round to play'.

And then, into the curtain call.

In the original draft synopsis I had expressed the hope that during the finale song, the doorbell might ring, announcing the return of the Tiger for a final bow. However, in rehearsal it soon became clear that there wouldn't be enough time for Daddy to change costume back into the Tiger. I had a sudden idea. Might the Assistant Stage Manager, who was also the male understudy, be able to appear as the Tiger at the end of the show? Matthew Dudley readily agreed, perhaps not realising that he would be climbing into an extremely sweaty costume! Health and Safety would have had a fit! But Matt gamely embraced the idea, and the audience were very excited to see the Tiger one more time. Many of them, particularly the adults, were mystified too! They had assumed, correctly, that the Tiger actor also played Daddy, yet here, in the final song, Daddy and the Tiger were both on stage! Once the show had proved itself, our producers, I'm glad to say, commissioned another Tiger costume for the understudy to wear, not only for this special moment, but also should he have to play the Tiger, if the main actor was ill or unable to appear.

Another ingredient I invariably employ in my shows for young children is audience participation. Breaking through the fourth wall and directly addressing the audience is something unique to theatre. The audience can hopefully feel part of the show they are watching, instrumental in helping the characters and developing the story. I like such participation to be creative, rather than, as in some pantomimes, a character coming on and asking, 'Did you have a nice Christmas?' The audience replies, 'Yes!' 'Can't hear you!' says the actor. 'You'll have to do it louder! Did you have a good Christmas?' '*Yes*,' shouts back the audience! Nothing really wrong with this approach, of course, but it can be somewhat patronising. So, when planning my Tiger synopsis, I included a short opening dialogue between the actors and the audience; then they invite them in the opening song to echo 'Hallo' and 'Hi'. I also gave them, in the opening scenes, regular invitations to count the striking hours on the clock.

When the Postman delivers the parcel for Sophie, she wonders what might be inside, and asks the audience for suggestions. This is designed to make the children feel that they can contribute.

The arrival of the Tiger is unashamedly pure pantomime! The audience can see him before Mummy and Sophie, and desperately try to alert them to the fact that there is a tiger at the door! It is the classic 'He's behind you!' routine from a pantomime, and it really does work. The children knowing something the characters don't know is truly empowering. And I don't believe that the children feel manipulated. They are so engaged, they want to help.

The Tigerobics section, as described earlier, encourages the audience to join in physically as well as vocally, and is really pure fun. This is followed closely by the departure of the Tiger, which yields a poignant lump-in-the-throat moment, as the children wave and call out 'Bye-bye, Tiger'. In the song, 'Sausages and Chips', the audience are invited not only to sing, but also to 'do the actions', learning from the actors how to echo the words of the song with movements.

Very often, the audience claps along to the final choruses of the title song. We never encourage them to participate in this way, because I feel that is rather like begging for approval! When the clapping arrives organically, simply through a desire to join in, I always get the warm feeling that we've won!

Once Judith had approved the synopsis, I set off to write the draft script and lyrics in my regular bolthole, room 208 at the Cooden Beach Hotel, Bexhill. For some reason I have always enjoyed writing near the sea. Once I got started, I decided that it was important to use as much of Judith's text as possible, because I realised that there would be many children in the audience who would know the story word for word by heart. So I gave a considerable amount of third person narration, straight from the book, to Mummy and Sophie. This used a technique I had learnt from David Edgar's brilliant adaptation of *Nicholas Nickleby*, directed so memorably by Trevor Nunn and John Caird for the Royal Shakespeare Company. Characters are able to talk about what happened to them by referring to themselves in the third person. The classic example often quoted from Edgar's adaptation of Dickens' novel is when Nicholas himself says, 'And Nicholas went to London!' He doesn't say, 'I went to London'. What I particularly like about this device is that the focus falls on the speaking protagonist, rather than a narrator. So children, who have a narrower range of vision than adults, don't watch the narrator rather than the character being described. This technique meant that much of Judith's text remains intact in the play, even using the past tense when describing action that is actually happening right now.

Sticking faithfully to Judith's storyline, having expanded the opening section, the first draft proceeded smoothly, and changed little in rehearsal. Once back home, I wrote the tunes of the songs, and visited Peter in Chipping Norton, where he did the basic arrangements and I recorded the songs for the interested parties to hear.

Meanwhile I had sent the first draft to Judith for her perusal and, hopefully, her approval. On March 10th, 2008, she phoned me. I jotted down some of her comments – something I often did over the coming years, not wanting to forget her witty remarks. To my relief, Judith said, 'The script is lovely, thank you so much... I can see why you've done the things you've done... it all works... things have come together so well, including the magic... I think I'm very lucky'.

I slept well that night!

Quite soon, we were into pre-production. I encouraged Susie, when creating her stage designs, to work in collaboration with Scott, who was able to inform her of the requirements necessary to make his magic work. Susie did her usual brilliant job, transferring Judith's illustrations to the stage, complete with the crayon-like decorations that are so distinctive in Judith's work. Indeed, as Judith recalls in her book *Judith Kerr's Creatures*, she was 'brought up short by the set, which looked exactly like the drawing in the book'. Susie's costume designs were also extremely faithful to Judith's illustrations, including, of course, the iconic tiger. Angie Burns, the outstanding wardrobe supervisor with whom Susie and I had first worked at Regent's Park Open Air Theatre on *Babe, the Sheep-Pig* and *Fantastic Mr Fox*, excelled herself in creating the costumes in the appropriate 1960s period style.

I had not worked before with Tony Simpson, our lighting designer, who cleverly created an atmospheric lighting plot, contrasting effectively the daylight sequences with the nighttime walk to the café. Tony, like all the creative team, stayed faithfully with the production over many years. Somehow, Judith's story inspired a feeling of affection and close involvement.

Our original cast featured Abbey Norman, a 4'10" bundle of energy as Sophie. Abbey has played the role on and off ever since. Devon Black was a lovely Mummy, who subsequently became a real mummy herself. Her two children, by a happy coincidence, went to the Judith Kerr Primary School in South East London. Alan Atkins was our magical first Tiger, also playing Daddy, the Milkman and the Postman. At 6'5", he set the benchmark for all future Tigers.

Rehearsals began in a church hall in Pimlico. Our company/stage manager was the ever-reliable Neil Hillyer, who had worked for me many times since leaving RADA. His assistant was Matthew Dudley, recently arrived from Australia, who was the same height as Alan, and proved a very capable understudy. Rachel Baynton was our versatile wardrobe mistress, who also understudied Abbey and Devon. The chemistry and commitment of this small but perfectly formed team proved invaluable once rehearsals got going, and I am eternally grateful to them, as well as the creative team.

Judith came to our first day of rehearsal. She clearly enjoyed the experience of the read-through, and meeting the team. She returned for our first run-through, and was particularly complimentary about Alan's Tiger, who was not, of course, wearing a costume, but expressed clearly the Tiger's emotions, occasional anarchic behaviour, and also his dignified yet friendly hauteur.

For the songs, Emma skilfully created appropriate dance routines, which always embellished the ideas expressed in the lyrics, rather than creating impressive choreography for its own sake. I loved the way she made the movement develop naturally within the storytelling. This included the use of mime, in the Daddy 'late for work' sequence, and the 'Tiger Waltz' we inserted to show the Tiger's delight and gratitude for his tasty tea. Peter, using my song tunes, wrote catchy incidental music to accompany the movement. He also, in his home studio, recorded backing tracks for all the music and songs. This was the first time, in forty years, we had ever used recorded music. Previously, a live musician would always be part of the team. But Nick Brooke and Kenny Wax, our producers, insisted on us using backing tracks. At first I resisted the idea, but I have to admit that, thanks to Peter's inventive and fun arrangements, I was eventually delighted with the result. And the actors rather liked the security of always hearing the same tempos.

Nick and Kenny also introduced me to the Sound Designer Andy Shaw, who proved to be a sympathetic and inventive creator of sound effects. With his creative partner, Jon Fiber, he came up with exactly the right eating and drinking sounds for the Tiger.

In rehearsal, I had the chance to record the radio presenter's voice for 'Tigerobics', and even to sing the song! So, whenever I see the show, I have to listen to my own singing!

One of the things I had requested from early on was to have Susie's kitchen set assembled in the rehearsal room from day one. In fact it arrived on day two! Very often we never see the actual set until we arrive in the theatre for the technical rehearsals. But with this play, I felt it was essential to rehearse on the set, complete with all the necessary doors and traps designed by Scott and Susie to facilitate the magic effects. Our work was made much easier having the real kitchen and props to work with so early in the rehearsal process. And Scott regularly visited us, to teach the cast how to work his magic tricks.

As rehearsals progressed, it became apparent that I hadn't allowed enough time in the script between the Tiger's departure and Daddy's return. The quick costume change needed another couple of minutes. So we introduced a short ballad version of the title song, sung by Sophie and Mummy, recalling with awe and amazement the extraordinary events they had just witnessed. This had the added bonus of establishing the title song before we then heard it at the end of the show, in its original uptempo version.

Our first performance took place at the Bloomsbury Theatre. We were all thrilled with the audience reaction. Judith later wrote, 'It is oddly moving to see a theatre full of three-year-olds spellbound by this singing and dancing version of a bedtime story I once told my little daughter so many years ago.' She also loved the fact that Susie and Angie had successfully delivered Sophie's iconic diamond-checked tights! I was particularly thrilled by the wonderful Tiger costume, designed by Susie and made by the talented team of Robert Allsopp and his associates. It looked amazing, and enabled Emma's regal movement to work as effectively as in the rehearsal room, when we didn't have the costume. One thing I hadn't really taken in until performances began was the fact that Sophie never leaves the stage, throughout the full fifty-five minutes of the show! And Mummy only disappears for a few seconds at the end, before re-entering in the finale song. Things are just as relentless for the actor playing Daddy, the Milkman, the Postman and the Tiger. Whenever he goes offstage, he is involved in an extremely quick costume change. The actors work extremely hard for their fees!

The audience reaction was very encouraging, first at the Bloomsbury Theatre and then on tour, and, by the time *Tiger* reached the West End's Vaudeville Theatre in 2011, the public and the press had taken the show to their hearts.

> '…a roaring success… consistently inventive… this *Tiger* is the cat's meow.'
>
> *(The Times)*

> 'It is perfect entertainment for pre-school children and brings all the mischief and humour of the original picture book to vibrant life.'
>
> *(Daily Express)*

> 'Wood, who directs as well as writing the show, has done an excellent job. There are cumulative rhymes and repetitive actions to latch onto and a chance to count, but this is fun not education, packed with joyful laughter and not a little amazement, and it is also framed in such a way as easily to introduce first-timers to the theatre.'
>
> *(British Theatre Guide)*

> 'I welcome this wholesome show because it will get a new generation into the habit of theatre-going.'
>
> *(Sunday Telegraph)*

> '…delightful'
>
> *(WhatsOnStage)*

It seems quite remarkable, and very rewarding, that since 2008, except during the Covid pandemic, the show has been touring and playing West End seasons almost non-stop. In 2012, we celebrated our nomination as Best Entertainment and Family show in the Olivier Awards. I treasure the memory of proudly escorting an excited Judith along the red carpet to the ceremony at the Royal Opera House. We didn't win the award, but Judith sent us all a customised card of congratulation anyway. Until her death in 2019, Judith continued to support the production and visit, to the delight of our various casts. She was very pleased that the play was so welcomed in the West End, first at the Vaudeville Theatre, then at the Lyric for several seasons, and the Piccadilly, and I know she would have been thrilled to know that we have so far played six seasons at the legendary Theatre Royal, Haymarket. She was surprised and excited when we started playing abroad, in Dubai, Singapore, Hong Kong, and even in Australia at the Sydney Opera House. In 2016 she wrote expressing her pleasure when the play went to China.

> Email from JK, 7th June, 2016
> *I have just had a happy, somewhat alcoholic lunch, with Nick Brooke, and he showed me pictures of the Tiger in China – amazing! It's quite different when you see the theatre and the posters in Mandarin and the queue of little Chinese children waiting to be photographed with the cast. Afterwards we walked a few steps down Shaftesbury Avenue to admire your name below* The Go-Between.

This was a reference to my grown-up adaptation of LP Hartley's book, which was playing at the Apollo Theatre, starring Michael Crawford.

It seems extraordinary that, as I write, *Tiger* has been roaring for seventeen years, apart from the enforced Covid break. I feel very fortunate and ever grateful to Judith for letting me adapt and direct her classic picture book for the stage, and, of course, I also thank Nick Brooke for having had the idea in the first place, and to him and Kenny Wax for co-producing the show.

In 2013, HarperCollins published *Judith Kerr's Creatures*, a splendid celebration of Judith's life and work. She had told me she was working on this lavishly illustrated memoir, but it wasn't until she kindly gave Jacqui and me a copy, on publication, that I found she had devoted two pages to the *Tiger* play, generously chronicling our collaboration and praising the creative team. I'm grateful to

HarperCollins for giving me permission to reproduce her comments in this book.

Over the years, as *Tiger*'s success continued, so our friendship grew. Jacqui and I loved escorting Judith on our regular trips to The Depot for Sunday lunch. We would arrive at her house in Barnes and be welcomed into the sitting room where, watched from his portrait on the wall by Judith's late husband, Tom, we would exchange news, perhaps discussing the latest *Tiger* auditions, or how Judith's new book was developing. Immaculately coiffured, Judith would always be stylishly dressed, often in trousers, sometimes wearing her tartan pencil skirt, in which, she would say, 'going to the loo is a major enterprise'. Then, before we set off, she would ascertain the location of Katinka, her beautiful cat, deliberating whether she would like to go outside or stay indoors. On one lovely, sunny day, Katinka insisted on staying in the bathroom. 'I don't know why, on a day like this', wondered Judith.

Driving to the restaurant, we always passed Barnes Pond. Judith once remembered spotting a young heron, alone and apparently confused. She thought it must have been dumped by its parents, so went to the fishmonger, who gave her some 'elderly fish', which she kindly threw to the young heron. To her dismay, the fish hit the unfortunate bird and knocked it over…

One day we drove by a tree that Judith told us she had planted for Tom, after he died. It was a lime tree, which would be good for wildlife. Judith had wanted to bury Tom's ashes with it, but had decided against, in case of foxes or other animals digging them up. She said she would scatter them among the trees opposite their house, on the edge of the common. Tom apparently used to look out at them a lot in his final years.

Arriving at The Depot, we would be warmly welcomed by our host, Jean-Francois, who treated Judith like royalty, often asking her to sign her latest book. He would unfailingly lead us to our favourite table overlooking the River Thames. Before looking at the menu, we would scour the far bank in an attempt to spy a heron, and when we were successful, Judith was sure it would bring us all good luck.

To accompany her meal, Judith would usually order a glass of her favourite Montepulciano. She told us that at home she sometimes enjoyed a tot of whisky, and amused us by telling us how, when she thought the battery of her compact Mercedes, parked outside the house, was running flat, she would sit in the car with the engine going, sipping a whisky and listening to Radio 4.

We were somewhat disappointed when The Depot was taken over by Rick Stein. The delicious Depot Sunday roast disappeared, and the predominately fishy dishes were not so much to our taste. But Jean-Francois was still there to greet us, and we loved our window table. Judith and I discovered that two starters and a dessert were very acceptable, and no longer ordered a main course.

Email from DW, 11th November, 2018
Dear Judith,

Lovely to see you, and what a good meal that was! I think we've got the hang of that menu now!!

Email from JK, 11th November, 2018
Dear David,

Yes, it was lovely. The tarte tatin, especially was memorable. But it seemed a particularly nice time, apart from the food, as well!

The next lunch was less successful!

Email from DW, 14th December, 2018
Dear Judith,

Lovely to see you yesterday. Shame about the fish pie! But we got a discount!

Email from JK, 18th December, 2018
Dear David,

Regardless of the fish pie, it was lovely.

Email from DW, 14th April, 2018
Dear Judith,
Today the Grand National took place… I never normally bet, but couldn't resist when I saw that one of the horses was called Tiger Roll. It won!!! And I won over £100!!! Hopefully this is a good omen for the 50th anniversary!!! [of the book] *And for the Piccadilly season and tour!!* [of the play]
David

Judith replied: Email from JK, 15th April, 2018
Congratulations! Not only a good omen, but now you'll be able to afford the Dover Sole at Rick Stein.

Jacqui and I would drive Judith home. Sometimes she would invite us in for coffee.

Email from DW, 6th May, 2018
Dear Judith,
Lovely to see you on such a beautiful, cloudless day! Thank you for coffee in the garden.

Email from JK, 16th May, 2018
Dear David,
We must do it again, and by next time I plan to have washed the moss off the chairs.

Occasionally we would lunch at Judith's other favourite restaurant, Riva. She once excitedly told Jacqui and me that recently she had been eating there with fellow author and illustrator Lauren Child, and realised that the Beckhams were at a nearby table – 'and David paid for our meal!' The Beckham children were great fans of her books!

During lunch we would often discuss aspects of Judith's work. In her self-deprecatory way, she would downplay her drawing skills. 'Trees and leaves I have no feeling for,' she said once. 'I love looking at them, but I can't paint them.' Another bête noire was buildings – 'I can't do buildings. They've got to be there, but they're not important in the picture, and if they're noticeable, they're wrong.'

When she was working on *One Night in the Zoo*, she was relieved to have finished the flamingos, with the large background expanse to fill, and was moving on 'to a giraffe and six rabbits – I thought of using squids, but they're not cuddly enough.'

Once we discussed economy in the writing of text for a children's picture book. Judith tried to use as few words as possible to tell the story, relying on the illustrations to do the bulk of the work. I hadn't realised that *Mog in the Dark* only used fifty-three words. Judith was delighted that many children told her this was the book that taught them to read. She was very aware that the teaching of reading in schools was pedestrian. Her son, Matthew, was given the *Janet and John* books, but found them boring, and instead cut his reading teeth on Dr Seuss. Judith recalled that 'the height of drama in *Janet and John* was – school uniform bought – Mummy bought a cap – Daddy bought a cap – John had two caps!' She was relieved that such reading schemes and children's picture books have significantly moved on.

Judith once criticised 'bad editors, who want to change something… They like being creative… That's the worst thing that can happen.'

But she had nothing but praise for her current publisher at HarperCollins, Ann-Janine Murtagh, who was ever supportive and encouraging. And she was heartily grateful to Ann-Janine for allowing her to retain the services of Ian Craig, her brilliant book designer, who had left HarperCollins to go freelance. Ian was a crucial ingredient in the creation of the 'look' of the picture books.

On March 17th, 2019, we had what was to be our very last lunch with Judith at Rick Stein. She hadn't been too well, but was still on sparkling form. Little did Jacqui and I know then that she would sadly pass away just ten weeks later. We talked about children. Judith was keen to hear how our grandson, Thomas, was getting on. He was now three and a half years old and beginning to enjoy creative play. Judith was reminded of playing with her daughter, Tacy. The most popular activity was The Big WaWas Game. Judith, on all fours, would crawl round the room and find, for example, a chair. She would react frightened. Tacy would calm her down, saying, 'Don't worry, it's a *chair*!' This reminiscence echoed my thoughts about the importance of empowering children. In theatre, a very useful device is to contrive it that the young audience know something before the characters on stage, and want to tell them, sometimes warn them. It's a classic element of traditional pantomime, of course. 'He's behind you!' In *Tiger*, we use it when he first appears, unseen by Sophie and Mummy. The audience enjoy being cleverer than Sophie and Mummy, and are delighted when they are proved right. There *is* a tiger! Judith noted that in the play, the audience become part of it. I agreed, suggesting that the audience is actually a character in the play, a character to whom I am often arrogant enough to give lines in the script.

The importance of 'empowering children' was a principle Judith utilised in her Mog books. 'They all have the same basic plot,' she told me. 'Mog does something but doesn't understand – the child readers *do* understand. Then things turn out OK, not thanks to Mog! The readers are empowered – they know more than Mog.'

Judith reflected that theatre was special because it offered the child audience the chance to be part of the story, whereas film allowed them to be simply 'spectators'.

This idea was in Judith's head, partly because the animated film version of *The Tiger Who Came to Tea* was in preparation. She said that she had enjoyed several conversations with the writer, Joanna Harrison, and hoped that the film would be faithful to the book. She admitted, with a smile, that a couple of ideas from my play were being used in the film. Daddy was to appear from the start, and the first ring of the doorbell would be, like in the play, Daddy returning, having forgotten his key. Judith also said that she thought the Milkman would be a character, like in the play, unlike in the book. I felt rather flattered that these ideas had found favour, and when I went to the launch of the television film in December, was pleased and relieved that Judith's story was indeed faithfully told, and that her illustrations had been beautifully reproduced.

Sadly, Judith never saw the completed *Tiger* film, but she approved of the unfinished versions that she was shown. By coincidence, the launch took place at the Odeon, Leicester Square, on Sunday, December 8th, the very day on which we were putting up the set in preparation for the opening of the play at the Theatre Royal, Haymarket. As I walked the short distance from the cinema to the theatre, I thought of Judith. Surely she would be happy to know that the television film and the play were both in full flight. Not only that, but thanks to the success of the film on television at Christmas, by January 2020, *The Sunday Times* children's book chart showed *The Tiger Who Came to Tea* at number three, fifty-two years after its publication!

I like to think that collaborating on the stage version of *The Tiger Who Came to Tea* helped Judith rekindle her creative spark following an inevitable fallow period during which she looked after her beloved Tom during his ill health until he died in 2006. After the sad time mourning her loss came what she called 'a new chapter in her life'. Her creative juices began to flow once more. Nine new stories were written, illustrated and published before her death in 2019. A remarkable tally.

Jacqui and I were often privileged to be given clues about her developing projects. What was so impressive was the variety and the innovation of her work, producing not only new picture books but also text-based novellas, a genre she had never previously attempted. She often spoke enthusiastically about 'The Great Haroosh', the magical moment when, after working out a story, 'all becomes clear'. The preparatory work was all-important to her, planning meticulously the beginning, middle and end. Once she knew where she was going, the real work began.

First came *One Night in the Zoo* (2009), a delightful fantasy in which Judith imagined nighttime goings-on amongst the animals, including the thin-necked flamingos, who left lots of background to fill in! The story moves along with admirable economy of text, using inventive rhyme. Judith often spoke of the importance of rhythm in picture books with very little text. *One Night in the Zoo* is a classic example of her skill. However, following the book's publication, Judith told me she wasn't happy with the light pastel quality of the printed illustrations – she felt that she hadn't used enough ink. Nicolette Jones, in her *Sunday Times* review, called it 'muted softness'. Judith felt this was a kind way of criticising the colour. After doing a book-signing, she remarked, 'we shifted lots of *Tiger*s – but people weren't interested in muted softness'.

Next came *My Henry*, in which Henry's widow, clearly a version of Judith herself, imagines exciting flights of fancy with her beloved husband. It is a humorous and tender tribute to her happy marriage. In her autobiographical celebratory book *Judith Kerr's Creatures*, Judith admits that 'This was a bit of an oddity, in that it also had a certain interest for grown-ups'. She hopes it is accepted, because she had always deeply disliked picture books, which, 'while claiming to be for children, are really self-consciously poetic for grown-ups'. She hoped that *My Henry* wasn't one of them. This reminded me of the time I told Judith I was adapting Sam McBratney's book *Guess How Much I Love You* into a play. Judith wondered whether this was a good idea. Her honest opinion was that this book was one of the 'self-consciously poetic for grown-ups' genre.

Next came *The Great Granny Gang* (2012), in which a gang of game elderly ladies defeat a gang of hoodies. Again using rhyme, Judith drew upon her diverse circle of feisty ladies and fused them with the modern phenomenon of young men wearing jackets with somewhat sinister hoods.

It was intriguing to learn that *The Crocodile Under the Bed* (2014) was a thoroughly reworked version of Judith's unpublished second book. Her young hero is called Matty, presumably named after her son, Matthew. It had been interesting to learn that 'Sophie', in Judith's first book, *The Tiger Who Came to Tea*, was originally called Tacy, after her daughter. The publishers decided that Tacy was too unusual a name and changed it to Sophie. They clearly approved of the name of 'Matty', who, feeling poorly and ill-tempered, misses out on a street party with his grandfather. But his luck changes when the crocodile under the bed sprouts wings and takes him off on exciting adventures on a jungle island. He plays with a chimp, rides a tiger, and uses the back of a giant snake to slide down. Imagination wins the day for Matty, as the street party has been marred by rain. Judith's love of drawing animals is abundantly evident. She often revelled at how the internet enabled her to Google references of every kind of creature in every kind of pose. I think it was when she was working on this book that, in a phone call, she complained, 'I'm trying to draw a bush. It's huge, this bloody bush!' and 'the monkeys are alright looking out – I needn't have put them in!'

On the phone in 2014, Judith talked about a new book she was working on, for six- to seven-year-olds. This was the first time she had written for this age group, following her picture books for the young, and, for older readers, the *Out of the Hitler Time* trilogy, which included *When Hitler Stole Pink Rabbit*. The new book turned out to be *Mister Cleghorn's Seal*, and it was published in 2015. The format was smaller than usual. The story was told in short novel form, with black and white illustrations interwoven within the text. The dedication read, 'To my father, who once kept a seal on his balcony'. This idiosyncratic tale about Mr Cleghorn finding an abandoned seal pup on a rock, and taking it home to his flat, was based on an incident in Judith's father's life. It is an enchanting story, humorous and touching. It triumphantly refutes Judith's oft-quoted 'I can't write'.

That same year, 2015, saw the publication of *Mog's Christmas Calamity*, based on the brilliant and extraordinarily successful Christmas television commercial for Sainsbury's. Judith had been sworn to silence about this advert, until just before it was released. She was amused when Jacqui and I reminded her that she always shopped at Waitrose! The advert brought Mog back to life. Judith had, to the surprise of many, killed her off twelve years before in *Goodbye, Mog*. Yet here she was again, causing festive chaos in a brilliantly produced animation film. The book ascended to number one in the British children's book charts. Judith was obviously pleased, but modestly announced, 'the book wasn't my story, and it was done in a great rush, and I hate the cover, but… you know, it's made a million and a half or something for Save the Children, and it's done a terrific lot for the rest of the books, obviously, so that's all good. But it was a different thing.'

Whenever Jacqui and I visited Judith, we were always aware of her cat, Katinka. She was often there in person, curled up in a chair, or Judith would tell us she was upstairs in the bathroom. Katinka's fur was mainly pure white, but she had an unusual dark, stripey tail. Judith would tell us how Katinka would climb up the wisteria and jump through the window in her bedroom, to wake her up. It was clear that she was more than a pet. She was Judith's devoted companion. So it was almost inevitable that Judith's next book was *Katinka's Tail* (2017), in which, in a dream, it becomes clear that Katinka's tail is magic. She leads Judith on adventures with other animals, and even flies with her to the moon and back. The fantasy element of the story enhances the very real connection Judith had with the beautiful cat who shared her final years.

Judith's last picture book proved, unusually, somewhat controversial. *Mummy Time* (2018) features her regular device in which fantasy springs from reality. A young mother sits on a park bench, chatting on her mobile phone to a friend. Her little boy, unseen by her, wanders off, meets a friendly dog, feeds the birds, then takes off on the back of a swan and experiences fun and danger before returning to his unconcerned mother. The text consists only of Mummy's part of the gossipy telephone conversation to her friend, and cunningly echoes the little boy's exciting activities. Judith gave us an advanced copy.

Email DW to JK, 5th August, 2018
Mummy Time *is brilliant! A real delight. It will be VERY successful, I know!*

But Judith was worried that her depiction of neglectful young mums on their mobile phones might prove unpopular – 'I hope they haven't turned against me,' she said. And in a newspaper article, she asserted that 'it wasn't supposed to knock mums'. She said to me, in a phone call, 'Toddlers are very boring sometimes. I see everyone on their phones and I wonder, if a herd of lions appeared across the street, I would be the only one to notice. But I hate people who use children's books to make political points'. Indignant mums did indeed criticise the book in online reviews. And I suppose it is true that, when reading the book to her child, a mum might feel rather guilty, and her child might feel insecure. To me, however, the story is a tribute to children's imaginations, rather than a criticism of young mothers' avid attachment to their mobiles.

When Judith told me about the book she was determined to finish 'before I die', she didn't want to give away too much, but said that it was based on real events in her family life. I inadvertently received a sneak preview, once she had finished the extensive text. She must have been emailing the typed script to her publishers, but mistakenly pressed a computer key that forwarded it to me. I never told her this had happened, but eagerly read her short novel, delighting in its wit and often sophisticated storytelling. Dedicated to her grandchildren, Tatiana and Alexander, *The Curse of the School Rabbit* is the tale of Tommy, his show-off sister Angie, and their parents, who take on the guardianship of Snowflake, an exasperating school rabbit, who pees on an important visitor, often escapes, and appears to put a curse on the family. Tommy's father, a 'resting' actor, and his uncle, a somewhat unsuccessful film director, become embroiled in the plot. Angie becomes very ill, and problems multiply until Judith wittily and cleverly ties up all the threads, creating a happy ending. Snowflake returns to school, and Tommy and Angie end up starring in a film with their father, directed by their uncle. Accompanied by exquisite black and white illustrations, the book is, I think, unlike anything Judith previously produced. Her last book stands out as a unique tribute to her versatility and fertile imagination, which never deserted her.

Reflecting on her own childhood years, Judith often regretted the fact that until later in life she had failed to understand how traumatic fleeing from Nazi Germany must have been for her parents. Her father all but lost his career as a theatre critic and found it difficult coping in England with another language. Her mother, considerably younger than her father, had her life turned upside down, and apparently attempted suicide. How anxious she must have been, accompanying nine-year-old Judith and her elder brother, Michael, as they travelled by train, fearful of their passports revealing their Jewish identity. In her novel, based on her childhood experiences, *When Hitler Stole Pink Rabbit*, Judith describes her escape almost as an exciting adventure. And indeed that is how she remembered it. She almost felt guilty in later years that she hadn't realised the immense danger the family was in. Her book, by the time we knew Judith, had become a set text in German schools. A German film company acquired the rights to film it, but, when the first draft of the script arrived, Judith was dismayed to find that the screenwriter portrayed her as an unfortunate child, a wretched refugee suffering deprivation and hardship. This, felt Judith, was so untrue. She regretted allowing the film to be made. However, I later understood that Matthew, her son, had spoken with the screenwriter and satisfactory changes were made. The film appeared and was critically well reviewed.

Her father, Judith remembered with affection, had 'a talent for happiness'. But she came to realise that he was not as passive as she described him in *When Hitler Stole Pink Rabbit*. She had since discovered, in his correspondence, just how much anti-Nazi propaganda he had been writing. Telling us about this reminded her of how, when they had reached comparative safety in Paris, she often feared that Hitler might be lurking behind the curtain in the lavatory.

When Jacqui and I told Judith how we had read books to our children, and that *The Tiger Who Came to Tea* was an all-time favourite, Judith remarked that bedtime stories were not something she remembered, even though her household was very literate. But she recalled her father telling her and her brother Michael stories from the Old Testament. The story of Adam and Eve was alright, but when he got to Abraham and Isaac, Michael had nightmares, and woke up screaming, 'I won't be sacrificed!', so her mother put a stop to it!

As a child, Judith recalled, 'I wished we had a cat'. Her deprivation was subsequently made up for once married – Mog was the first of the many cats that became part of the family, and became immortalised in so many of her stories.

Theirs was not a religious household. Apparently, from the age of five, Judith would tell people that her family were 'free thinkers'. She told us how she had tested the existence of God once. At breakfast they had a nice white roll each, only one. One day she asked God to give her *two*. Miraculously there was, for some reason, one roll left over, and she was allowed to eat it. However, in thanks, she offered a drawing to God, by throwing it up in the air. God didn't accept it, so she decided He didn't really exist.

As a child in Berlin in the late 1920s and early 1930s, Judith said she had much enjoyed being taken to the theatre. She particularly loved a production of *Emil and the Detectives*. Regular theatregoing in later life with Tom stopped when he became incapacitated. She told me she didn't go to the theatre for a long time. But, after he died, she began seeing plays with a friend, and was once again enchanted by the experience, 'even if the play wasn't that great. I loved the red of the auditorium, the curtain etc'.

Judith enjoyed music. She told us that her father had taught her to play Brahms' 'Lullaby' on the piano. I once sent her a CD of me singing some of the songs I had written for my children's plays. She amused me by ringing up one day, saying that she had enjoyed listening to them, but had to stop when she found that she was colouring in her backgrounds rhythmically in time with the music!

Judith fondly remembered her mother successfully teaching her algebra and simple division. She had made it seem sensible, using an apple, which she divided into halves, quarters and eighths. She approved of this practical application to the teaching of mathematics. In later years her mother, after all the problems and trauma the family had been through, said to Judith, 'Maybe you'll have the luck'. Judith never forgot this, and indeed knew that she *had* had the luck, especially when she took her first book, *The Tiger Who Came to Tea*, to Collins, the first publisher she approached, and they took it. Lucky, indeed. She stayed with Collins, later HarperCollins, throughout her long career, and, early on, made the unusual decision not to use a literary agent to negotiate her contracts.

Frank Cottrell Boyce has pointed out that many children's writers can't wait to get rid of the parents in their stories, so that they can concentrate on the adventures of the children. Enid Blyton, Arthur Ransome and CS Lewis are prime examples. But, for Judith, the family unit, united and enjoying life together, was a predominant feature in her work. Her ever-popular series about Mog features a thinly disguised version of her own family. Mog's exploits are always closely within the domestic lives of the parents and children. The books celebrate the family unit. And, in her conversations with Jacqui and me, it was apparent how proud she was of those children, now they had grown up. Matthew's writing achievements were regularly praised, as was the work of Tacy, who was not only a skilled prop maker for films, but also painted remarkable pictures of hugely magnified insects, one of which graced the wall of Judith's sitting room, and also a sensitive portrait of her mother that lived in the hall. Judith's love of her children – and grandchildren – was such that she seriously considered not paying for a private operation, because 'I always think the money belongs to the children'.

Judith sounded like a very sensible teenager. She told me that, aged sixteen, she was kissed by a boy. When asked another time for another kiss, she replied to him, 'I don't think we should make a habit of it!'

Judith always showed interest in our family. Grandson Thomas was often given presents, especially when a new piece of *Tiger* merchandise came on the market. His toy *Tigers* went down particularly well, but he was reluctant to wear his *Tiger* fancy dress costume!

When we moved house, Judith thoughtfully dropped us a line…

Email from JK, 23rd September, 2017

I thought of you on Thursday, wanted to wish you happy dreams in your first night in your new house, but then realised that it

was after midnight, and either you'd be having them or not, and my wishes wouldn't have much influence.
Love, Judith.

Once she came and spent Easter Day with us.

Email from JK, 15th August, 2016
I think Thomas is LOVELY!

Email from JK, 15th August, 2016
PS... and so is his Mum.

In her eighties and early nineties, Judith's energy and lust for life were prodigious, and often put Jacqui and me to shame. She loved her daily walks along the river, often crossing Hammersmith Bridge before catching the tube into Central London to purchase art materials. When we were invited to Nick Brooke's 50th birthday celebration in his Shaftesbury Avenue office, I suggested we might hire a car there and back. Judith pooh-poohed the idea, insisting that we caught a bus to Hammersmith Tube Station then take the Piccadilly line. This we did, and she insisted on returning the same way. She regularly spoke at book festivals, including Hay and Edinburgh – she thought nothing of flying up to Scotland and back the same day. I once had the privilege of interviewing her at the Wimbledon BookFest, but her interviewer of choice was Nicolette Jones, the *Sunday Times* children's book critic. 'I know her now,' Judith enthused. 'She makes it so easy'. We were interviewed together about the *Tiger* play for the Society of London Theatre's Kids Week. This took place in blazing sunshine on the stage of the Open Air Theatre, Regent's Park. It wasn't a comfortable experience, but Judith embraced, as usual, the opportunity to talk to children and their parents about her work.

Seven Stories, the Centre for the Children's Book in Newcastle, created a splendid exhibition of Judith's work, including her childhood pictures, smuggled from Berlin by her mother when they escaped the Nazis in 1932. Judith was genuinely moved by the scope and thoroughness with which Sarah Lawrance and her team had put together this celebratory tribute. I went up for the launch, and, as usual, was moved by Judith's witty and honest replies to Sarah's questions. Her gratitude to Great Britain for so warmly welcoming her refugee family, making it possible for her to live what she insisted was a 'very lucky life', was something she often spoke about, notably when she received the Peter Pan Award (2006) for a lifetime's service to children's arts. Her acceptance speech at the Action for Children's Arts presentation event at the Waldorf Hotel brought many of us to tears. Her humility and modesty were genuine and heartfelt. When I was flattered to receive the same award (by then called the JM Barrie Award) some years later, Judith not only attended, but spoke warmly about our collaboration.

Email from DW, 9th November, 2017
Thank you so much, Judith, for coming today and for saying lovely things!!
David

Email from JK, 9th November, 2017
I didn't say nearly enough lovely things about you. Next time you win a prize I will write them all down in advance on a bit of paper to make sure that I don't leave any out.
Judith

When Judith received another Lifetime Achievement award, this time from The Book Trust, I went to the presentation at London Zoo, where Judith was photographed by the tiger enclosure, did several television interviews, and stood chatting to admirers for a considerable time.

Email from DW, 7th July, 2016
Dear Judith,
Attached is a photo I took of Clare Morpurgo, displaying that exciting poster!! Lots of love, David.

Email from JK, 8th July, 2016

Dear David,

Thank you so much for the photo. I had never seen the poster. It's lovely. The whole thing was a total surprise – I had no idea that it would be so big. And they give you money, too. Love to you both, Judith

Judith loved parties. She genuinely enjoyed meeting and talking to people, rarely if ever sitting down. Jacqui and I enjoyed her 90th birthday celebration at the Wallace Collection, organised by HarperCollins, who celebrated her achievements at other events, once at the Savoy, once memorably at their offices in the City. The Tiger from our play arrived by boat, and was greeted by Judith on the landing stage. Another photo opportunity! When Judith and her son, Matthew Kneale, both had new books published, Jacqui and I attended a joint launch at the London Library. Judith sparkled with pride at Matthew's achievement.

Jacqui and I felt privileged to be invited by Judith to accompany her to the Sandown races, where she was doing a book-signing. We were all entertained royally – literally, in the Royal Box! And we much enjoyed being part of the celebratory lunch party after Judith received her much-deserved OBE. This took place in the restaurant at the top of the National Portrait Gallery, with magnificent views of Nelson's Column and other famous landmarks.

The Story Museum in Oxford, of which I was a proud trustee, invited Judith and me to an event at the Oxford Playhouse, talking to children after a performance of *The Tiger Who Came to Tea*. At the age of ninety-four, Judith gamely arrived, posed with the Tiger for more photographs, and enchanted her young audience.

Email from DW, 27th October, 2018

Lovely to see you today, Judith. Thank you so much for venturing forth to Oxford! The Story Museum were delighted! And the event seemed to go well. Thank you, too, for letting me share

your car home, which was a real treat!!
David.

During the journey back to London, she excitedly told me that on the way, her driver had asked, 'Would you like some heat in the car?' He had pressed the appropriate knob, which warmed her seat 'like a pad – marvellous!'

In 2018 I published a short memoir, *Filming If…*, to celebrate the 50th anniversary of Lindsay Anderson's much-praised film, in which I had played a rebel schoolboy. I told Judith, who, extremely honestly, remembered seeing the film when it first came out, and hating it! But she was gracious enough to read my book…

Email from JK, 28th June, 2018
I very much enjoyed your account of the filming of IF… *Must try to watch it again, now that I know what it was about.*
Judith.

The Oldie magazine organised a celebratory screening of the film at the Curzon, Soho, preceded by lunch at Brasserie Zedel. Jacqui and I invited Judith, who agreed to come. Valerie Grove, who was chairing a Q&A with me after the screening, so enjoyed meeting Judith that she asked to write an article about her in a forthcoming issue of *The Oldie*. Harry Mount, the editor, and James Pembroke, the magazine's proprietor, were also charmed by Judith, and, as a result, gave Judith one of the annual *Oldie* Awards.

Email from DW, 11th September, 2018
Dear Judith,
Thank you so much for taking the time to join us for the IF… *screening. It was lovely to see you, and I know* The Oldie *folk were thrilled you came. Hopefully you didn't hate the film quite as much as 50 years ago… but I won't be upset if you did!*
David.

Judith's enviable energy was also splendidly evident in Alan Yentob's brilliant BBC Imagine documentary called *Hitler, the Tiger and Me*, filmed as a celebration of Judith's 90th birthday. There was a sequence showing Judith speedily ascending, even skipping up, the staircase to her workroom at the top of the house. When Jacqui and I jokingly accused her of showing off for the camera, she told us with satisfaction that several takes had been required! The informative and moving programme took Judith back to Berlin to see the home she was forced to flee at the age of nine, when her father, Alfred Kerr, the distinguished writer and theatre critic, and outspoken opponent of the Nazis, was on Hitler's death list, and the family managed to escape. At our next lunch Judith was clearly pleased with the reaction to the programme. She was surprised, she said, to be 'accosted in the street' several times by people who recognised her from the programme. She had clearly found the experience of revisiting her childhood home quite emotional. The house, unsurprisingly, looked quite different now, although the garden and the steps leading to the front door were exactly as she remembered them.

Judith's positive approach to life and her optimism were endearing and often uplifting. When Tom, her husband, died, after such a long and happy marriage, her grief was without doubt all-consuming. Jacqui and I first got to know her when she was emerging from her overwhelming sadness. She said, philosophically one day, 'the world is full of widows'. And indeed she began to enjoy once again the company of her widowed friends, particularly the actress Geraldine McEwan, who had recorded the audio book version of *The Tiger Who Came to Tea*. When Katinka killed a mouse and brought it indoors, as a present perhaps, Judith wistfully told us that she buried it in the garden – 'There's only so much one can do for a mouse'. When her house was burgled, Judith didn't dwell on the unpleasantness of the situation. She told us how impressed she was with the policeman who came to take her statement – 'he was so careful,' she said, 'that when crossing out, he used a ruler!' She calmly coped with malfunctioning hearing aids, and had no hesitation in having her cataracts removed.

She said, with a smile, that she had wanted stronger glasses, 'but there aren't any!' She once told us she had been worried that her memory was failing. There was a particular word she couldn't remember. But when the word came back to her, it was 'dementia', and she was hugely relieved that this meant she didn't have it…

Judith revelled in the new lease of creative life she discovered in her final years, but, as she grew older, it naturally took its toll. By then she was much in demand for interviews and events, often travelling miles in a day with her much-loved publicity person, Philippa Perry. Once, on the phone, she admitted to me that she was exhausted. She said she was displaying every symptom of overwork 'but it's not the work that exhausts me'.

She had a brave and humorous attitude towards death, which I don't think she feared. On a ledge by her front door there was a signed instruction to not resuscitate her if unconscious. And she was an ardent supporter of assisted dying. She felt that one should be able to say, when appropriate, 'It's been lovely, but now that's it! Then you simply press a button…'

Judith could joke about death too. She told us that when she was writing and illustrating *Goodbye, Mog*, the book that surprised everybody when Mog was killed off, 'I had this funny dream. It was my funeral. The children were there. Afterwards they said, "Now what shall we do? Let's go to McDonald's!" They've hardly got me underground, then they go off and eat junk food!'

Another time she was talking about clearing her attic, then taking stuff to the dump at Kew. She had noticed that 'If you go to the cemetery, you turn left, and to the dump, you turn right… Rather depressing!'

In the summer of 2016, Judith had to have an operation on her hand. When she returned home, she phoned to tell us about how things had gone. Her bravery and stoicism were again much in evidence. She told us that her hand was in a sling. 'So I can't work.' But she really wanted to share her surprise and gratitude for the way her operation had been conducted. 'They gave me a local anaesthetic…

it makes you sleepy… then they do their work… then to the recovery room… then on a trolley back to my room and bed, for a cup of tea… then a rest for a while… then someone showed me the lunch menu… I had a great omelette and crème brûlée (I thought of Jacqui)… and I had to wear special disposable knickers!'

Even in early 2019, when we were aware things were getting more serious, she tried to make light of the fact that she was having various tests, going to 'a great professor in Harley Street', and that she was not eating much. 'At least I'm getting money out of Bupa,' she joked, 'and at least I'm losing weight.' This, to Jacqui and me, was not something to smile about. Judith certainly didn't have any weight to lose, let alone the half a stone she told us she had lost since last summer. But she still had the energy to attend the Oldie of the Year Awards on February 2nd at Simpson's-in-the-Strand. Judith received the award for The Oldie Tigress We'd Like to Have to Tea, and her acceptance speech included a spirited rendition of her Tiger, which included what appeared to be the roaring pounce from the play's Tigerobics sequence. And the following month, Judith enjoyed posing with her Royal Mail postbox in Barnes to celebrate World Book Day, 2019. The painted postbox faithfully featured text and artwork from Judith's best-known picture books, *The Tiger Who Came to Tea* and *Mog the Forgetful Cat*, and she was clearly delighted with it. She told Jacqui and me about it at what sadly was to be our final Depot lunch on March 17th, when her conversation was as animated and amusing as ever.

On May 11th, 2019, Judith telephoned me for what was to be the last time. She said she was 'not feeling too brilliant', surely a euphemism for saying that she thought the end was in sight. She had lost more weight. A tumour had been diagnosed, but she said 'they can't get at it'. It was difficult to reply positively, with hope, when Judith said, 'I can't believe I've become this person'. I said goodbye, trying hard not to make it sound like a final goodbye, put the phone down and stayed silent and thoughtful for quite a while. Matthew kindly rang twelve days later to tell us the sad news that Judith had died the day before, of ovarian cancer.

Next day, and all week, deserved tributes were rife. Judith's photo was on the front pages of *The Guardian* and the *Evening Standard*. Fulsome, affectionate obituaries appeared in all the newspapers, and the television stations all reported the sad news of the death of this legendary and much-loved writer and illustrator. ITV News went to Hexham, where the *Tiger* play was running, and filmed an excerpt to insert in a major story. And I was flattered to be interviewed about working with her, on the BBC News Channel. And the cartoonist Pilbrow published a poignant cartoon called *Judith Kerr's Wake*, in which sad mourners at a tea table (in black and white), are joined by an even sadder Tiger (in colour).

On February 19th, 2019, Judith had written to our producer Nick Brooke, accepting his invitation to attend a performance of the *Tiger* play at New Wimbledon Theatre on June 15th. Sadly, this was not to be.

Ian Craig, Judith's book designer, told me that, when they were working together on *The Curse of the School Rabbit*, which was to be Judith's last book, she told him of her plans for the next one. It was to be about a child, aged four or thereabouts, who had sailed to England from the Caribbean on the *Empire Windrush*. Such a story would have been not only relevant, but would have echoed her own arrival here as a child refugee. Her death has robbed us of what I'm sure would have been a special story.

On June 3rd, 2019, we all said our final farewell to Judith. Her funeral at Mortlake Crematorium was, as I think she would have wished, a simple, non-religious, unshowy celebration of a very special woman. Family, friends and colleagues gathered in an atmosphere of shock. We all, perhaps, had believed that Judith was indestructible. Beethoven recordings began and ended the service, which was introduced by Philippa Perry, Judith's much-loved PR person. Matthew spoke affectionately, Tacy read from *When Hitler Stole Pink Rabbit*, and tributes and readings were given by Ian Craig, Judith's trusted and revered book designer, Lauren Child, the children's author/illustrator much admired by Judith – the admiration was mutual – and, finally,

Judith's nephew Sir Timothy Kerr. As we all filed out, I realised that the coffin was still in view. Sometimes the coffin slides away in vision, sometimes a curtain is discreetly drawn around it. On this occasion, neither happened. As we exited, turning our backs on the coffin, I found myself feeling guilty that we were leaving Judith all on her own.

Back at the house, the guests mingled in the garden. Her much-valued neighbours, the broadcaster Peter Snow and the composer Howard Goodall were there, as well as Sarah Lawrance, who had done so much to promote Judith's work at Seven Stories in Newcastle. The *Tiger* play was represented by producers Nick Brooke and Philip Noel, as well as Jacqui and me. As we stood chatting, remembering Judith, I thought of our coffee in the garden on the mossy chairs. Before leaving, I took a couple of photos of Judith's iconic kitchen, although there were caterers in there, so I didn't get a great shot! I took another photo of Judith's front door, knowing that this would be the last time we would be visiting. Farewell, Judith. It was an honour to know you and to have had the privilege of collaborating with you.

Afterword

A happier occasion was held by HarperCollins on November 13th, 2023, at the Savoy Hotel, to celebrate Judith's centenary year. A large assembly of family, friends and industry fans enthusiastically toasted Judith's memory; Charlie Redmayne, HarperCollins CEO, made a heartfelt tribute. Matthew spoke with love and humour, and Tacy read some of her mother's words. A party atmosphere that Judith would have loved. And I would have loved to share with her the *Netmums* review of our play that had been published three months earlier. Zoe Craig analysed in affectionate detail the structure of the play, exploring how it works for its young audience. Judith, like me, would have been delighted by this understanding appraisal of our collaboration.

Judith Kerr at work in her studio at her home in Barnes, 2003
© Associated Press / Alamy Stock Photo

Coco Pops! Young Matthew Kneale at the kitchen table © Nigel Kneale

Front cover of DW's family copy of *The Tiger Who Came to Tea*, First paperback edition (1973)

DW and Judith Kerr outside her house in Barnes © Jacqui Wood

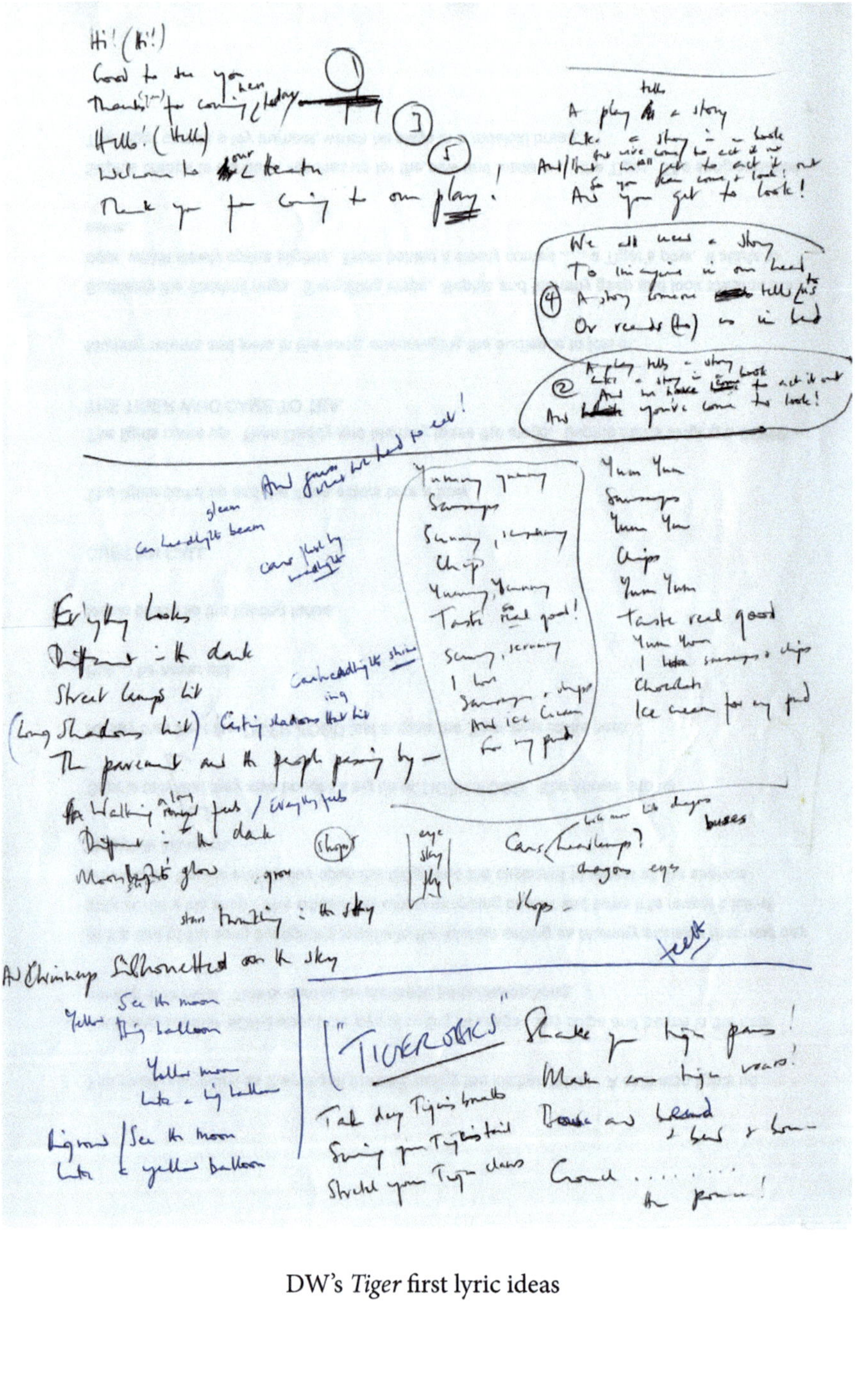

DW's *Tiger* first lyric ideas

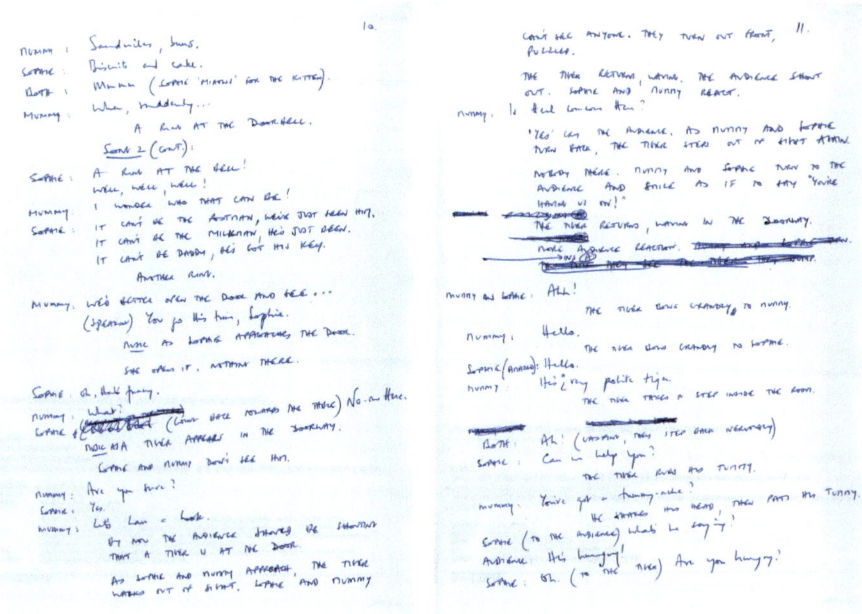

10.

MUMMY: Sandwiches, buns.
SOPHIE: Biscuits and cake.
BOTH: Mmmm (SOPHIE 'MIAOWS' FOR THE KITTEN).
MUMMY: When, suddenly…

A RING AT THE DOORBELL.

Song 2 (CONT.):

SOPHIE: A RING AT THE BELL!
WELL, WELL, WELL!
I WONDER WHO THAT CAN BE!
MUMMY: IT CAN'T BE THE POSTMAN, WE'VE JUST SEEN HIM.
SOPHIE: IT CAN'T BE THE MILKMAN, HE'S JUST BEEN.
IT CAN'T BE DADDY, HE'S GOT HIS KEY.

ANOTHER RING.

MUMMY: WE'D BETTER OPEN THE DOOR AND SEE…
(SPEAKING) You go this time, Sophie.

MUSIC AS SOPHIE APPROACHES THE DOOR.

SHE OPENS IT. NOTHING THERE.

SOPHIE: Oh, that's funny.
MUMMY: What?
SOPHIE: (LOOKS BACK TOWARDS THE TABLE) No-one there.

MUSIC AS A TIGER APPEARS IN THE DOORWAY.

SOPHIE AND MUMMY DON'T SEE HIM.

MUMMY: Are you sure?
SOPHIE: Yes.
MUMMY: Let's have a look.

BY NOW THE AUDIENCE SHOULD BE SHOUTING THAT A TIGER IS AT THE DOOR.

AS SOPHIE AND MUMMY APPROACH, THE TIGER WALKS OUT OF SIGHT. SOPHIE AND MUMMY

11.

CAN'T SEE ANYONE. THEY TURN OUT FRONT, PUZZLED.

THE TIGER RETURNS, WAVING. THE AUDIENCE SHOUT OUT. SOPHIE AND MUMMY REACT.

MUMMY: Is there someone there?

'YES' SAY THE AUDIENCE. AS MUMMY AND SOPHIE TURN BACK, THE TIGER STEPS OUT OF SIGHT AGAIN.

NOBODY THERE. MUMMY AND SOPHIE TURN TO THE AUDIENCE AND SMILE AS IF TO SAY "YOU'RE HAVING US ON!"

THE TIGER RETURNS, WAVING IN THE DOORWAY.

MORE AUDIENCE REACTION.

MUMMY AND SOPHIE: Ahh!

THE TIGER BOWS GRANDLY TO MUMMY.

MUMMY: Hello.

THE TIGER BOWS GRANDLY TO SOPHIE.

SOPHIE (AMAZED): Hello.
MUMMY: He's a very polite tiger.

THE TIGER TAKES A STEP INSIDE THE ROOM.

BOTH: Ah! (GASPING, THEY STEP BACK NERVOUSLY)
SOPHIE: Can we help you?

THE TIGER RUBS HIS TUMMY.

MUMMY: You've got a tummy-ache?

HE SHAKES HIS HEAD, THEN PATS HIS TUMMY.

SOPHIE (TO THE AUDIENCE): What's he saying?
AUDIENCE: He's hungry!
SOPHIE: Oh. (TO THE TIGER) Are you hungry?

DW's handwritten pages of the original *Tiger* script

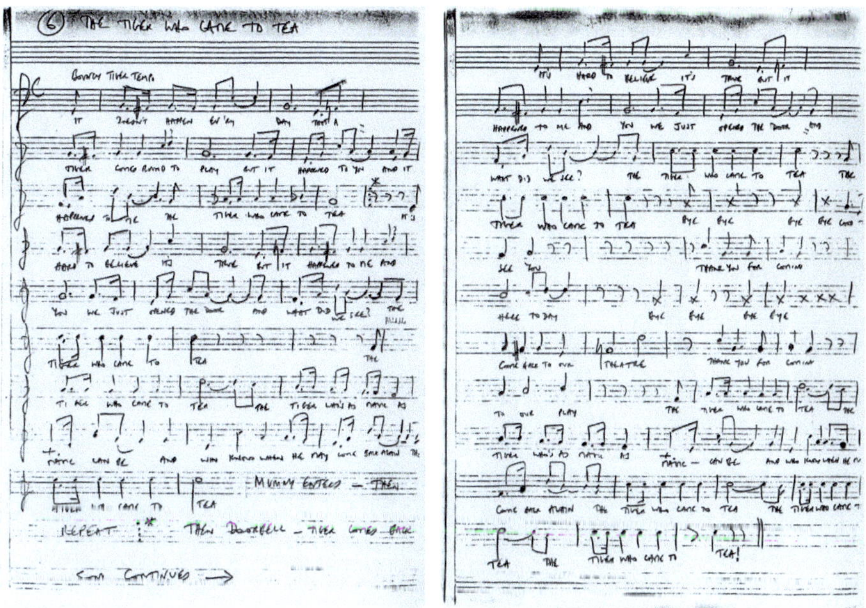

DW's first music score for the *Tiger* title song

Susie Caulcutt's set design model for Tiger
© Cultural Heritage Digitisation, London / Ken Jackson

Susie Caulcutt's set for *The Tiger Who Came to Tea* © Robert Day

On stage, Judith Kerr takes tea with (L to R) Jenanne Redman (Mummy), Alan Atkins (Daddy/Tiger), Matthew Dudley (Tiger understudy/ASM) and Abbey Norman (Sophie), Vaudeville Theatre, 2011 (Photographer unknown)

Sophie hugs the Tiger – in the book and in the play! Illustration: Reprinted by permission of HarperCollins Publishers Ltd © (Judith Kerr) (1973). Photograph: Sophie (Jocelyn Zackon) and Tiger (David Scotland) © Robert Day

Reviews

The Tiger Who Came to Tea

Editorial Staff | London's West End | 8 July 2011

Dramatist David Wood has had some practice turning much loved children's books into plays so it is no surprise that he has produced a lively and faithful adaptation of Judith Kerr's classic storybook *The Tiger Who Came to Tea*.

This 55-minute show at the Vaudeville Theatre tells the story of Sophie and her mum visited by the big cat with a very big appetite, just as they are about to have their tea.

The play is written first and foremost for children. They are included in the action right from the start when the three actors mingle amongst them; throughout the play they are encouraged to join in the songs. This can of course get a little tedious for adults, but it definitely kept the younger ones amused. There are some attempts at education with counting featuring prominently, but it is the physical comedy, which gets the children laughing.

Movement director Emma Clayton deserves praise; there are some great slapstick sequences which had the young audience in fits of giggles; and there were some sleights of hand which even had a few of the adults wondering how they did it.

Set and costume designer, Susie Caulcutt did not stray far from Judith Kerr's illustrations; all the cast members were dressed exactly as in the book. And the cardboard kitchen was almost exactly the same.

Abbey Norman manages to play the little girl Sophie very convincingly, which is always difficult when adult actors play children. Jenanne Redman plays Sophie's mother with enthusiastic energy but it is Alan Atkins as Sophie's father, the milkman, postman and the tiger who gets the most laughs. As daddy his great comic timing and flaying limbs turned breakfast time into a Chaplinesque routine as he manages to put the tea cosy on his head and almost put his shoes in the toaster. And his polite tiger, helped by Clayton's movement direction, was delightful.

Judging by the shouts and laughter of the mostly pre-school audience they were entertained for the full duration and hopefully it will lead their parents to dig out the original to read to them.

Joanna Ing

★★★★★

The *WhatsOnStage* review of the first West End season of *Tiger* at the Vaudeville Theatre, 2011 © WhatsOnStage

Tiger card from Judith Kerr to DW and the cast to congratulate them on their Olivier Award nomination, 2012

"Earlier that year I had given a talk at the Jewish Book Festival. It was weird, because it was held in a hotel across the road from where we had lived when we had first come to London and where we had been bombed out. There were lots of questions, so it went on for quite a long time, and I was feeling tired and vaguely haunted by memories at the end, when I was handed a letter with what seemed a wild suggestion.

A theatre producer called Nick Brooke wanted to turn *The Tiger Who Came to Tea* (which takes about three minutes to read) into a one-hour stage play. At first I just thought it was ridiculous, but then I thought, why not, and made an appointment to go and see him. He was clearly very professional, and totally serious. It still seemed a mad idea, but I was having tea with David Wood and his wife Jacqui the following week, and I asked him what he thought. David, of course, has written just about every bit of children's theatre there is, and when he said, rather to my surprise, that he thought he could make it work, we agreed to give it a go.

We met a few times to talk about the sort of thing it should be, and then he wrote it, and there it was – fifty-five minutes of theatre, using the story just as it was, but with songs (composed by himself), and magic and lots of audience participation. He also directed it – it was all done on a shoestring – and when I went to an early rehearsal,

Below: Scenes from the stage version of *The Tiger Who Came to Tea*

I was brought up short by the set, which looked exactly like the drawing in the book. There were two young actresses playing Sophie and her mother, and a very good young actor called Alan Atkins playing the tiger, the father and three other characters, and the whole thing just felt effortlessly right. It opened at the Bloomsbury Theatre in August and it was an immediate success. It toured on and off and then in 2011 it came to the Vaudeville Theatre in London for the summer season. And in 2012, when it opened at the Lyric, it was made nominated for an Olivier award!

It was a huge piece of luck for me. It was wonderful to make contact again with drama, which, since my BBC days, I had always loved. And it is oddly moving to see a theatre full of three-year-olds spellbound by this singing and dancing version of a bedtime story I once told my little daughter so many years ago. I wished Tom could have seen it, but it was nice to remember that David had once acted in one of Tom's plays, and that Tom had told me how very good he had been."

Above (pages 61 and 62): extract from Judith Kerr's *Creatures*, her memories of working with DW on the stage adaptation of *The Tiger Who Came to Tea*. Reprinted by permission of HarperCollins Publishers Ltd © (Judith Kerr) (2013)

London (West End)

The Tiger Who Came to Tea

Theatre
Lyric Theatre, London
July 2-September 7
Reviewer: Francesca Whiting

It is no easy task maintaining the attention of toddlers and young children for almost an hour, but David Wood's stage adaptation of Judith Kerr's much-loved picture book succeeds in capturing the imaginations of every child present.

With its beautiful illustrations and gentle humour, Kerr's book has been a hit with parents and children since it was first published in 1968. Wood's production manages to capture its inherent mischief: the tiger in particular is an inspired creation. He's presented as a dandy who retains impeccable manners as he devours every morsel of food and drink in the house.

The show is interlaced with short song and dance sequences. One highlight is Sophie (Abbey Norman) and her mum's (Jenanne Redman's) dance with the elegant, tail-wagging tiger (Matthew Dudley). The audience is invited to join in with the singing on several occasions.

Part of the enjoyment of the book is the illustrations' snapshot of life in 1960s London: the kitchen units of this era, Sophie's mother's chic clothes, the old Routemaster bus. Much of this has been woven into the stage adaptation: the props, costumes and designer Susie Caulcutt's simple kitchen set whisk you back to this period.

While the theatre programme advises that the show is for the ages of three and above, my two-year-old son was hooked for the entire 55 minutes.

The action moves at such a fast pace that it's perfect for young children, while parents can sit back and enjoy its eccentric charm.

★★★★★ **Packed with song, dance and humour, children and parents will enjoy David Wood's stage adaptation of Judith Kerr's picture book**

Authors: Judith Kerr (book), David Wood (adaptation)
Directors: David Wood, Emma Clayton
Design: Susie Caulcutt (set and costume), Tony Simpson (lighting designer), Shock Productions (sound design), Peter Pontzen (musical director), Emma Clayton (choreographer)
Technical: Nick May (production manager), Angie Burns (wardrobe supervisor)
Cast: Abbey Norman, Matthew Dudley, Jenanne Redman
Producer: KW and NB Ltd
Running time: 55mins

Top left: Judith Kerr's dedication in her book Creatures, 2013

Top right: Clare Morpurgo at the presentation of The BookTrust's Lifetime Achievement Award to Judith Kerr, 2016 © DW

Left. The Stage review of *Tiger*, July 2014 © The Stage

Judith Kerr with DW and *Tiger* cast members, past and present, when DW was awarded the Action for Children's Arts J M Barrie Award, 2017 (Photographer unknown)

First Tiger visit to China, 2017. Chinese promoters' team with (L to R) Ashley Tucker (Mummy), Jacob Jackson (understudy Tiger/ASM), Abbey Norman (Sophie), Harry Holmes (Daddy/Tiger) and Katie Arundell (understudy/wardrobe) © Graeme Reid

Judith Kerr and DW with the *Tiger* company at an Oxford Playhouse event in 2018, organised by The Story Museum, to celebrate the 50th anniversary of the publication of *The Tiger Who Came to Tea* © Adrian Cassidy, The Story Museum

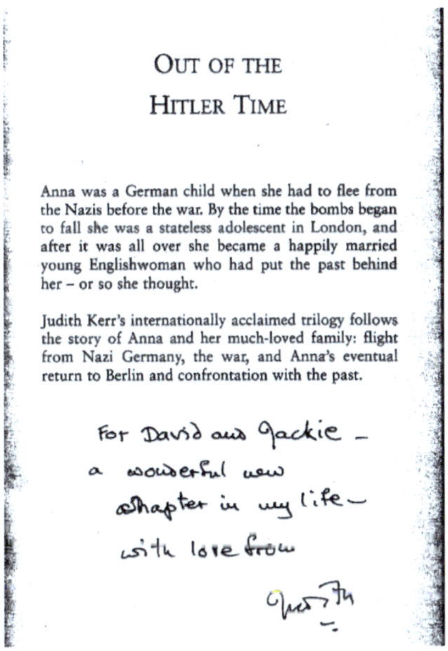

OUT OF THE HITLER TIME

Anna was a German child when she had to flee from the Nazis before the war. By the time the bombs began to fall she was a stateless adolescent in London, and after it was all over she became a happily married young Englishwoman who had put the past behind her – or so she thought.

Judith Kerr's internationally acclaimed trilogy follows the story of Anna and her much-loved family: flight from Nazi Germany, the war, and Anna's eventual return to Berlin and confrontation with the past.

For David and Jackie –
a wonderful new
chapter in my life –
with love ~~from~~
Judith

Judith Kerr's dedication in her book *Out of the Hitler Time*

Judith Kerr (demonstrating Tigerobics!) at the Oldie of the Year Awards, 2019 © NEIL SPENCE / Alamy Stock Photo

Left: Judith Kerr with her celebratory postbox in Barnes, 2019 © Paul Davey / SWNS

Below: Judith Kerr's celebratory postbox in Barnes, 2019 © Paul Davey / SWNS

Judith Kerr and DW enjoying lunch at The Depot, Barnes, 2019 © Jacqui Wood

Jacqui Wood and Judith Kerr, The Depot, 2019 © DW

Private Eye marked Judith Kerr's death with a tribute by the cartoonist Giles Pilbrow, 2019 © Giles Pilbrow

Why The Tiger Who Came To Tea is the BEST show for kids ... EVER!

Zoe Craig, Netmums Associate Editor (Local), 22 Aug 2023

I've seen *The Tiger Who Came To Tea* live on stage FOUR TIMES now, and I've decided it's the greatest stage show ever created for under 8s. Here's why...

Are you planning a trip to see *The Tiger Who Came To Tea* live on stage? You're in luck! I think it's a near-perfect piece of theatre for kids. Read on to check if this musical play will suit your kids, in this 'all you need to know' review.

I've seen A LOT of theatre shows aimed at kids. But for the last few years, I've come back to the same show each time: *The Tiger Who Came To Tea*. Here's why I think it's such a brilliant musical for kids under 8.

1. The gentle beginning

The house lights are still up. Three smiling characters appear on stage, slowly, gently, waving and greeting the audience. They're our actors. We're encouraged to shout hello! Already your kid is engaged in the show, before it's even begun. Kids and grown-ups in the audience then join in the welcome song, where it's explained we're about to see a story told on stage. What a perfect beginning.

2. The comedy

What do under-8s love? Laughing. Particularly at funny grown-ups being silly. And this show will make them laugh. There's visual gags; slapstick; physical humour and more from Daddy, the Milkman AND the Postman...

Before THAT moment – the arrival of the Tiger – your kids will already have been giggling, sniggering and chortling away. They're feeling, I'm sure, safe and happy in their seats as the theatrical magic unfolds...

3. The structure

What else do little kids love? Structure. Tick, tock, tick, tock, time moves on, literally, as the clock moves. We all count (everyone can shout out the numbers!) and it's time for another snack… which will be interrupted by another ring at the door, another character.

There are little surprises here and there, but they all fit into a simple, safe structure: perfect for little kids already experiencing sensory overload on their trip to the theatre.

4. The suspense

So, no spoilers here, we ALL know what's coming. A TIGER! It's on the poster! It's in the title! We've read the book! But WOW, the phenomenal way that Tiger appears on stage. No jump scares here. Anything 'scary' is dialled right down. We're in control: we even see him BEFORE the characters on stage. We need to shout to tell them he's there!

If you're worried your kid will be scared of the Tiger, show them pictures beforehand. Talk it through. And then trust that once they're screaming at Sophie and her Mummy to JUST TURN ROUND and see him too, I'm pretty sure they won't be scared of the Tiger any more.

5. That Tiger

What can I say? He's HUGE! Stripey! Colourful! Furry! And completely gorgeous. Who can resist falling in love with such an incredible stage presence?

All the kids I know who have seen this play have LOVED that Tiger. Silent, but SO expressive; cheeky and totally charming; he really is something very special.

6. The songs

The songs in *The Tiger Who Came To Tea* are also wonderful: clear and simple; short enough to keep your kids' attention; and beautifully sung by the cast.

There's not one but TWO opportunities to get onto your feet, dance, sing and join in. Again, these seem to come at just the right moment when any littler audience members are getting restless after sitting still.

- Swing your tiger tails, stretch your tiger claws, and roar your tiger roars with the Tiger
- Then later, in the cafe, you stand up again, do the actions, and sing along about 'yummy, yummy sausages, scrummy, scrummy chips', and all the rest

When the stars come out and the family sings about how children see the world transformed 'in the dark', I always get something in my eye.

And I defy you to come away without singing, 'It's hard to believe it's true, but it happened to me and you; we just opened the door, and what did we see?

'*The Tiger who came to tea*!' I was stunned to hear how my kids, aged just 4, had picked up the songs' words perfectly after the show.

7. The stage magic

The Tiger devouring the buns! Those disappearing sandwiches! Slurping down all the orange juice! When the Tiger empties the contents of the cupboard and the fridge! The self-filling shopping basket! Magic.

Seats: If you have a nervous kid, sitting further back in the stalls, or even upstairs where possible, it might feel safer for the moment that big Tiger reveal takes place. We found free booster seats at the side of the stalls.

Interval: There's no interval, so get your snacks ready before the show starts!

Text: ©Netmums, the parenting community you can trust through the highs and lows of family life

Production images: © Robert Day

Flyer (front & back) for the Summer Season of *The Tiger Who Came to Tea* at Theatre Royal, Haymarket, 2024 (Spot the date typo!)

PHILIPPA PEARCE

TOM'S MIDNIGHT GARDEN

Tom's Midnight Garden flyers – Unicorn production at the Pleasance Theatre, London (2002) & Unicorn Theatre (2005)

PHILIPPA PEARCE

Philippa Pearce OBE was born in 1920 in Great Shelford, near Cambridge. She was educated at the Perse Girls' School in Cambridge and then (on a state scholarship) at Girton College, Cambridge, where she read English and then History. During the War she worked as a Temporary Civil Servant, and afterwards joined the School Broadcasting Department (Radio) of the BBC, working there as a scriptwriter and producer for thirteen years. In 1958 she became an editor in the Educational Department of the Clarendon Press (OUP) in Oxford, before returning to London as Children's Editor at André Deutsch Ltd (1960–7). Alongside this part-time position, she was writing and producing for radio, both for adults and for children, book-reviewing (mainly for *The Guardian* and *The Times Literary Supplement*), lecturing and storytelling. *Tom's Midnight Garden* was published in 1958 and went on to join the pantheon of children's classics. Philippa married Martin Christie, a fruit-grower, in 1963, and they had one daughter, Sally. Martin died soon after her birth and, in 1973, Philippa and her daughter moved into the country to live in Great Shelford, where Philippa had grown up. They lived very near the Mill House and its garden, upon which Philippa closely based the settings for *Tom's Midnight Garden*. The local Cambridgeshire countryside and the river nearby appear in her other books, including *Minnow on the Say*, *A Dog So Small*, and in some of her short stories. In 1993 Philippa became a Fellow of the Royal Society of Literature, and in 1995 she received the honorary degree of Doctor of Letters from Hull University. She was awarded the OBE 'for services to children's literature' in 1997. She continued to write up until her death in 2006.

Key Players

Philippa Pearce	Author
David Wood	Author/playwright/adapter
Tony Graham	Artistic Director of Unicorn Theatre/Director of the play
Laura Cecil	Philippa Pearce's literary agent
Frank Whitbourn	Theatre expert and mentor to DW
Chris Moxon	Administrative Director, Unicorn Theatre
Stephen McNeff	Composer of the music for the play
Sally Christie	Philippa Pearce's daughter who worked in children's publishing, and became a children's author herself
Ben Norland	Sally Christie's husband

How it all began...

It was all thanks to Tony Graham, then the Artistic Director of Unicorn Theatre for Children. We were sitting in a room at the Tate Gallery, waiting for an Action for Children's Arts board meeting to begin. Tony suggested the book *Tom's Midnight Garden* by Philippa Pearce as a possible subject for stage adaptation. I, somewhat arrogantly, dismissed the idea, saying it had already been done. Tony was sure that it hadn't, and indeed he proved to be correct. I was probably thinking of the BBC Children's Television adaptation. To be honest, I had never read the book, but recognised it was a classic, with a very well-known title. I made enquiries and found that the stage rights were indeed available. Surprised, but rather excited by this news, I read the book, loved it, and wondered why the story had never been staged. Was Philippa Pearce not interested in a theatre production? Did she feel that the necessary two time zones might make it impossibly tricky to stage?

It was encouraging when Philippa agreed to meet me. She invited me to lunch on 11th December, 1998. Philippa greeted me at the door of her picturesque cottage in Great Shelford, near Cambridge. She was a sparkly, friendly host. She was then seventy-eight years old. I was delighted to find that she was an inveterate lover of the theatre, who travelled regularly to London to see productions by the National Theatre and the Royal Shakespeare Company, and was intrigued by the possibility of *Tom* being adapted. I explained my initial thoughts, using costume more than set design to illustrate the 1950s and the Victorian periods. I also told Philippa how important it was for me to see the story through the young boy Tom's eyes. Over lunch, Philippa told me the cottage she was living in was but yards away from the Mill House where she had lived as a child, and which was indeed the setting for *Tom's Midnight Garden*.

Philippa was very entertaining and witty, and I was amused when she offered me some 'Stinky Bishop' cheese, which ignorantly I thought was a family expression rather than the name of a real cheese! Once Philippa had given the go-ahead for me to do some work, I told her I would do a treatment or synopsis, which she would be the first to see and, I hoped, approve. She seemed genuinely interested in the prospect of a play, and I sensed that she would always be a positive participant in its creation. This proved to be the case, as our correspondence confirms. Philippa's comments and suggestions were extremely helpful, and we rarely had a serious difference of opinion. She was, however, a little concerned about some of the flowery language I had taken from the narration in the book and put into Tom's mouth as he told his story. I told her I thought this was reasonable dramatic licence, and she graciously agreed to see how this would work in performance.

The Unicorn production went into rehearsal. I attended several sessions and was very impressed by Tony's direction and the attitude of the actors, who clearly loved the story. Stephen McNeff had composed some hauntingly appropriate music, which was played live by talented actor-musicians within the company. The play opened at the Pleasance Theatre in north London. Philippa and her agent, Laura Cecil, came to a special performance on a Sunday afternoon. We waited for the play to start, but frustratingly the stage lighting refused to work. I was concerned that much of the atmospheric quality of the production would be lost, but thankfully the cast were magnificent, and it became clear how strong Philippa's story is. The audience were involved and captivated in spite of watching the play under harsh working light and with the house lights full on!

The play later toured and went to New York, only days after the horrific events of 9/11. My wife Jacqui and I were humbled by the resilience of the New Yorkers, who not only brought their children to see the play, but gave it a great reaction.

To my delight, Philippa and I continued to meet regularly, often for lunch in her favourite Ely restaurant. I introduced her to Jacqui, who often accompanied us. And Philippa introduced me to her daughter Sally and son-in-law Ben, and their two sons Nat and Will. I treasured our meetings, and together we took part in the occasional Q&A session after performances of the play, particularly when Birmingham Stage Company toured it. I was privileged to read her new book, *The Little Gentleman*, pre-publication. In her letters she had written about the discipline she needed to complete the book, adding that once it was finally finished, 'I shall frisk'!

Philippa died unexpectedly in 2006, aged eighty-six. Not long before, we had both attended a special children's book event at Roehampton University. That was the last time I saw her. I was privileged to attend her funeral; the crematorium was absolutely packed with her family, friends and admirers. Later on, I was delighted to be invited to be one of a group of Philippa's circle, who wished to arrange a regular Lecture in her name. Homerton College, Cambridge, where Philippa had regularly talked to students – including my daughter Katherine – offered to host the event, and Julia Eccleshare, Victor Watson and I shared the inaugural Philippa Pearce Lecture, which has since become an important annual celebration, featuring top children's authors discussing children's literature as well as remembering Philippa's genius.

Happily, the play lives on, and has had several prestigious productions, notably at the Theatre by the Lake, Keswick, and the Minack Theatre in Cornwall. Many amateur and school productions have also been mounted. Philippa's story will never date, and hopefully the play will have a long life too. Philippa became a dear friend, and I much miss her.

DW

'AN EXPERIMENT WITH TIME'

Correspondence with Philippa Pearce 1998 – 2006

24. XI. 98

Dear David Wood,

Here is the map, as promised.

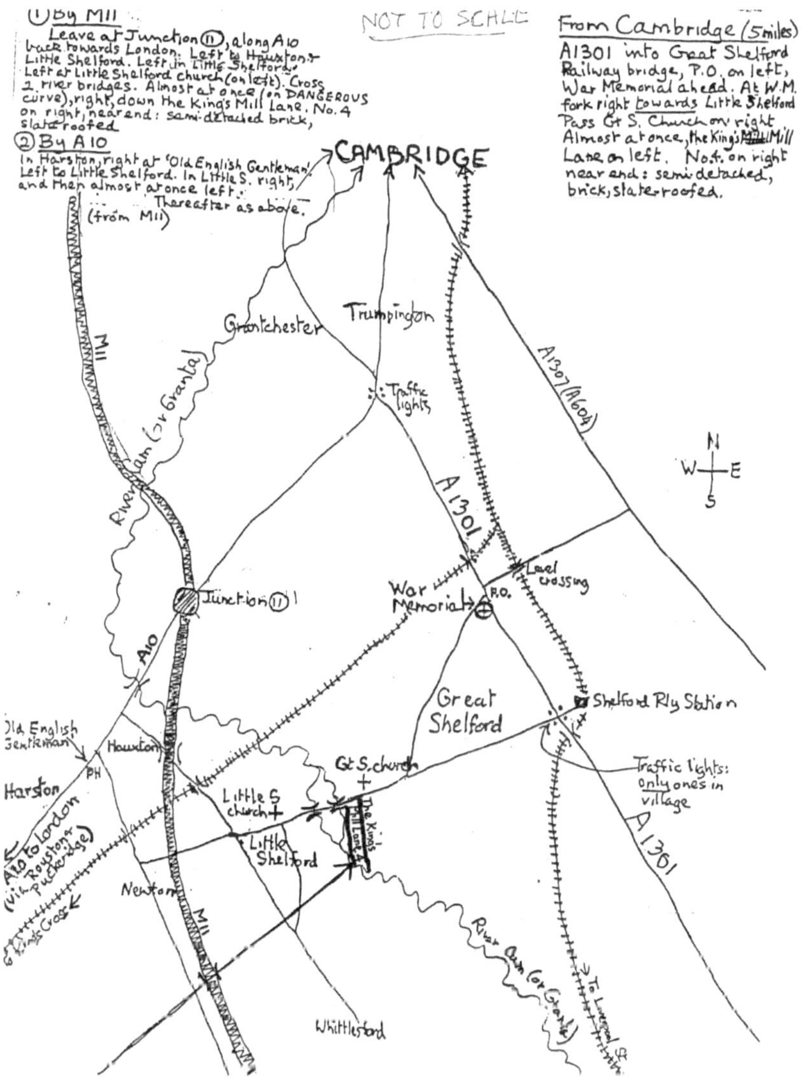

Looking forward to seeing you
on Friday December 11 (for lunch)
soon after 12 noon. Talk then.
In haste
All good wishes
Philippa Pearce
Do telephone if there's any problem

14 December, 1998

Dear Philippa Pearce,

I so enjoyed meeting you. Thank you so much for the splendid lunch and for giving me so much of your time. Also, I was thrilled that you were able to come and see the MAGIC AND MUSIC SHOW on Sunday.

If you feel able to entrust me with the job of adapting TOM'S MIDNIGHT GARDEN for the stage, I would do my utmost to keep faithful to the spirit of the book, sending you ideas and a draft synopsis before getting down to the script. Ideally I would try to find a theatre who would present the first production. Certainly it is worth trying The National and the RSC.

I hope very much that we might meet again soon. Greetings from my daughter, Katherine, who sat next to you once in the dining hall at Homerton!

Thank you so much for giving me a copy of DREAD AND DELIGHT. I have already read the Barbara Griffiths story – occasionally a child comes to help on stage who would warrant the same treatment!

Please accept copies of THE GINGERBREAD MAN and*

* Since its first production in 1976, my musical play *The Gingerbread Man* had become very popular, enjoying West End seasons, repertory theatre productions and UK tours.

THEATRE FOR CHILDREN,[*2] *with my thanks, admiration and every good wish.*

Yours sincerely,

David

Encs.

19.i.99.

Dear David,

You must think I am very rude – indeed, I AM very rude – not to have replied earlier to your letter of December 14. Especially I should have thanked you for the 2 books, which I read – I read Theatre for Children very earnestly indeed.

What you wrote chimed in, of course, with what we discussed when you were here; and I do feel at ease with your approach. I should like to be consulted on the adaptation, in the way you suggest. But I have a strong feeling – touch wood, of course! – that we shall not be in serious disagreement.

I have already told Laura[*3] (as you probably know) that I would like things to go ahead, and she is in touch with OUP.[*4]

So it only remains for me to wish you A HAPPY NEW YEAR (and drop in for lunch any time; it was most enjoyable for me).

Philippa

25 January, 1999

Dear Philippa Pearce,

Many thanks indeed for your kind letter of January 19th*. I certainly wasn't thinking that you were rude! I thought you should have a few weeks in which to read my book, before replying to my letter! Anyway, I'm delighted that you are happy*

---

*2 This is the book I wrote with Janet Grant, *Theatre for Children: A Guide to Writing, Adapting, Acting and Directing* (Faber 1997).

*3 Laura Cecil, distinguished children's book agent, who represented Philippa Pearce.

*4 Oxford University Press, the publishers of *Tom's Midnight Garden*.

for me to have a go at TOM'S MIDNIGHT GARDEN. I promise you that I will do my best to be faithful, and to keep you in touch with all developments, synopses, first draft etc. etc.

You may be interested to know that Unicorn Theatre are very keen indeed to present the première, possibly in the year 2000 or 2001. Tony Graham, the Artistic Director, is a fan of the book, and indeed it was in a conversation with him that the idea of approaching you first came up.

I suppose it could be argued that we should have a stab at the National, for the Cottesloe, before committing to Unicorn. On the other hand, Unicorn specialises in work for the target age group, and it might be best to join forces with them from the outset. What do you think?

Unicorn is having to move out of the Arts Theatre in a couple of months' time. They are doing a season at the Pleasance Theatre, in north London, and meanwhile are trying to find a more permanent home, or, indeed, to get enough funding to build their own theatre. So I'm not quite sure where TOM'S MIDNIGHT GARDEN would open…

I have just finished adapting Roald Dahl's THE TWITS – a very different undertaking! The book is really rather unpleasant, but children absolutely love it, and I can see that the subversiveness is very appealing. The play will open at the Belgrade, Coventry, in March.

Meanwhile things seem to be quite busy here, trying to plan ahead, and also preparing my Collected Editions for Methuen Drama.

Next time I am anywhere near Cambridge, I will hope to see you. I much enjoyed meeting you and our conversation. And I was delighted that you were able to come and see the MAGIC AND MUSIC SHOW.

All good wishes.
Yours sincerely,
David

8.ii.99

Dear David,

Thank you for your letter of January 25th about the Tom's Midnight Garden project.

As far as the National (Cottesloe) versus the Unicorn goes, I really think you have so much more experience in this whole area that your opinion is the one that matters.

I have only top-of-the-head observations to make. There is always an element of dismissive snobbery about children's literature, which probably extends to children's theatre, I suspect. Would the National feel this about a play already associated with the Unicorn? For that reason only, might it be better to try the National first?

But you say the Unicorn 'are very keen indeed': that is tempting. Only a magician such as yourself can really see the potential of birds in the hand and birds in the bushes.

Do keep me posted on all this, when you have the time – and do call again when you're anywhere near.

All good wishes

Philippa

15 February, 1999

Dear Philippa,

Many thanks for your letter of February 8th.

Tony Graham, who runs the Unicorn, has invited me to a meeting on February 26th to discuss things further.

I might mention the idea to the National before the meeting, just in case. You are quite right in saying that children's theatre is seen by many in our profession as being in the second or third division! In fairness, however, the National have been doing more productions for children in recent years than ever before…

I will keep you up to date, of course!

Meanwhile, my adaptation of Dahl's THE TWITS goes into rehearsal on March 1st. Fingers crossed!

I have been busy correcting the most appalling set of proofs I have ever seen! Methuen are doing Collected Editions of my plays – two volumes with four plays in each. There seemed to be half a dozen mistakes or more on every page! Apparently the typesetter was chosen because they were extremely fast (and, I suspect, inexpensive!). The result has been hours of ploughing through hundreds of pages. I'm sure it will be worth it in the end.

We have been invited to take a production of THE GINGERBREAD MAN to Dubai for a week! This involves rather a lot of advance planning, particularly the transportation of the set and costumes in a container, by sea, three weeks before we even begin rehearsals! I have a cast who have done it before, so hopefully everything will come together well. I have never been to that part of the world, and, apparently, this will be the first time a children's play has been performed there. Maybe it'll be the beginning of something...

I do hope you are well and as busy as you would like to be!

All good wishes.

Yours sincerely,

David

Five months then went by, during which I worked on an initial treatment and synopsis of the play, keeping in touch with Philippa from time to time.

18.VII.99 from Philippa Pearce

Dear David,

Thank you for the up-date. <u>Very</u> nice to think that things are still going forward – and (because I've a small job in hand at the moment) not <u>too</u> fast.

I look forward to your treatment/synopsis.

All good wishes for the Collected Plays

And to you

Philippa

05 October, 1999

Dear Philippa,

This is just to let you know that I went to the National Film Theatre on Sunday and saw the film of TOM'S MIDNIGHT GARDEN.

I know you were disappointed, and part of me didn't really want to see it! But then I thought I ought to see how they had approached the material.

On a positive note, I must tell you that the very full house thoroughly enjoyed it. It got applause at the end! And the children were certainly listening, which is always a good sign.

I was not very happy with some of the special effects, which seemed too cartoon-like, if you know what I mean. And I got rather annoyed by the "development" of Uncle Alan and Aunt Gwen – their apparent yearning for a child seemed somewhat twee to me. This often happens when film producers try to develop characters that so-called star actors are going to play!

My main worry was that TOM seemed far too old. Would you agree with me? I know you never specify his age in the novel, but it seemed very odd to me to see this confident 14-looking-year-old being spoon-fed medicine by his Aunt!

Do you agree? How old do you feel TOM is? My own feeling is that he is too young to notice or understand that Hattie is growing up. In many ways the whole point is that he has no sexual awareness yet and therefore her blossoming relationship with Barty goes completely over his head. In the film, however, he appears to be developing feelings more than friendship for Hattie. But maybe that is just simply because he is being played by someone a little old for the part.

Having said all that, I'm not sure what will happen in the stage version! Will it be possible to find a real boy of the right age who has the sensitivity and skill to "carry" the whole piece? I'm not sure! Or do we need an older "boy"? Very interesting!

I have just finished my first draft of SPOT'S BIRTHDAY

PARTY, which the Oxford Playhouse will be presenting next spring. This is for pre-school children.*

Now I intend to think a lot about TOM, in the hope of having a synopsis within a few weeks. Fingers crossed!

I do hope you are well and have enjoyed a happy summer.

My teaching in Chicago seemed to go well, in spite of intense heat over there!

All good wishes.

Yours,

David

November 23 1999

Dear David,

I feel miserably guilty as I write to you. I'm used to guilt because of replying late; but this is worse.

I CANNOT find your last letter, so don't know what I ought to be writing back. Please excuse me.

Certainly, you'd seen the film of TMG, and – to my unsurprise – were not much impressed by it. Yes, I suppose the boy was too old, but he was growing all the time, in an almost frightening way.

I don't think you much liked the modern 'framing' of the story – and I thought the epilogue quite ludicrous.

Something that really annoyed me was their treatment of the skating to Ely. One saw a pair of skating feet going to and fro – to and fro – as though to say: 'Well, time passed, and they got there'. Whereas I'd always heard that one of the advantages of film is that it can open up a story – scenically, landscape-wise. And what I'd wanted to convey was leaving the rather cosy, safe, enclosed garden for the wide spaces of the Fens in winter – and the exhilaration of that.

---

* Spot, the endearing puppy, featured in several novelty books created by Eric Hill. I was granted permission to create a stage play from the books, aimed at a very young audience.

I'm sure your letter also spoke of what progress you were making on the project as a whole. But I can't remember any detail.

If you ever could spare a minute to send me a copy of your last letter… But I hate to suggest that trouble.

In extenuation of my wrong-doing (Is extenuation the right word?), I must tell you that I have been awaiting the birth of a second grandchild. And he's arrived, and all's well – Hurrah!

I'm going to London to see him to-morrow. I suddenly felt it was now or never to write to you in confession.

Many apologies again.

Philippa

29 November 1999

Dear Philippa,

Many thanks for your letter of November 23rd. Please don't feel guilty! I have been in America for nearly a month, so haven't worried about not hearing from you!

Am enclosing a copy of my last letter, although there probably isn't much in it you have missed out on!

I agree with all your comments about the film version of TMG. The modern framing of the story just made things too tricksy, in my opinion. And, yes, the skating to Ely was, forgive the pun, skated over. The exhilaration and the freedom that Hatty experiences in that episode of the book is a wonderful evocation of her spreading her wings and growing up. The filmmakers totally missed that.

I have started work on the stage version. It is quite a challenge, but I always knew it would be! One of the problems is knowing how the character of Tom can be played properly by a genuinely young actor. One of the questions I asked in my letter was how old you had imagined Tom was? I see him as no more than eight or nine, whereas in the film he seemed far too old to be complaining about the bars on the window and too old to be behaving as petulantly as sometimes the director obviously requested. I'm beginning to feel that in the play there should be as little scenery as possible. To keep on changing scenes and to go backwards and forwards in time, location-wise, could well be cumbersome. It may be we can achieve a lot through the imagination, which is partly what theatre is about! Certainly I feel I want to emphasise the almost supernatural aspects, using the ticking of the clock, the house talking to Tom, the sudden violence of the storm and the magical journeys back and forth as the genuinely theatrical elements of storytelling they really are.

I have now read the book many times and it is still as haunting as ever. It is a privilege to work on it.

Very soon I hope to be in touch with you to discuss things further.

Meanwhile, my adaptation of Roald Dahl's THE TWITS has reopened, this time in Cardiff, and seems to be working very well. My radio adaptation of SWALLOWS AND AMAZONS went out on Radio 4 over the summer and seemed to get some nice reviews. And my teaching and lecturing in America was most enjoyable. Also I was able to take my own British production of THE GINGERBREAD MAN to a theatre in New York State, where it was received very warmly.*

I do hope you are well and that we meet again before too long.

All good wishes.

Yours sincerely,

David

In early 2000 I delivered the first draft of the script to Philippa. Her first response was on the telephone. She was very supportive and enthusiastic, but told me she had several points and suggestions to make, in a letter. I was surprised and, indeed, flattered to receive her next letter, which showed how much thought she had put into her initial reaction to the play.

---

* Twenty-five years earlier, I had written the screenplay for the 1974 film version.

10.ii.2000

Dear David,

This is the letter to confirm – and somewhat extend – our recent telephone conversation about your play-script based on *Tom's Midnight Garden*. I'll go through the points, mostly minor, as they crop up, page by page.

page 5 (Uncle A's penult. speech) '…as long as you're infectious…' should be (I think) 'as long as you may be infectious'

page 7 Tom's torch (bottom) Important that this should be taken away for good? It shouldn't be an available alternative to moonlight later. (And note its use on your **page 83**)

page 9 (middle) 'Twenty-four hours… Twice twelve…' True but confusing, suggestion there might be two extra hours available every day.

page 11 first speech (Tom) This is one example of many which raises quite a large issue. By using the wording of the original narrative in speeches (or letters) you have given these a non-realistic, literary tone (e.g. 'thick beetle-browed yew trees'). You may have calculated that at certain times this heightened speech is justified by the whole atmosphere created. Something I can't properly judge (see also comment on **page 39**). Even so there are some things which would seem outside Tom's experience or knowledge e.g. **(this page)** 'a fan of peacock feathers' and **(page 12)** 'a housemaid'

page 16 bottom '…Different season…' This anticipates the winter episodes unnecessarily, I feel. Better to omit, and let the scope of the time-shifts build up gradually?

page 17 (middle); see also **page 29–30.** Since writing the book, I've come to feel uneasy about my invention of the King of the Fairies episode, simply because I once received an abusive letter from a group of (older?) girls playing on the double-entendre of 'fairies'. Please think about this. If you still decide to keep the reference, it might help to give a name i.e. Oberon. I like the way you extended the significance of the note on page 30 ('I wanted them to help me escape.'), although what Hatty really wants now is friends rather than escape, which comes later.

page 18 (middle) I realize your need to cut down on the number of doors, and not to have greenhouse and orchard-to-potting-shed, but the conflation raises problems. Greenhouse doors are seldom, if ever, of solid wood; usually wood below, glass above: will this make Tom's transportation (I have just made this word up cf. defenestration) awkward?

page 19 (middle) 'a scream upstairs in the house' This seems rather misleading, as if co-incidentally something horrific is happening indoors. There should be a link between the sight of the tree falling and the cry e.g. 'Someone was watching from the house and was scared out of their wits.' (The book says: 'Tom heard something – a human cry – an "Oh!" of the terror he himself felt. It came from above him – from the window of one of the upper rooms.' p.56)

page 21 (top) 'Like a caged tiger…' This image seems wrong to me. I should have thought Tom might be restless in the daytime; but also subdued, even apathetic, longing for the night.

page 22 and later 'terrier on a lead' Perhaps it doesn't matter; but one would not normally have a dog on a lead in one's own garden.

page 24 (top) 'That wouldn't work.' This doesn't sound right (to me) for a late Victorian child.

page 25 (bottom) 'scrumping' This usually means stealing fruit from someone else's orchard or garden.

page 31 (Tom involved in apple throwing and catching) We've already discussed this.

page 33 Goose-feathers. I'm afraid you can't have these in the greenhouse. They belong only to the potting-shed, where Abel would pluck the goose and store the feathers in a sack for the making of pillows, feather beds etc.

page 34 Tom: I've read in the Bible about Cain and Abel. Suggest enlarge to '…about Cain's killing Abel.' Would tie up better with Hatty's account?

page 35 (bottom) 'forest outlaws' Better say Robin Hood, whom every child knows?

page 38 Tom and Hatty: The secret passage! For clarity, add 'through the hedge'?

page 39 (middle) Hatty's speech in reverie sounds so high pitched (see my comment on **page 11**). There is also a contradiction in it: in one line the river 'reaches the sea'; in the next it has an 'endless journey'

page 44 (top) The idea of a guardian angel looking after the dead parents sounds to me out of character (for Tom) and out of (his) period.

page 52 (very top) 'bringing the wood' Sounds too vague? Planks would be needed, but too heavy for Hatty. Perhaps 'bits of planking'?

page 53 Abel: '…that he haunt me not' Why bother to point out a mere typing error (haunt for hurt)? But – in my bitter experience – because the error makes sense, it can survive, to plague everybody.

page 57 Clock ticking 'like a human heart-beat… (Tom) Please, let it be Hatty's heart!' Again (see **page 11**) this (almost directly from the book's narrative bottom page 133) sounds to me rather too literary for boy's letter and speech.

page 58 For the period, James would not be 'carrying files' but 'office-ledgers' (see p.135 of book)

page 67 Is it going to be possible for Hatty to 'hide in the shadows of the clock' if she's carrying an oil-lamp?

page 68 Hatty… 'I'm meant to be resting.' Better just say 'in bed'. This helpfully opens the possibility that she wouldn't have been welcome to the family meal, anyway.

page 69 (bottom) We've already discussed the problem of Abel's being in the garden so late.

page 78 I'd like it to be clearer that the minds of Tom and his uncle work in totally different ways. Tom is seduced by his imaginings; his uncle tries to stick to pure reason. (It's true that, in the book (page 164), Uncle A is the one who first mentions Rip van Winkle, but only immediately to dismiss the legend as 'not very illuminating', in favour of 'a new point in Time which we'll call A'.)

page 80 (top) Probably better just to mention pollution, without specifying cause – which nowadays is as much from farming as industrial?

page 84 The skates would be screwed to the boot-heels and secured further down the foot by straps. It would help if Tom could say he '...rubbed the rust off Hatty's skates and oiled the leather <u>of the boots and the straps</u>.'

page 85 Tom: '...Onward, onward etc' Again. Very literary. See my note to **page 11**.

page 86 Tower-keeper's speech. King's Lynn and the sea should come at the end, as climax?

page 92 Echoing sound of dustbins. Not certainly identifiable? What about adding to Uncle A's speech on **page 93**: 'It wasn't burglars. <u>Only dustbins knocked over...</u>'?

page 97 Tom's first speech Not explicit enough. Suggest: '... Hatty was a girl <u>in Queen Victoria's reign. That began in 1837.</u>'

page 98 (nearly middle) '...a scream. Upstairs!' See my point on **page 19**. Could Mrs B answer: 'It was me! <u>I was so frightened / startled</u>. Next day...' By the way, could you omit the year (1895), which would make courtship and marriage happen so very quickly? I don't feel we need a date here, anyway.

page 99 Mrs B's first speech. For absolute clarity could we have, 'We turned <u>this</u> house into flats'?

page 101 top. I worry about Peter and secrecy; that seems to me more important than Abel's history. Here's a possible re-write:

Mrs B: And bring your brother, the one I saw at Ely.

Tom: Peter. I will – and Peter can keep a secret.

Mrs B: Our secret. etc etc

****

Oh, dear! My comments and suggestions have run on; but I hope you will see how minor they are, almost always. For your script as a whole, I have real admiration. Thank you for what you have done.

With all good wishes, (*typed letter unsigned*)

P.S. I have decided to send you – to give you a taste of the flavour of Uncle A's reasoning – a photocopy of the pages upon which I based the Time discussion on page 164 of *T.M.G.*

The pages Philippa refers to are from a book by JW Dunne called *Nothing Dies*, published in 1940.[x] The author (1866–1949) was a successful English aeronautical engineer, who designed some of Britain's early military aircraft. He experienced a series of strange precognitive dreams, leading him to re-evaluate their meaning and significance. He wondered whether dreams could be a blend of memories of past and future events.

26 April 2000

Dear Philippa,

RE: TOM'S MIDNIGHT GARDEN (the play)

The last few weeks have been enjoyably hectic, directing SPOT'S BIRTHDAY PARTY for the Oxford Playhouse. I'm glad to say that the production opened very successfully and is now on tour until July. Sadly it doesn't come to Cambridge! Aimed at two to six year olds, a notoriously difficult age, we seemed to have pitched it just about right. And the popularity of the SPOT character, created by Eric Hill twenty years ago, guarantees interest. I am very conscious that the vast majority of children

[x] These pages are included in the Appendix at the end of this book.

coming to see the show are entering a theatre for the first time in their lives. It is so important to get it right for them. The worst thing would be to put them off for life!

I was able to take a few days off over Easter. My wife, younger daughter and I went down to Cornwall to stay with my mother-in-law, and I had time to go through your letter of February 10th.

First of all, I'm very pleased that you have reacted so positively to the script and that its structure has not given you cause for concern. As I think I told you, structure is, to me, incredibly important. Moulding the story to work theatrically is the challenge! Sometimes accommodations have to be made and events have to be telescoped or transported to a slightly different time or location, and this can sometimes cause concern for the creator of the original material. I was very happy to find that none of your comments reflected this aspect of the adaptation.

Thank you, too, for taking the trouble to read the adaptation so carefully. Your comments are all very much appreciated.

I'm assuming that you have a copy of your letter – if not, let me know, and I will send you one!

I would like to go through all your comments with you, before finally making the necessary alterations. You will find that there are two or three things where I am still unsure how to best proceed! It may be useful, if you could bear it, for us to meet and discuss these areas face to face. Or a phone call might be enough.

Anyway, first let me go through the points where I am in total agreement with your comments…

Page 5 – "…as long as you're infectious…" – has been changed to "…as long as you may be infectious".

Page 7 – the question of the torch! On reflection, I have decided to remove the torch altogether. It is true that a torch is a very theatrical object/device, which I thought would be particularly effective on page 83. However, its validity there is outweighed by the argument that a torch could be useful to

Tom when leaving the flat and descending the stairs. I have substituted a bed-side lamp, which Tom uses to read on page 7. Uncle Alan simply turns this off. On page 83, Tom uses it to cast light towards the cupboard, when searching for the skates. I hope you agree that a bed-side lamp can be turned on without as much likelihood of discovery as a main bedroom light. And it will give an atmospheric look to the scene in almost as theatrical a manner as a torch light.

Page 9 – I take your point about "twice twelve". I have changed Tom's line to, "After twelve o'clock comes one o'clock." This seems to work quite nicely and is not as confusing.

Page 16 – I have taken out "Different season." as you suggested. However, the rhythm of the line seemed to need an extra phrase. So I have changed it to… "and every night different. Different time of day. Different weather. But always there. Always real!"

Page 17 – I am reluctant to lose the "note to the fairies" episode, partly because it helps depict Hatty's use of an imaginary world to offset her loneliness, and also because I feel it gives Tom the chance to be somewhat dismissive of Hatty's apparently girlish nature. If Tom becomes too involved with her too quickly, it feels somewhat glib. I can certainly add the name Oberon. I wonder also if I might extend further the significance of the note by giving Hatty a line like, "I wanted them to be my friends. I wanted them to help me escape." This combines my addition with your comment on it. It seems to me it strengthens the whole idea. We are able to see Hatty's desperation, and Tom is, to some degree, able to sympathise too. What do you think? While thinking about this section, I noticed that I had made it possible for Tom to remove Hatty's note from under a stone and then replace it. I don't think it is possible for him to do that, is it?! I don't think there is a problem about this, because she can simply place one corner of the note under a stone, leaving the "address" visible.

Page 18 – you quite rightly picked up my amalgamation of

the greenhouse door with the orchard door. I think, however, I am going to have to leave this. It is highly likely that the set will not realistically depict the greenhouse door, with its wooden bottom half and its glass-paned top half. It may well be that there is a simple door frame to suggest it – in which case, Tom's mime as he goes through the door will be even more theatrical, in my opinion. I hope you can accept this anachronism.

Page 19 – my suggested re-write of the first sentence of the letter read by Peter is: "the fir-tree crashed to the ground, Peter, and I heard a horrified scream. I think it came from a window up above me." I hope this does the trick.

Page 21 – I agree that the "caged tiger" image is not appropriate. The line could easily be cut, but I wonder whether there is another animal image that would work for us. My first thought is, "Like a caged bear, loping and moping about the flat." Maybe a bear is too large an animal. There must be a nice image to suggest Tom's restless, yet subdued behaviour.

Page 22 – I had to smile about your comment concerning the "terrier on a lead". You are absolutely right, of course. The reason I smiled was that I realised that the only reason I had used this idea was that I was thinking of how the director of the production would achieve the idea of a family dog accompanying the boys in the garden. Especially, of course, when he growls at Tom. In my mind I supposed that it might be possible to do it with a puppet dog, which could be controlled, as it were, on a lead! I have now removed all reference to a lead, which reads much better. However, in the introductory notes, I have suggested that one way of making the scene work might be to use a puppet, which would indeed be on a lead.

This leads me to a more general thought. It may well be that in the "story-telling staging" I have suggested, where we are not trying to realistically depict the scenes in the story, it would be inappropriate to use puppetry, which might be too specific in the wrong way. For instance, I think it would be very imaginative and effective for the geese to be imagined rather than, however cleverly, played as puppets. Similarly, the wren. But I do wonder about Pincher. The style of the play might be better served by an actor miming Pincher, rather than the use of a puppet. This is quite an interesting debate, which I will probably develop further with the director at Unicorn.

Page 24 – I have happily reverted to the line you employ in the book! "It would be no good. I can't run as fast as they can."

Page 25 – scrumping. You are quite right, of course. This word means stealing fruit from someone else's orchard or garden. I have re-written the sequence as follows :-

"HUBERT: No. We're going to the kitchen-garden.
HATTY: What for?
EDGAR: Apples.
HATTY: You were told not to pick any apples."

I think this works. However, on page 30 there is another reference to scrumping, which I would like to keep. Edgar says, "Or you'll tell Mother we've been scrumping I suppose." In this context, I feel the word is appropriate, because it suggests stealing, albeit from one's own garden, but when one has been told not to! This may sound like a semantic quibble, but, to be honest, I like the word "scrumping" and would love to get it in somewhere!

Page 33 – Goose-feathers. You are right, of course. But I must say I am sad to lose the goose-feathers, which make a nice theatrical moment. I think I will have to cut them completely, unless I insert in this sequence, which is really a narrative sequence, a mention of the potting-shed, which could lead to the goose-feathers being thrown, even if we do not actually see anything resembling the potting-shed… The problem is they come, at present, as a climax to the guided tour of the garden, and would not work so well if they were inserted before the arrival at the greenhouse. Am still thinking about this one!

Page 34 – I have amended the line, as you suggest, to "…about Cain's killing Abel." In fact I wonder if I can omit the apostrophe *'s' and simply say, "…about Cain killing Abel.", which is easier to say and is, I don't think, grammatically incorrect. Or is it?!*

Page 35 – forest outlaws. The phrase is one that you use on page 85 of the book. However, I agree that Robin Hood would be clearer. How about the following exchange?…

"HATTY:	*My cousins used to make these. They played at being forest outlaws. Robin Hood, Little John… I always wanted to join in.*
TOM:	*Why didn't you? You could have been Maid Marian.*
HATTY:	*They said I was too young. And then, when I was old enough, they said they were too old."*

I quite like this. Do you?

Page 38 – I am reluctant to add "through the hedge", because the hedge has been mentioned in the previous line. Also, "the secret passage through the hedge" is mentioned on page 32. I think it should be clear.

Page 44 – the guardian angel idea – I rather liked this idea, but was careful to make it not understood by the Young Hatty. But if it seems out of place to you, I think it will have to be cut. Is there anything else Tom could say about the angel? Something comforting? I feel that he should say something to try to comfort the Young Hatty. Any ideas?!

Page 52 – I have adopted your "bits of planking" idea. Thank you.

Page 53 – I, too, have had typing errors continue through drafts and publisher's proofs unspotted until too late! Be assured that haunt has reverted to hurt.

Page 58 – files have been replaced by office-ledgers.

Page 67 – I have amended the stage direction to: "SHIELDING THE OIL-LAMP, SHE HIDES IN THE SHADOWS OF THE CLOCK OR RETREATS UP A FEW STAIRS. TOM JOINS HER." I think this should be possible.

Page 68 – "resting" has been changed to "in bed". Thank you.

Page 69 – I'm sure you understand that I need Abel to come back to the greenhouse in the evening. I have inserted a line for Abel on page 70, to explain this. After Hatty has told him he made her jump, he now says: "just checking the furnace in the heating-house, Miss Hatty." Then he sees Tom and mutters his prayer. Hope this is acceptable.

Page 80 – Pollution. I would rather like to keep the idea of pollution coming from factories. It is very faithful to the book! When you wrote this, in the 50s, I'm sure it would not have been true to say that farming caused pollution. It seems to me that this is a period detail which is quite acceptable. Hope you agree.

Page 84 – I have added "of the boots and the straps" as you suggest.

Page 86 – I have reversed the Tower-Keeper's speech as follows: "Over there, ladies and gentlemen, you can see the spires of Castleford, over here the city of Peterborough, and in that *direction lies King's Lynn and the sea."*

Page 92/93 – I have added "Only dustbins knocked over..." as you suggest.

Page 97 – I have changed the line to "Hatty was a girl in Queen Victoria's reign. That began in 1837." – as you suggested.

Page 98 – I have changed Mrs. Bartholomew's line as follows: "It was me! I was watching from the window! Frightened! Next day, Midsummer's Day, Barty and I were married." I hope this does the trick.

Page 99 – I have amended the line to "We turned this house into flats", as you suggested.

Now we come on to the areas I would like to discuss with you in more detail...

First of all, the question of heightened language, especially those mentioned by you on pages 11, 39, 57 and 85. I quite understand the point you are making. Indeed, it was as you surmised – I felt that it was legitimate to make the language more literary whenever the characters were, as it were, narrating their own story/situation.

At one point I had thought that it might have been best to employ straight-forward narration, whereby a narrator other than the protagonist would be able to tell the story, sometimes using your narrative passages from the book. But it became apparent that it was not necessary to do this. It actually felt better not to have a third party, or even several third parties, actually telling the story, rather for the story to tell itself, and for sometimes the information to be given in the letters to and from Peter and also in sequences which I can only describe as self-narrative, in which Tom and Hatty narrate "out front", without actually going into the third person. I far prefer this method, because it keeps the focus in the right place. The temptation to look at a narrator, when in fact he or she is not the most important person, is considerable when watching a play. Children particularly find it difficult not to look where the speech is coming from!

Also, I do love some of your descriptive passages. "Thick beetle-browed yew trees" is literary, yes, but very rich, and it would be a great shame not to use it! Similarly, the idea of "a fan of peacock feathers" or "a housemaid" does not seem too far away from Tom's experience. On page 26 of your book, you actually say that "Tom had seen housemaids only in pictures". This suggested to me that he knew what they were called and the sort of things they did!

Again, on page 39, I feel that Hatty ascends a higher plane when she describes the journey of the river. I really feel it works like that! It may be that she is voicing thoughts she could not in reality voice, but I don't think we should be frightened of occasionally veering into the poetic! Also, the contradiction you point out concerning the river in one line "reaching the sea" and in the next having an "endless journey" seems to me to echo your own description! On the top of page 89 of the book, you say that "she envied the waters their endless journeying". That is where I took the phrase from. In other words, the river may reach the sea, but the water has an endless journey, which continues once it reaches the sea via the river.

On page 57, I love the idea of Tom thinking of Hatty as he listens to the clock ticking like a human heart-beat. I quite accept the fact that in the book you are able to say this in the narrative, but he would not voice it himself. But in the play I feel that he can say this, as though he is voicing his innermost thoughts. You are absolutely right that it is "too literary", but, in a way, I feel that is the whole point of using it! It just gives an extra moment of insight. And I don't think it becomes a false moment. Again, the poetry of the whole idea makes it, to me, legitimate…

"Onward" on page 85 perhaps goes a little too far! Maybe it could simply become "On, on." Yet I would still defend the basic idea of using heightened language in this context.

On a different tack, I would like to discuss page 101 with you – the idea about Peter and secrecy. I looked back at the book and found that you did not really worry too much about Peter and secrecy! I'm sure it is implicit. I honestly don't think it is necessary for Tom to assure Mrs. Bartholomew that Peter can keep a secret. I also rather like the idea of tying up the Abel/Susan strand.

While discussing this, I would also like to ask you a wider question about the scene between Tom and Mrs. Bartholomew. Tony Graham of Unicorn Theatre is a little worried that the scene is too long. He feels we need to wind up the proceedings a little sooner, and perhaps not tie up all the ends so carefully. I'm not sure I agree with this, although I can understand that the scene is a little wordy, with no action, and may not hold. I would love to know what you think, and whether there are any areas that you feel would be more suitable to cut than others…

Page 78 – the whole notion of Time and the conversation between Tom and Uncle Alan. I'm trying to get to terms with this! I think I understand what you are saying. Maybe this is another area we can discuss.

Page 31 – you quite rightly told me on the telephone that I couldn't have Tom catch an apple! I am still thinking of how to change this. I still want Tom to help Hatty "against" her cousins, so that they (Tom and Hatty) become a team. I realise another thing. I actually have them shaking hands at the end of that scene. I suppose this is impossible too! Having said that, there are places in the book where Tom puts his arm around Hatty. And also, on page 117, they appear to be releasing frogs together! But I do understand the central premise that Tom cannot pick up things. Maybe the apple drops to the ground and Tom simply whispers to Hatty its whereabouts. Or maybe I will come up with a better idea. Or maybe you might help me out by thinking of something!

I think that is it! I hope I haven't gone on too long. But I so value your contribution that I feel it well worth while writing down my thoughts, rather than just presenting you with a second draft for further comment.

Please let me know whether you would like to chat on the phone or whether I could come and see you again. Or, if you have no time to discuss these thoughts more fully, please feel free to say so, and I will do my best to resolve the problems and then present you with another draft to read.

Thanks again for reading the first draft with such care. I'm delighted that you feel it is "getting there"!

All good wishes, and looking forward to hearing from you.

Yours sincerely,

David

I decided to pass on some of Philippa's comments to Tony Graham, the Artistic Director of Unicorn Theatre, who would be directing the play. He and Chris Moxon, the theatre's Administrative Director, needed to be kept up to date.

02 May 2000
Tony Graham
Unicorn Theatre

Dear Tony,

TOM'S MIDNIGHT GARDEN

First of all, when discussing with Elly information for your schools' brochure, I discovered your opening date is September 30th. This is just to say, well in advance (!), that I will not be able to attend that first performance, because I am performing at Eastbourne for the International Brotherhood of Magicians Convention. However, I might be able to come to the Sunday, 1st October, performance.

An update on the second draft… Philippa Pearce sent me a list of suggestions, many of which I have already incorporated. They were all tiny details, but perfectly legitimate.

There remain two or three somewhat bigger quibbles which I am hoping to discuss with her. For instance, she points out that it would be impossible for Tom to catch the apple. I need to find another way of Tom helping Hatty at that point. She is also questioning some of the heightened language in the narrated passages. She worries that they are too sophisticated for Tom and Hatty. I am resisting her on this. I believe that we can go into a more poetic vein when we are narrating, even if the actors playing Tom and Hatty are doing the self-narration. Nearly all the actual words are very faithful to the book and I think work well. A good example is Tom's first description of the garden. I hope you agree with the stance I am taking.

I will probably have to cut the goose feathers, because Philippa is adamant that these would have been kept in the potting shed, which is not an area we are planning to see on stage! I suppose I could make it part of the narration that they went to the potting shed, even if we do not see them going there. What do you think? Do you like the theatricality of the goose feathers being thrown like snow? Or will it simply make a mess on the stage which will be a damn nuisance for the rest of the act?!

Philippa also wants me to look at the discussion about the nature of Time between Tom and Uncle Alan. I will do this, although, to be honest, I think the way it is described in the book is rather complex, in fact, to be honest, rather unnecessarily complex! I have tried to simplify it a bit. Anyway, we'll see...

I'm intending to deliver the second draft by the end of May. Will this be okay? I can assure you there are no big structural changes. Philippa is very happy with the way the play "works".

I will look at the final scene to see if I can make a few cuts, as you suggested.

I do hope the tour is going well.

All good wishes.

Yours,

David

9 June, 2000
Tony Graham & Chris Moxon,
Unicorn Theatre
TOM'S MIDNIGHT GARDEN

Dear Tony and Chris,

Yesterday I spent the day with Philippa Pearce. I am now in a position to complete the second draft. I hope to do it within the next couple of weeks. Will that still be in time for the Peggy Ramsay application?*

Tony, I'm glad to say that I managed to convince Philippa of some of the points you and I agree on. I don't think anything we have done will cause you problems.

Interestingly, she feels that we should use no puppetry whatsoever, but imagine all the animals, including the dog. Certainly I believe that we can do the geese with just a sound effect. Maybe we should extend that to the dog.

I am faxing through an article in the current edition of THE BOOKSELLER. Typically, there is no mention of the forthcoming

---

* My play agent for many years was Tom Erhardt, who worked with the legendary Margaret ('Peggy') Ramsay. After her death in 1991, the Peggy Ramsay Foundation was established, through which her Estate was used for charitable purposes relating to playwriting and production.

play adaptation, only the film. I think the Unicorn office ought to write or e-mail THE BOOKSELLER pointing out that the play opens only weeks after the film.

You will be interested to know that Philippa is very excited about the play. I have a feeling that, if asked, she might do some sort of publicity for you. Certainly she will want to come to see the play. She is an avid theatre goer. She especially likes going to the National. However, she lives near Cambridge, so we might have to arrange transport or something. As I have already told you, I cannot be there on September 30th. I suppose there is no need for me to be there on the same day as Philippa, but it would be nice for me to be able to escort her. Maybe we could pick a date after the press performance…? What do you think?

All good wishes

Yours,

David

10 May 2000
From Tony Graham
Artistic Director
Unicorn Theatre

Dear David,

TOM'S MIDNIGHT GARDEN

Thanks for your letter. Glad to hear that you're performing at the IBM* Convention on September 30th – quite an honour – and thanks for your apologies in advance. We'd be delighted to see you whenever it suits you.

I totally agree with your stance on the narration issue. Maybe Philippa does not quite appreciate the difference between a narrative voice in theatre and a voice in role – two significantly different voices. I would have thought that this distinction is one of the most common literary devices and that, as you

* The International Brotherhood of Magicians, British Ring, at whose 2000 Convention in Eastbourne I performed part of my *Magic and Music Show*.

suggest, the device on stage would capture the precise tone and inflection that she creates in the book. I'm sure you can persuade her how "storytelling" theatre works at its best.

On the feathers issue: I feel she's being a bit literal. You may be right that, in practice, a stage full of feathers could be a nuisance. But it's one of those things that needs to be tested in rehearsal/tech. Curiously, we do a "lots of feathers in the forest" moment for Jemima* and that's early on in the first half – they are not especially a problem and you're not aware of them after that moment. There may be other ways of doing it – but at the moment, I like the theatricality of floating, flying feathers. See if you can persuade her. Again, it's a classic case of the difference between a reader's imagination and the theatrical licence one needs in order to find the correct image/symbols on stage.

Good luck on the Time issue. Once again, I'm with you. Ideas on stage need embodiment in action not long, complex discourse.

Second draft by end of May is fine. Any tightening on the final scene would be much appreciated.

We've been approached by the Education Department of the BFI to get involved in a Tom's Midnight Garden event on October 8th at the NFT. They will be screening the Willard Carroll movie at 11.00am. At 1.30pm they want a "Page to Screen and Stage" discussion with speakers from both the movie side and our stage version. I have committed to it, but if you're available and interested, you would be obviously the key player. What do you think?

It was good to see you yesterday. I'm glad you met Steve McNeff. Hopefully, he hasn't convinced you of the need for a full-scale orchestra at this stage. My inclination is still towards one cello. Steve wants three actor-musicians. We meet on Friday…

All the best,

Tony

---

* Tony's Unicorn Theatre production of *Jemima Puddleduck*.

15 May 2000

Dear Tony,

Many thanks for your letter re: TOM'S MIDNIGHT GARDEN. I'm delighted that you agree with me on these issues.

So far, Philippa has not responded to my long response to her comments. The good thing is that there is nothing major in a structural sense that needs addressing. Just the odd little changes here and there, which I don't think you will object to.

I agree with you that a few floating, flying feathers could be a nice theatrical moment, and, quite honestly, who the hell cares where they come from! However, I don't want to ruffle HER feathers too much!

At the moment, October 8th is very free in the diary, and I will pencil in the event at the NFT. I think it's quite a good idea to have a discussion about the movie and the stage versions.

The movie was meant to be released a few months ago, but got delayed. It now seems to have got delayed again. I managed to see it at a one-off screening at the NFT some time ago. I thought the actor playing Tom was far too old and there was a strange device whereby we met Tom grown-up, complete with family, which really didn't add anything. It means that there were not two time zones, rather three, which was somewhat clumsy in my opinion. To be honest, the audience seemed to quite enjoy it, and, clearly, there were things that the movie could do extremely visually and tricksily, that we cannot do. However, I do think that the way we can be imaginative in fact enhances the magical, haunting quality of the story.

I was pleased to meet Steve, who was very complimentary about the adaptation. I will leave you to fight it out with him over how many musicians you use! I'm sure that simplicity will be the keynote!*

I will do my best to get the second draft to you by the end of

* Stephen McNeff, composer of the music for the production.

May. However, I feel I must wait until Philippa responds. I think I will have to nudge her if I hear nothing within the next week or ten days.

I'm glad to say that SPOT'S BIRTHDAY PARTY opened well in Oxford and is now touring. It will be at Richmond week beginning 29th May, and Hammersmith for two weeks, opening Wednesday 26th July.

Am doing THE LIGHTHOUSE KEEPER'S LUNCH at the Oxford Playhouse, just for a week during the week beginning June 26th. A forty-minute piece for two professional actors and sixty children.

Look forward to seeing you soon.

With all good wishes.

David.

I prepared a second draft of the script, incorporating most of Philippa's suggestions, and sent it to her for her perusal. She replied with some more useful ideas.

1.vii.2000

Dear David,

Here is the letter I said I would send after reading your second draft. I do think it goes very well, so I have only a few comments to make, usually quite minor. Plus some appreciative applause.

page 24 and probably elsewhere: Abel crosses himself. I think he should, if possible, always have Tom within view when he does this, so that the significance can begin to dawn on the audience. Such a pity that there doesn't seem an opportunity for it when Abel, with Hatty in his arms, faces Tom (page 54).

page 19 and elsewhere: Wow! and Double wow! This is an anachronism for the 1950s, although to be appreciated by contemporary children. I leave you to decide.

also page 19 and elsewhere: ...BACK DOOR... Although this is only in a stage direction, I'd prefer GARDEN DOOR. In a house of any pretension, the Back Door was the Tradesman's Entrance, with easy access to kitchen etc (even if the Door was actually at the side of the house!). The Garden Door for family and friends.

page 49…TOM BRINGS DOWN HIS HAND THROUGH HER WRIST I think you must have told me of some illusionist trick which I've now forgotten.

page 75-6 Aunt G. seems almost incredibly stupid not to have checked at all on Tom's apparent absence. I suggest a slight re-writing (underlined) which might also provide a nice dramatic effect:

AUNT GWEN Alan, it's serious. Tom isn't in his bed. He's gone.

UNCLE ALAN Hang on, hang on. Are you sure? Have you checked his room thoroughly?

AUNT GWEN Well, no…

ETC ETC

Then, in the Stage Direction, you could indicate the two adults peering into Tom's bedroom. The curtains are across the window, so that the room is dim and the bed looks empty to them. They switch on the light, and then they realise that Tom is slumped on the floor on the far side of the bed, leaning against it, with only the top of his head showing.

But, David, if you don't like my idea, junk it.

page 87 middle I'm afraid of the situation not being quite clear to the audience. Would it be too laboured to enlarge the speeches something like this?

TOM Peter, look at the postcard I sent you. The tower of Ely cathedral. We're here!

HATTY Let's go inside. Let's climb the tower.

and (rather similarly) page 88 line 5:

TOM (GOING TO HIM) Peter! You looked at my postcard from Ely! (OR: my Ely postcard)

and (again, for rather similar reasons) page 95 line 4.

UNCLE ALAN It wasn't burglars. Only dustbins knocked over in the backyard. Please go back to bed.

page 99 5 lines from bottom This is really important, although I want you only to change night to evening in Mrs Bartholomew's speech. She is, of course, remembering the story which Tom experienced in the garden (page 19 of your script). In my book (page 55–7) this is a night-scene; you have elided it impressionistically into a daytime scene. I think we could cover the apparent inconsistency by the word-change I suggest.

page 103 Lovely! But we now have two endings. I suggest that the vertical handclasp is visible to the audience (of course!) but not to Aunt G. and Uncle A. Then, without pause, it turns into a hug visible to all.

I know you're always busy. Please don't bother to write back on this. I rely on your judgement.

With all best wishes –

Philippa

P.S. I omitted one point:

Bottom page 12 THE ACTORS MIME EATING.

Would it not be better if they did (virtually) eat. So much has to be mimed, and this doesn't need to be.

After I had finished the first draft of the script, I had sent it not only to Philippa but also to my mentor, Frank Whitbourn. Frank had been the director of a residential summer drama course I was lucky enough to attend at the age of fourteen, and became the first person I asked to read all my plays. I valued hugely Frank's supportive comments and insightful criticism. A record of our half-century of correspondence was published as *Frank Exchanges* (The Book Guild, 2023). Here is Frank's response to my adaptation of *Tom's Midnight Garden*. I felt it was so helpful and interesting that I forwarded it to Philippa.

From Frank Whitbourn
7 Feb. 2000
(I can't quite believe this!)

Dear David,

I don't know Philippa Pearce's book (published by O.U.P. I notice, that's a hall mark of quality) so I have necessarily approached Tom's Midnight Garden as an original play in its own right.

I find it spell-binding. Clearly it aims at an audience older than those for whom most of your past work has been designed. Are they Tom's contemporaries? He seems very mature for his age, Peter too, but the letters are a very successful way of maintaining the narrative and the degree of literacy Tom displays is acceptable under the terms of poetic licence. Both characters are convincingly established and my belief is that if characters in a play or novel are convincing then any activity in which they take part will be credible too.

As you say, the fluency of the narrative is essential and therefore you are quite right to offer no act divisions, or any interval (the older spectators shouldn't need 'to be excused', should they?), because any such interruption could break the spell which is cast from the very first moment of Mrs Bartholomew's entry down the stairs to wind the clock, the symbol of Time, and the chorus of off-stage voices. Absolutely gripping. I find myself wondering whether it might be best for these to be recorded by other actors than those in the play, but perhaps they should be represented as presences surviving in the house. In your introduction you ask 'Is it a ghost story? Is it exploring the supernatural? Is it about the power of the human spirit? Does it suggest that an old house can retain memories of the past? Is it about time? Is it about freedom?' And you rightly answer 'It is about all these things. And what makes it a classic is that it is also believable.' It creates in the words of Coleridge (I think) 'a willing suspension of disbelief'.

So I am a little troubled by the suggestion of the introduction of puppets for the geese and other animals. Could not these be boldly imagined? If the actors see them, the spectators will see them also. I recall Charles Laughton as Macbeth. The ghost of Banquo did not materialise at the banquet table, but we, the audience, saw him because Laughton saw him. And Sybil Thorndike feeding chickens in Uncle Vanya at Chichester convinced us that they were there because they were there for her. And Dickens (though I never saw him reading) in the same way established the reality of Sykes and Nancy in his terrifying representation of the murder in Oliver Twist. I did see Emlyn Williams however, and he pulled off the same magic.

All this supports your belief in the necessity of simplicity in the setting. The introduction of revolves or wagons would be shattering. As I was reading I found myself visualising a setting with a central Victorian staircase leading to the 'first floor back' on an upper level, with Tom's bedroom central too, so that it might dominate the action along with the clock, fitted with bed, cupboard and 'practical' door for him to prop open with his slipper. And I suppose a table for the breakfast scene on the same level, like the bedroom, a permanent part of the 'minimalist' set.

Then I began to picture a front door in a wall to my right (stage left) through which Uncle Alan would bring Tom to stay, affording a glimpse of the street beyond, extending perhaps behind a gauze wall. Though so much is established by verbal description I felt that a limited visuality would not come amiss.

On the other side was the door to the garden. Now, in such a Victorian house, this would have been a 'garden door' from a lobby where those going to the garden would change into outdoor shoes or put on galoshes. Victorian houses did not provide direct access from living-rooms to the garden, though

Georgian houses allowed a way out through tall sash windows for persons prepared to stoop a little. The 1850s house, just demolished, across the way from us, had a very prominent door leading to the garden and the park. So I visualised just such a door, a 'practical door' for Tom's way into the garden. And it seemed to me if this ponderous and prominent means of ingress and egress were set in a wall of gauze similar to that on stage left (my right) the sudden misty lighting up of a view of the garden might provoke the sort of gasp of surprise achieved by the sudden appearance of the magic wood at the end of the first act of Barrie's Dear Brutus. (An apparition as cunningly prepared for in his text as the disappearance of his heroine on the 'Island-that-likes-to-be-visited' in Mary Rose. And the appearance of Buckingham Palace in B.F.G.) This would allow Tom, having stepped out through the door, to make his way back for extended action in the central stage area, round the lower end of the gauze flats. The action in the garden is going to require as much space as possible and Abel and his greenhouse – to be imagined and mimed – will have to be there also, will they not? Likewise the cathedral tower.

I happen to have been reading recently Revelation, so I enjoyed the use of it and its wonderful language (for which James the First's bishops should probably get more credit than the author – whoever he was, nobody really knows though some fundamentalists believe they do – of the original). The compilers of the New Testament were in two minds, I gather, about admitting it to the canon, but happily accepted it as they accepted the erotic Song of Solomon for the Old. As literature, if not as Holy Writ, both works have so much going for them. The images in Revelation with its Four Horsemen, Angels, trumpeters, golden throne and glassy sea are a kind of unscientific fantasy run mad. Magnificent!

The garden door, perhaps draped or colour-glazed, as it probably would have been, might well be added to establish the Victorian scene. And perhaps a telephone table by the front door would clarify the presence of the 20th century on that half of the stage.

But I have rambled on enough and detained you too long with my impertinent comments and fancies. I may get hold of the book, or I may not. It might disappoint me after experiencing such a spell-binding text as you have presented me with.

It is absolutely beautiful. I trust that you will direct it when it is staged. Don't let anybody else muck about with it for heaven's sake, or the Four Horsemen may descend upon Unicorn Theatre straight from the A.V.!

Thank you for it and the privileged pre-view. Love as ever (Mary calls 'And from me') to you and all yours, not forgetting the Internet!

Frank

P.S. What a splendid start for the Millennium you've provided. Who needs that disastrous Dome?

An Afterthought, after struggling to 'proof-read' the illegibility of the above, is it not perhaps a play as much, or even more, for adults than children? Like Peter Pan?

P.P.S. And after 'proof-reading' with difficulty I do apologise for this miniscule and not-easily-decipherable miniscule hand. I do, I do, I do!

F

2.vii.2000

Dear David,

The return of this letter from your friend, Frank – with many thanks indeed.

I found the comments, suggestions etc quite fascinating – although some of the theatrical technology baffled, of course. How lucky you are to have someone – a friend – so intelligent and aware and with such great experience!

(And how lucky he is having you, too.)

And you sent me (I think) the original letter. So now you have it back to treasure.

By the way, Sally is thrilled at the prospect of Spot's Birthday Party. Spot is a top fictional favourite with Nat, who is 3 years old next Saturday. So Sally plans that she and I and Nat will attend in due course. (I am looking forward to the sunflower coup de théâtre.)

A lovely prospect! Thanks!

Great haste

Philippa

10 July 2000

Dear Philippa,

Many thanks indeed for your letter and for the several very valid and useful points you make.

I will incorporate them into the next draft, or simply give them to the director to incorporate in rehearsal.

I know that Unicorn are hoping very much that you will come and see the production. It opens on September 30th, but unfortunately I will be performing my MAGIC AND MUSIC SHOW on that day! Unicorn wonder if you and I could both go together on either October 14th or 15th (Saturday or Sunday). I think they will be officially inviting you in due course.

The performances will be at the Pleasance Theatre in north London. As I think I told you, Unicorn is no longer at the Arts Theatre.

I would be very happy to meet you off the train at Kings Cross and escort you to the theatre! Maybe we could even have a bite to eat first… Have a sunny summer!

All good wishes.

Yours,

David

30 August 2000

Dear Philippa,

On Tuesday I went to the first day of rehearsals! The company were very enthusiastic about the whole project and I hope very much that rehearsals will progress well.

The music composer has come up with some interesting sounds and a nice theme. Three of the cast will also be playing cello, flute and violin, which I think will sound very good.

I enclose some copies of the leaflet. It doesn't mention all the schools' performances, which go throughout the week, just the weekend ones.

Hopefully you will be able to come on October 14th or 15th as discussed, and I can escort you to the theatre!

One thing came up at the rehearsal, something which I'm ashamed to say I had never thought about. The actress playing Aunt Gwen asked if Castleford was really Cambridge. I suppose she must be right. Or is she?!

I do hope you are well and have been enjoying the summer.

All good wishes, as ever.

Yours,

David

08 October 2000

Dear Philippa,

I have now seen two performances of TOM'S MIDNIGHT GARDEN. On the whole I am delighted with the production, which succeeded in holding a very difficult audience of nine year olds virtually rapt throughout. Most of the children had never been in a theatre before, and most were from widely different cultural backgrounds from the world of the book! But the beauty of the story and theatricality of the production seemed to work very well. Advance booking is excellent and the response has been tremendous. There have been a couple of newspaper reviewers in to see it, but, to my knowledge, no reviews as yet.

I'm looking forward to seeing you on Saturday 14th. My wife and elder daughter (the one you once apparently sat next to at Homerton!) are coming too.

I suggest it is best if we meet at the theatre. It is in a most unlikely place for a theatre! You turn down North Road, off the Caledonian Road, and Carpenter's Mews is a tiny turning on the left. In fact it is not really a turning at all, certainly not for cars! The theatre is up some outside steps. But before you ascend, if you are there a little early, you could pop into the restaurant on the right hand side of the courtyard. We might have a quick drink before we go in, if we have time. Otherwise I will meet you at the top of the stairs before going into the auditorium. I look forward to meeting Sally again – we sat opposite each other at lunch at an IBBY Conference a year or two ago.

I understand they are giving us a little tea party afterwards, which is nice.

I do hope you are well, and look forward to seeing you on Saturday.

All good wishes,
Yours,
David

On October 14th, 2000, Philippa, accompanied by Laura Cecil, her agent, met me, my wife and our elder daughter at the Pleasance Theatre in Camden. As more and more audience members arrived, I realised that the small foyer was uncomfortably full. The auditorium doors remained closed until only ten minutes or so before curtain up. Eventually, we were all allowed in, only to be informed that the lighting system had completely failed. The cast would have to perform in basic working light mode, and the house lights would have to stay on. My heart sank. Tony's production was full of atmospheric lighting. However, to the great credit of the actors, and of Philippa's

story, I was mightily relieved that the performance was well received. But it was ironic, to say the least, that this should have happened when Philippa was watching the play for the very first time.

17.x.2000

Dear David,

I resolved not to write to you until I could tell you that I was seeing your (our?) TMG play again with the proper lighting. I've booked for the very last performance (Nov 4), to go either with Sally or with her partner, Ben Norland (also of Walker Books), who's very interested in this kind of project.

But I was amazed and delighted last Saturday even at the lighting-less production we attended. One could see how good the play was in structure and coherence and performance.

I thanked you then, and thank you again now – and congratulate us both!

Philippa

24 October 2000

Dear Philippa,

Many thanks for your letter. Delighted to hear that you are intending to go on November 4th. I will be going to see that last performance too, so look forward to seeing you there.

It is very pleasing to know that the Arts Council have seen fit to give Unicorn money to tour the production. Hopefully it will have another London run too.

You may remember that Puffin decided they did not want to publish the play. I am currently talking to Samuel French Limited, who publish all my plays in acting editions, in the hope that they will make an offer to publish the play in time for the spring tour. This is asking rather a lot, perhaps, but it would be so useful for teachers bringing parties of school children to see the play to have a copy easily at their disposal.

I'm wondering whether Oxford University Press might be interested in publishing the play, but this is probably unlikely. I think I will speak to Laura Cecil about this.

See you soon!

All good wishes.

Yours,

David

26 October 2000

Dear Philippa,

RE: TOM'S MIDNIGHT GARDEN – THE PLAY!

I'm delighted to tell you that Vivien Goodwin, the Managing Director of Samuel French Limited, saw the play yesterday and immediately got in touch to say that Samuel French would like to acquire the amateur rights and publish the play, copies to be made available by the spring, to coincide with the Arts Council tour!

I'm extremely pleased about this and hope you will be!

Our various agents will be getting in touch with each other, I'm sure!

All good wishes and looking forward to seeing you on November 4th.

Yours,

David

CC Laura Cecil

20 November 2000

Dear Philippa,

RE: TOM'S MIDNIGHT GARDEN

I have been preparing the so-called definitive version for Samuel French.

Here is a copy for your perusal. If there is anything you want changing, please let me know!

Tony's production added one or two words here and there, but he and I felt there was no need to incorporate these into the published text. However, I have reinstated Mrs. Bartholomew's lines about her two sons dying in the Great War.

When Aunt Gwen and Uncle Alan discover Tom has gone, I have offered a compromise to make her look a little less stupid! It is not quite my original version and not quite your suggested amended version – as I say, a compromise!

I do hope you have not been badly affected by all the extraordinary weather. Hope, too, that you have a lovely Christmas, and that we meet up again before too long.

All good wishes

Yours,

David

Encs.

5.xii.2000

Dear David,

You will have had my slightly hysterical message about the S. French script of Tom's Midnight Garden, which you kindly sent for my comments. 'Slightly hysterical' because I could NOT get down to reading it for the number of friends and relations who wanted 'just to drop in before Christmas'. They've come, they've gone and now I have read it.

Rather an anti-climax, because I found nothing in it to comment on, anyway – except page 94 (bottom) of the script, where Tom calls Hatty's name three times, 'piteously'. In both the performances I saw I missed hearing the name in the general row of dustbins, surreal voices etc. Therefore one missed the significance of Mrs B.'s 'Someone was calling' and, later to Tom, 'You called a name.'

Perhaps 'piteously' is misleading, suggesting weakness. Vocally the call should have (I think) the strength of wild despair or desperation. That's partly why I suggest the addition of 'Where are you, Hatty?' So that here the text would read something like this:

TOM (CALLING WILDLY) Hatty! Hatty! Where are you, Hatty? Hatty! Hatty!

Anyway, see what you think.

Meanwhile, I've not yet said how pleased I am at the S. French enterprise. And probably in time for the Spring tour, too!

Here's to us both in 2001, and in the meantime –

HAPPY CHRISTMAS!

Philippa

10.i.2001

Dear David,

Thank you for having done that tidying up with S. French.

You may be startled that I bother to write specially about that. I'm <u>really</u> thanking you for your Christmas card, and at the same time pointing out that with the new millennium I have <u>entirely</u> given up the sending of Christmas cards.

(The relief!)

It's quite surprising how many generous friends <u>still</u> send me cards. And I'm at liberty – and leisure – to write back or (mostly) not.

I expect you had a good family Christmas; we did.

You'll already have many irons in the fire, I know. I hope all goes well. And to you and all the family

A HAPPY NEW YEAR

Philippa

15 January 2001

Dear Philippa,

Thanks for your letter of January 10th. How civilised to give up

the idea of sending Christmas cards! We would love to do that, but feel it will be necessary to wait a few years before we dare take the plunge!

The tour of TOM'S MIDNIGHT GARDEN opens on March 30th at the Cochrane Theatre in London. Have you been sent a schedule? I only have a rough date list of theatres, with no times of performance. We must liaise on if and when you would like to visit the production and I will try to come on the same day.

I managed to complete an adaptation of FANTASTIC MR FOX (Dahl) before Christmas. This was a sudden commission from the Belgrade, Coventry, who will be producing it in March/April. It will be quite interesting, because they will augment their six professional actors with local amateurs, both adults and children.

THE TWITS (also Dahl) had a very successful season at the Warwick Arts Centre. It is this production that starts touring next month, right the way through to July, which is satisfying!

Am currently marking time a little before plunging into the next adaptation. I'm spending a few days at Arts Educational, the drama school in West London, giving mock auditions to final-year musical theatre students. It is always enjoyable meeting students and seeing what they can do.

I do hope you are warm enough in Cambridgeshire – it is extremely cold here!

All good wishes for a peaceful and successful 2001. Hope to see you soon!

Yours,
David

24.i.2001

Dear David,
Thank you for your letter of the 15th.

No, I haven't had a schedule of the <u>Tom's Midnight Garden</u> tour. I'd like one, of course, in case it became accessible to friends and relatives. But for myself – no, I find I don't need to see it again for a bit.

But what about your Spot play? To much disappointment, my grandson (3½) had to miss it in 2000 (?) in London. Is it appearing again anywhere else in the foreseeable future? Please don't forget this inquiry.

Good wishes to you all

Philippa

30 January 2001

Dear Philippa,

Many thanks for yours of January 24th.

I heard good news yesterday – TOM'S MIDNIGHT GARDEN's visit to the New Victory Theatre, New York, is confirmed. October 17th to November 4th. I am delighted – it will be the first time anything from my pen has been seen "on Broadway"! And, of course, it's all thanks to your splendid story. I'm very pleased that the Americans who came to see the Unicorn production appreciated the story so much, despite, or maybe because of, its Englishness!

Now, on to SPOT'S BIRTHDAY PARTY. The tour is meant to start in the autumn, in October if all goes according to plan. No details yet, however. The producers want to take it into the West End for Christmas, which would be the ideal place for your grandson to see it. But no confirmation yet! We will make a note to contact you in due course.

All good wishes, as ever,

Yours,

David

During the succeeding months, the proofs of the Samuel French acting edition of the play arrived, and I spent time checking and correcting them. I was very pleased that this published script would be available for amateur companies and schools to produce.

I was admittedly a little bit disappointed that Oxford University Press didn't want to publish an educational edition of the play to tie in with their publication of the book. But at least the play would be in print and available.

13 June 2001

Dear Philippa,

RE: TOM'S MIDNIGHT GARDEN – THE PLAY

I am busy correcting the proofs of the Samuel French acting edition.

There are a few little textual changes which crept into the Unicorn production. Sometimes these were planned, to add clarity. Sometimes they were impetuous actors' ideas!

But I think all of them are worth consideration, and I certainly don't want to include them without your agreement.

I have enclosed the relevant pages of the typescript, with my handwritten amendments for your consideration. I have numbered them, so that I can refer to each amendment in this letter...

1. *We found that when Tom looked at the book and reacted, it wasn't really clear why he was expressing disgust. So we put in the line about the Ideal Book for Girls. This may seem like using a sledgehammer to crack a nut (!), but it certainly got a good reaction from the audience and made the intention perfectly clear.*
2. *These lines, which are really straight from the book, were inserted to give the actor playing Peter time to change, having just exited as Edgar. This was really a logistical problem caused by me not giving enough time in the first place. But, as often happens in these cases, I rather liked the insertion, which played rather well.*
3. *Tom whooped in Red Indian-style on the mention of the word "wigwam". I rather liked this, because it gave the scene added energy and excitement. Do you agree?*
4. *Dale, the actor who played Tom, suggested adding "little girl", to try to make even clearer the fact that this is Hatty, but some*

years earlier. With the same actress playing the part, it could have been (and probably was) confusing. Would you mind adding "little girl"? Let me clarify that! The problem was, because the same actress played the SMALL HATTY, it looked as though Tom knew it was her (because he recognised her)! Adding "little girl" helped the audience realise he didn't recognise her.

5. *It was impractical for Aunt Grace to be brushing her hair throughout the scene. There just was not enough time to re-dress it. And it was a wig, anyway! In the production, she said she was "dressing for dinner", which seemed fine. Do you agree?*
6. *When we discussed the word "wow", we agreed that it was probably anachronistic, but nevertheless worked rather well in the context. During the tour, Tom and Peter started saying the word on the tower of Ely Cathedral. I rather liked this, because it somehow brought them together, tying up their amazement at the various happenings. What do you think?*
7. *This is not a textual change. In the production, Susan carried a coal scuttle, not kindling wood and newspaper. I think this probably makes sense, because a coal scuttle is more easily associated with lighting a fire. Do you think I could change this in the stage directions?*

I look forward to hearing from you. Please feel free to ring me or drop me a line. Or maybe I could come and see you!

I'm hoping that we can return the proofs quite soon, so that a second set can be prepared, and copies sent to both of us for a final perusal.

All good wishes, as ever,
Yours,
David

ps.

8. *They omitted 'Just over the embankment', because it seemed irrelevant – the 'gig' (two chairs) were already in position on stage as he said the line! Is this all right with you? D.*

18.vi.2001

Dear David,

In response to your letter of June 13 about last-minute corrections to the text of T.M.G. in the S. French edition:

1. *(page 4 of play-script) 'the Ideal Book for Girls' OK*
2. *(page 36) insertion OK*
3. (page 33 – sic) OK. (bean wigwam: war whoop)
4. (page 44) – 'little girl' OK
5. (page 59) – 'dressing for dinner' OK – rather regretfully: the family have slipped upwards socially into Forsyte-Saga-land. (Worse still in the film.) The book envisaged a very middle-middle class family, not at all stylish. For example, their family business takes them to market in a pony and trap.
6. (page 88) 'Wow!… Double wow!' By now you know my aversion to this. It's American, and an anachronism for the 1950s. Worse, it will – like all slang – become dated – with the wrong date.

However, I could not suggest an alternative that you – and young audiences – would like.

So I had to trust to your ingenuity. In the meantime, if all else fails, OK.

I'm so glad to think you and your family will be in New York for the next production. You must tell me all about it.

All the best

Philippa

01 October 2001

Dear Philippa,

As you may have heard, TOM'S MIDNIGHT GARDEN has been nominated for the Equity Award for Best Children's Show in the Awards given by the Theatre Management Association. Am enclosing an article from the Stage. The Awards are presented on Sunday October 21st.

I am delighted about this. We are up against the Young Vic with THE THREE MUSKETEERS and the Liverpool Playhouse with A CHRISTMAS CAROL. Personally I wouldn't mind betting that the Young Vic win the Award! But you never know! It is very pleasing to have been nominated!

Neither Tony Graham nor I will be able to attend the Awards Evening, because we will both be in New York, where the play opens at the New Victory Theatre. After the appalling events on September 11th, we wondered if the whole thing would be cancelled. But they seem determined to carry on, and rehearsals start today.

I do hope you are well and have had a good summer. We went to San Diego for a Children's Theatre Conference, then travelled around on the West Coast. Now I'm preparing to revive my adaptation of Dahl's THE BFG and to direct the 25th anniversary production of my play, THE GINGERBREAD MAN.

The Samuel French edition of TOM'S MIDNIGHT GARDEN is, I understand, virtually ready – it is hoped that copies will be on sale in the New Victory Theatre, New York, during the run. I hope the publication will lead to further productions of the play.

Hope to see you soon.

All good wishes, as ever.

Yours,

David

CC Laura Cecil

11 October 2001

Dear Philippa,

I hope by now that you, like me, will have received a copy of the playscript of TOM'S MIDNIGHT GARDEN, which Samuel French have just delivered. I hope you think it looks nice. Simple, but nice! Acting editions are no more than tools, really, but hopefully they can look reasonably attractive too!

Tomorrow, Friday, I am going to a run-through of the play, featuring the third Mrs. Bartholomew! The rest of the cast remain the same. Next day they leave for New York. Hopefully they will have a happy time, in spite of the ever-present shadow of the events of September 11th.

Jacqui and I fly over to New York on Saturday 20th and will see the show a couple of times during the following week.

The Theatre Managers' Association Awards will be announced at a ceremony on October 21st. Fingers crossed for TMG!

All good wishes, as ever.

Yours,

David

14.x.2001

Dear David,

I'm a slow correspondent, so I'm answering <u>two</u> letters from you.

To begin with, many congratulations for the nomination of <u>TMG</u> for the Award. (My book, yes; but <u>YOUR PLAY</u>.) I shall try to catch the announcement next Sunday.

And thank you for making sure (as I think you must have done?) that a copy of the Sam. French playscript reached me. As you say, half way between a tool and a book, but looks most craftsmanlike. I'm glad to have it.

And you're off to New York so soon! I do hope that all goes well, and you have as much success Over There as here. I shall want to hear about it when you get back.

As usual, warmest good wishes –

Philippa

Card, dated 30.x.2001

Dear David,

MANY CONGRATULATIONS!

You were so modestly doubtful of any chance of finding favour with the Theatre Managers (and I'm sure they're tough judges) – and now this!*

Some time you must tell me about the play in New York. Then – no doubt at all – I shall have to congratulate you all over again.

I no longer send Christmas cards, so – unless you think it's intolerably early – I'll wish you all a H.C. now.

Ever

Philippa

For some reason I didn't write to Philippa about the New York trip in October. Maybe I told her about it on the telephone. Jacqui, my wife, and I were somewhat daunted by the idea of going, following the recent horrors on September 11th. However, we were received with tremendous warmth – I think New Yorkers were relieved that visitors were beginning to return – and the play was very well received. A few schools cancelled, due to the fact that they were over the other side of the bridges leading to Manhattan Island, and parents quite reasonably didn't want their children to be stuck the wrong side, should the bridges be attacked. A very positive review of the production appeared in the *New York Times*. The visit was, of course, a sobering experience, too. We took the cruise round the bottom of Manhattan Island, from where one could see smoke still rising from Ground Zero, plus the cranes and arc lights.

16 April 2002

Dear Philippa,

I heard last week that the Library Theatre, Manchester, will be doing TOM'S MIDNIGHT GARDEN as their Christmas play. This is good news, because they are a very good company, who take great care with their children's work.

---

* The Unicorn Theatre production of *Tom's Midnight Garden* had won the Theatre Managers' Association Equity Award for Best Show for Children and Young People 2001.

Maybe I have already told you that the Questors Theatre, Ealing, will present what I think is the amateur première of the play, again for Christmas. I wonder if you will be staying with Sally at that time. If so, maybe we could all go and see the production together!*

I do hope you are well and enjoying the coming of spring. Things are busy here. I am about to revive SPOT'S BIRTHDAY PARTY. Maybe this will be the time for your grandchild to see it! In London, the show will play at the Peacock Theatre during the week beginning September 2nd. Let me know if you would like me to organise tickets. Again maybe we could all meet up!

Meanwhile, I have THE BFG on tour. Business seems to be good. Also a production of my adaptation of JAMES AND THE GIANT PEACH is touring – not my own production this time – it is produced by Birmingham Stage Company.

I'm off to New York for a few days soon. Various meetings. I find New York an exciting place. Last time Jacqui and I went, it was, of course, to see TOM'S MIDNIGHT GARDEN, and only two or three weeks after the tragic events of September 11th. Things will be virtually back to normal, I suspect.

It would be nice to meet up again. Maybe I could come and see you sometime soon – could I take you out to lunch?

All good wishes, as ever, from Jacqui and myself.

Yours,

David

31.i.2003

Dear David,

My system of <u>not</u> communicating with friends until <u>after</u> Christmas has more or less broken down. <u>I can't now remember what I've done</u>, chiefly because there's no deadline to keep me up to the mark.

---

* Sally Christie, Philippa Pearce's daughter.

But I know I owe you thanks for sending me those reviews of the Manchester production of TMG. I really wish I had made the effort to go – especially as you might have been there.

But, since May last year, I've been concentrating as far as possible to the exclusion of outside attractions, however tempting – in order to work on a full length book for children. I was amazed – at my age – to find an idea gripping me – insisting on my dealing with it. I've been very slow – slower than usual, I think – but the end is in sight. I've written nearly ¾ and should have finished by the summer.

Then – as a friend of mine used to express it – I shall frisk.

Meanwhile, we are deep in snow; my little grandsons out of school because school is shut. Have you heard of a lazy wind? Rather folksy. It can't be bothered to blow round you: it blows straight through you. We have ours from the north.

Love to you all
Philippa

05 February 2003

Dear Philippa,
Many thanks indeed for your lovely letter. I'm so delighted to hear that you are beavering away on a new full-length book! This is really exciting news. But I won't sound too effusive, just in case it puts you off your stroke! I don't know about you, but I find it very difficult to get too enthusiastic about things too early, because I always fear that the rug will be pulled from under my feet if I "show off"! It's a shame really, because sometimes one feels like jumping in the air with excitement, but a little, rather boring, voice of reason echoes in one's head and a warning light goes on!

But every good wish for the new book!

Yes, I have been delighted with the success of the Manchester production of TMG. It was very exciting, as good as the Unicorn production, yet very different! I am trying to persuade the producers of the forthcoming tour to use one of the two existing productions rather than to do a third. I feel it might be tempting fate to do yet another one – and it would be a shame if it wasn't as good as the first two, yet was touring all round the country! We will see.

Your Cambridge snow is something I knew about, because a meeting I was due to attend in Birmingham at the weekend had to be cancelled, because one of the delegates was coming from Cambridge! I hope it hasn't inconvenienced you and the family too much. I'm sure your grandsons are enjoying themselves!

You may have heard that I am due to work with Ben soon on a book for Walker. This will be an adaptation of a Dick King-Smith book, for young children to perform in school. Am looking forward to it.

Am also doing Philip Pullman's CLOCKWORK and starting on Jamila Gavin's CORAM BOY, so I have my work cut out for the year!

All good wishes, as ever. I hope very much to come and see you before too long – but I think I will keep away from Great Shelford until you have rested your pen after completing the final page!

With love,
David

18 September 2003

Dear Philippa,
I'm delighted to tell you that TOM'S MIDNIGHT GARDEN, the play, has been nominated for another award!

In fact it is the same award as it won two years ago, but a different production. This was the splendid Manchester Library Theatre production I told you about.

How are you? Your new book must be in production now, unless you are having to do any tinkering! Looking forward to it enormously.

Things are busy here, with various productions at home and abroad. Last month Jacqui and I went to New York, where the Americans kindly gave me a Distinguished Writing Award for SPOT'S BIRTHDAY PARTY. Remarkable, really, because the play has never been seen in the States! Nice though!

We look forward to seeing you again before too long.

Meanwhile, let us celebrate the nomination! Thanks, as ever, for letting me adapt your classic novel.

With love and best wishes from us both,

Yours,

David

23.ix.03

Dear David,

I shall have to try to think up new ways of congratulating you on awards for your TMG on stage. As usual, I'm very pleased – for both of us, indeed. (And for yourself alone: very nice about Spot's B'day Party in the U.S.!)*

Quite unconnected with all this, I noticed, in the cutting you sent me a reference to:

'The Story of the Little Gentleman, Catherine Wheels' Theatre Company in association with Brunton Theatre, Musselburgh.'

You see, the story I've just finished is ALSO to be called The Little Gentleman, and obviously one must beware of a clash or confusion of literary identities. Do you know anything of this stage-work, or know who would know?

My book is still only in the earliest stage of production –

* The excellent Library Theatre, Manchester, production of *Tom's Midnight Garden*, directed by Roger Haines, had won the Theatrical Management Association's Equity Award for Best Show for Children and Young People.

probably 'tinkerings' (your word) yet to come, an illustrator to be chosen etc.

This coincidence (above) worries me.

Love to you all,

Philippa

19 May 2004

Dear Philippa,

Having heard you talk at Bromley about THE LITTLE GENTLEMAN, my appetite was whetted, and I was really keen to read it!

Having resigned myself to waiting until publication at the end of the year, I happened to be corresponding by e-mail with Laura, and she suggested I might ask Francesca at Puffin if I could have a sneak preview!

Feeling a bit guilty, going behind your back, as it were, I contacted Francesca, who very kindly sent me a set of proofs. I have just read your splendid new opus in one sitting! I couldn't put it down. It has an air of mystery, yet the relationship between Bet and the mole is written with such warmth, that the reader gets totally involved. At any rate I did!

What a clever idea. And I love the mix of history and present day (just as I love it in TOM'S MIDNIGHT GARDEN, of course).

The mole is very endearing, because he is not sentimentalised one jot. His frustration and occasional grumpiness are very attractive "negative" features, which you use to great effect.

Although I don't see this one as a play, not at a first reading, anyway, something tells me it might end up on television or film, and most definitely radio!

On film, one could actually see the historical scenes, plus get an idea of the mole's incredible journey. And, of course, the shrinking of Bet could be very easily and effectively realised.

My admiration and many congratulations on a delightful book, which I'm sure will be extremely well received by critics and public alike. I am going to read it again soon, but Jacqui has bagged it next!

We both hope very much to see you soon, and send our very best wishes.

With love and a big "well done", and thank you for giving me a happy afternoon reading in the garden!

Yours,

David

30.v.04

Dear David,

What a lovely letter to have from you about The Little Gentleman! (I need something to sustain me between finishing a book and holding it in my hand as a book. All the usual Best Butter from the publisher is no good, because they have a vested interest in the project, anyway.)

I can't tell you properly how glad I am that you – and Jacqui, I hope – really like the story. Moreover, you see in it some of the very things that I most hoped would slip into the sympathetic imagination of the reader.

Thank you –

Love

Philippa

The next major production of *Tom's Midnight Garden* was mounted by the Birmingham Stage Company, directed by Neal Foster. This production embarked on two long UK tours and a season at London's Bloomsbury Theatre. It played to rewardingly large houses of school children and family audiences.

12 December 2004

Dear Philippa,

The Birmingham Stage Company tour (the production we saw in Bromley) has been very successful, even though you and I were not entirely happy with it! A second cast took over some months ago. The tour is finishing this week. Apparently they are extending by a week or two, to take the production to Dubai!

Meanwhile, Tony Graham tells me that he is seriously considering a revival by Unicorn Theatre within the next couple of years.

I do hope you are well, and hope to see you soon.

All good wishes,

Yours,

David

cc Laura Cecil

30.i.05

Dear David,

I've so much to thank you for. – I mean, of course, apart from the adaptation (re-creation?) of TMG for the stage. What a success that has been! And periodically you've been popping interesting notices into the post for me. Thank you for all that.

In all, 2004 was a very good year for me, as I hope it was for you. Especially for you, perhaps, since I realise that you usually have several projects on the go at the same time.

I forget whether you ever met Judith Cheston, who did publicity etc for the Birmingham theatre people? I was most impressed by her. She followed me (on the telephone) like a bloodhound for (telephone) interviews with local papers everywhere. She was also very polite and considerate. When I finally met her, I thought her a remarkably nice person.

If reviews indicate, The Little Gentleman should be doing

well. I only grieve that you simply cannot make a play out of him. Too small? Too reclusive? I should have had more forethought.

I hope that 2005 may bring us together again on some occasion, and the best of it, anyway, for you both.

Philippa

26 April 2005

Dear Philippa,

Much looking forward to seeing you on May 10th.

Do you know The Ticker Arms in Whittlesford? It sounds rather good.* **(*I meant the Tickell Arms – DW)**

If you have no objection, I will book us a table there for lunch.

Do hope you are well.

See you soon.

All good wishes,

Yours,

David

11.v.05

Dear David,

The roses from your garden are coming out (which of you gardens? I can't see either of you managing to fit that in) but I don't need them to remind me of lunch at the Tickell Arms. Such a treat – a grand treat (almost grandiose: you had to change your shoes)!

But most of all I enjoyed our conversation during that lunch-'hour'. Nice food is lovely; but real conversation is glorious.

So thank you so much for everything.

Love to you all

Philippa

P.S. You whetted my interest in your Gingerbread Man. If it is put on again anywhere, please let me know.

18 May 2005

Dear Philippa,

Thank you so much for your lovely card.

I, too, thoroughly enjoyed our lunch. The meal was really excellent, and I feel that the change of management has probably made the Tickell Arms more welcoming than it was last time you nearly went! Indeed, I am very glad I changed my shoes! Maybe I should have worn a tie too!

Later that evening I went to the Pentacle Club meeting and heard my friend Geoffrey Durham give an excellent lecture. As a result of my attendance, I have now been asked to deliver my own lecture this time next year! This is a talk I have done for the Magic Circle in London, all about magic for children. So, if agreement is reached, I will be able to take you out again!

But, hopefully, we will meet before then, particularly at the opening of the new Unicorn Theatre in November, when, I hope, TOM'S MIDNIGHT GARDEN will once again work its magic.

Please don't feel you have to read all the enclosures! But you did express interest in THE GINGERBREAD MAN, so I have sent you a copy of the play, as well as a copy of the storybook version I wrote some years after the play was first put on. THE GINGERBREAD MAN will be thirty years old next year! It has been very good to me, with productions all over the world. The book version was on Puffin's list for about ten years, and when they decided to stop reprinting, I did it myself! Quite a few copies get sold when I visit schools. I hope you like it.

We also talked about THE SEE-SAW TREE. So I have enclosed a copy of the play, plus the manuscript of the book version that everybody turned down!

It was lovely to see you. Do hope you have a happy and relaxing summer, and that we meet up again before too long.

Jacqui sends her very best wishes too. She is the gardener of the family! Although I do mow the lawn!

Jacqui has just won the Tutor of the Year Award at the Adult

Education College she teaches at. We are delighted at this well-deserved honour!

With love, admiration as always, and all good wishes,

Yours,

David

8.vi.05

Dear David,

Thank you so much for your letter of congratulations on the (long) listing of The Little Gentleman. I am still gratefully inhaling the delicious scent of a little bouquet of flowery compliments such as yours. (I expect no more for the future: the present honour is enough. To be set among so many young, sparkling stars!)

Yes, I had your batch of Wood-work and was about to write to you, but I have been reading it intently. (Not just conscientiously – although I think I do that, too.) I became fascinated by the difference between the plays and the novels-from-the-plays. This seems to me particularly obvious for The Gingerbread Man. I'm glad you had some success with the novelisation, but not surprised that the play was such a much more resounding one. Even in the script, the words really seem to dance off the page into one's imagination. (I suppose the songs make a lot of difference, too.)

I'd love to see The Gingerbread Man on stage some time.

Your mention of Cromer brings to me memories of family holidays at West Runton. Beeston's Hump then seemed almost mythic. Sheringham was exciting and sophisticated. (Did we ever reach Cromer? I don't remember.)

I think we had a whole fortnight. My father could only get down at the weekends, but he came laden with (home-grown) poultry, vegetables and fruit. Otherwise – and I cannot think this arrangement survives anywhere – our landlady provided no food. My mother supplied everything raw (so to speak) and the landlady cooked it.

I shall look forward to seeing you (I'd love to hear you) on the Pentacle occasion, perhaps.

Thank you for your kind words on Sattin Shore. I feel it needs kind words – I'm conscious of a curate's egg effect – the details of which I won't burden this letter with (oh dear! grammar rickety!).

Congratulations to Jacqui! That kind of honour in education represents such a combination of intelligence, hard work and humanity.

Love to you both

Philippa

19.6.05.

Dear Philippa,

Many thanks for your 8th June letter – your inclusion in the Guardian long/short list is thoroughly deserved – I have read one or two of the others & think you knock spots off them!! Let's cross our fingers, anyway.

Very interested to read what you say about adaptation – it is certainly true that I am much more at home with the play format than the book! The use of audience participation is something I like (though it must be positive or creative – not 'Are you having a nice Christmas?' 'YES!!' Or 'He's behind you!'), and to find a substitute for the storybook version is always problematic! And I fear I'm a better story acter-outer than a story writer! If a production of THE GINGERBREAD MAN can be organised for its 30th anniversary in 2006, I'll make sure you see it!

Much enjoyed your Sheringham memories – fascinating to think that the landlady cooked rather than provided and prepared the food – it reminds me of my kindergarten in the early fifties – my mother gave me a jar of scotch broth or stew, which the school heated up for ½d!

Some day you must elaborate on your enigmatic lines about SATTIN SHORE! I much enjoyed it – and the other day Ailsa, the daughter of the much respected writer Geraldine McCaughrean, told me it was one of her most favourite books (she is now 14, I think). Was it not sufficiently appreciated? Critically? Or sales-wise?

I will keep in touch re the Pentacle Club event – no date as yet!

This week we go to Italy – for a wedding in Lucca, which I'm told is lovely. In July we go to Chicago for a children's theatre conference. In August we tour my MAGIC AND MUSIC SHOW in Scotland!

Do hope you haven't been too hot – it's been baking in London!

All good wishes from Jacqui & me –

With love –

David

03 August 2005

Dear Philippa,

Many thanks indeed for your kind card. My response is a little late, because Jacqui and I have been in Chicago for a week, attending a children's theatre conference. We had a good time, and they even performed my adaptation of THE BFG as part of the conference.

Several people came up and said nice things about TOM'S MIDNIGHT GARDEN, remembering it from when it played in New York.

Delighted to hear that you are still pottering on the computer! Sometimes following up leads on the internet can prove very interesting and time-consuming!

Next week we leave for Scotland, where I am doing a few performances of my MAGIC AND MUSIC SHOW. This summer is very busy, which is rather nice!

The other day I was delighted to hear that the University of Chichester were to give me an Honorary MA. To be honest, I had no idea that there was a University of Chichester! It is one of those new ones, created from training colleges in the area. And Chichester was where I was at school, so it is rather appropriate. I am looking forward to the ceremony in October.

I met up with Tony Graham the other day. Apparently building of the new Unicorn Theatre is going well. Hopefully there will not be any delays! He is much looking forward to directing TMG. Nearer the time we must discuss whether or not you would like to come and see the production in the brand new theatre with me. * *Maybe Sally and Ben might like to come too. Are the two boys old enough yet?*

Hope to see you before too long.

Love and best wishes from all of us.

Yours,

David

19.VIII.05

Dear David,

Corresponding with you is a terrible temptation: I enjoy it. But tomorrow Helen (other g'mother) and I are off to Southwold for a week's bucket-and-spade holiday with Sally's family. So I must be brief.

Congratulations on the Chichester Hon. M.A. You deserve it, of course. I assume that you never bothered to acquire an Oxford M.A.? I got a Cambridge one, because it gave the right to borrow books from the Univ. Lib. I simply paid £5.

* On November 24th, 2005, the brand-new Unicorn Theatre in Tooley Street, near the Tower of London, opened its doors for the first time. I was honoured and delighted that the very first production in the brand-new theatre was my adaptation of *Tom's Midnight Garden*. The revival of Tony Graham's original production at the Pleasance Theatre, in North London, was warmly welcomed.

(A foreign acquaintance, to whom I told this, rather naturally asked me how much I had paid for the B.A.)

Can the system still survive?

I still congratulate myself on our T.M.G. being the opening production of the Unicorn. I still don't know what Sally feels about the 2 little boys attending. Otherwise Sally and Ben and I would love to come, I think.

MUST STOP!

Love to all

Philippa

30 August 2005

Dear Philippa,

Hopefully you had an enjoyable week in Southwold. Am I right in thinking that Jill Freud, wife of Sir Clement, runs her summer repertory theatre in Southwold? I wonder if you went to see a play. Do hope you had good weather and that the children enjoyed themselves, and that Sally and Ben got a bit of a rest!

Things have been hectic here. Following our Chicago trip, Jacqui and I embarked on a mini-tour of Scotland. I was performing my MAGIC AND MUSIC SHOW. We visited some lovely theatres and enjoyed the audiences. Alnwick, on the Northumberland coast, which we visited on the way up to Scotland, boasts a lovely Playhouse. And the Byre Theatre, St. Andrews, which was recently completely refurbished, indeed rebuilt, I think, was quite delightful. As was the town itself, complete with its magnificent beaches and famous golf courses. Then we had three days "holiday" at St. Fillans overlooking Loch Earn. This was very enjoyable, particularly when we zoomed off to Pitlochry for the day – and visited the theatre and saw a rather good production of an adaptation of KIND HEART AND CORONETS.

After a show in Peebles – in a delightfully converted church – we performed our last show in Kirkcaldy, in a theatre called the Adam Smith, which, although I had often sent my children's plays there in the past, I had never visited in person. Another delightful venue.

The weather was kind too except on the one day that I spent at the Edinburgh Book Festival, launching LADY LOLLIPOP, my adaptation of Dick King-Smith's book – the one that Ben designed. This was a very happy occasion, with a full house watching 30 children perform the play.

Since our return, we have been to the Isle of Wight with my mother, who enjoyed the trip. She is a few years older than your good self! Each year we try to give her a short break, and for the last 3 years the Isle of Wight has proved ideal.

Now we are preparing to go to Menorca for just a week before coming back to reality!

One of the first things I do upon my return is to attend a press conference for the new Unicorn. I think it is taking place in the new building, which is coming on apace, I hear.

I have told Unicorn that you are keen to attend a performance of TOM'S MIDNIGHT GARDEN. I am sure they will be in touch soon to discuss a date and a time. It may well be that there is a special celebratory opening performance to which we will all be invited.

In your letter you asked me if I had ever bothered to acquire an Oxford M.A. The answer is no! I could have paid for one, but it always seemed to me to be a bit of a cheat! Your reason for accepting a Cambridge one – it gave you the right to borrow books from the University Library – is a very reasonable one! I don't think I was offered the same privilege!

I think the system still survives at Oxford and Cambridge. Rebecca, our younger daughter, who went to Oxford, has resisted the acquisition of an M.A., rather like me! Katherine, the one who went to Homerton, has never mentioned the possibility.

I seem to be all behind with my work. But maybe it is good to have a rest now and then! Richard Fowler, the illustrator and paper engineer with whom I work, and I have recently done two novelty books for a packager. One of them is, apparently, already in the shops in Spain and France, but no British publisher can be found! It's a strange world, the children's publishing world isn't it? And it gets stranger every year, I think.

I have two or three adaptations I am meant to be working on, but have managed to relegate them to the bottom of the pile… I must take a deep breath and get started!

I hope very much to see you before too long, possibly at Unicorn. The magic lecture I have been asked to do in Cambridge won't be until next year I fancy.

Jacqui and I send you our very best wishes, as ever,

With love,

David

3.i.06

Dear David,

I was just settling down to thanking people for their Christmas cards (It can go on into February!), when your letter came with the enclosure of reviews of T.M.G. on stage.* So I can thank you twice over in one letter.

I don't know how you find the time to be so kind as well as being so professionally, creatively busy. But in this your whole family is the same, I believe.

I hope – and expect – that you had a happy Christmas. So did we – a really happy one, by which I mean no quarrels and no illnesses. Even the new puppy had only one accident, and we were able to keep the kitten away from the baubles on the Christmas tree.

* At the new Unicorn Theatre.

Sally is driving me up to the Unicorn on the 15th for my 'conversation' with Julia Eccleshare. I do hope I don't say something stupid – or forget something in a ridiculous way e.g. J.E.'s first name.

I shall keep a sharp eye open in case you are there, but don't really expect you to be.

It would be rather late to wait, on the off-chance, to wish you a happy New Year – so I'll do it now –

To all Woods, may they prosper and be proliferous (I've just looked it up in the dictionary) in a HAPPY NEW YEAR.

Love to you all

Philippa

In October 2005, I was asked by the BBC to write the script for a play to celebrate the 80th birthday of Her Majesty Queen Elizabeth II. The play was to bring together as many iconic characters from British children's literature as possible, linking them into one story. It would be performed at the Children's Party at the Palace, a major event for two thousand children and one thousand adults, to take place in Buckingham Palace Gardens on June 25th 2006. The play would be screened live on BBC1 television. Working on this unique project took up seven months of my life! Maybe one day I will write about it… The play was called *The Queen's Handbag*, and to my relief was very well received. I was very grateful to Trevor Nunn for directing the starry cast.

15.ii.06. (Postcard)

Dear David,

Many congratulations! It has only just dawned on me that the D.W. of the Buckingham Palace party must be YOU! How splendid! You'll be run off your feet and at the same time take everything in your stride. Don't let any royals try to boss you about.

*The very nicest restaurant I know, to which one day I shall take you. Only English cooking, and second helpings offered.

Love Philippa

28 February 2006

Dear Philippa,

Do hope you are well!

It seems a long way away, but this is to let you know that I am scheduled to deliver my lecture on children's magic to the Cambridge Pentacle Club on the evening of Tuesday, May 9th.

I would love to meet you for lunch on that day, if convenient!

Maybe you could put it in your diary and we can liaise nearer the time…

The Buckingham Palace event is, as I knew it would, taking up quite a lot of time! I will tell you about it when I see you!

All good wishes,

As ever,

Yours

David

4.iii.06

Dear David,

I had already put June 25 (David Wood/B'ham Palace) BBC 1 in my diary. (Well, June 25 was already there…)

And now I have put your name and lunch against May 9th. Is this when I can treat us to lunch at the Old Fire Engine House in Ely? I hope so. (To wait until after the Queen's birthday is a nuisance.)

Any chance that I could hear you at the Pentacle Club?

If possible, I'd like to include Sally* in our lunch party –

* The Old Fire Engine House, Ely, a picture of which was on the front of the postcard.

altho' she'd have to leave early to meet the little boys out of school.

∗and always, of course, Jacqui, if she were free

Love to you all

Philippa

9 March 2006

Dear Philippa,

Many thanks for your letter of March 4th.

Yes please! The Old Fire Engine House would be perfect on May 9th!

And it would be great if Sally joined us.

Unfortunately Jacqui won't be available on that day – she teaches on a Tuesday. So sadly she will miss out on the Ely lunch!

I'm sure it would be absolutely fine for you to come to the Pentacle Club. It sounds rather splendid, but I am afraid the meetings of the Club take place in a school hall on the outskirts of Cambridge. I will have more details soon. The starting time is, I think, 7.00pm.

After our lunch, I will need to get to the hall by 5.00 or 5.30 to set up. Would you be able to get a cab? Or might Sally like to come too?!

It would be good – and flattering – to have you in the audience. Most of the people there will be amateur magicians, possibly with their families.

The Buckingham Palace event is beginning to take up quite a lot of time! It is all very complicated, checking with the copyright holders, agreeing content, trying to get actors to commit etc. etc. Hopefully it won't become a nightmare!

Last week we had a meeting with the Disney people, which seemed to go quite well. It seems they might even allow Winnie-the-Pooh to appear on screen with Paddington and Rupert! That will be a first, and a last, I should think! Normally Disney characters are not allowed to sully themselves with any characters other than their own brand!

Let me know if all the above works for you. Much looking forward to seeing you.

All good wishes from Jacqui and myself.

Love

David

25th September 2006

Dear Philippa,

Things seem to be ridiculously busy at the moment, but most of the activities I am involved in on a day to day basis are enjoyable ones, so I have no complaints!

Directing BABE, THE SHEEP-PIG in Regent's Park proved to be a delightful experience, in spite of the oppressive heat in the rehearsal room, and in the open air, once we put the show on the stage! Everyone seemed very pleased with it and I have been asked back to direct another one next year. I think we will probably do FANTASTIC MR FOX, which could work well in the open air.

Last week the tour of my adaptation of Dahl's DANNY THE CHAMPION OF THE WORLD opened at the New Theatre, Cardiff, so I went to see it. It's a nice production, and the audience seemed to love it. Fingers crossed for a successful tour!

Then I went to Oxford for a meeting about the proposed Story Museum, which is a similar idea to Seven Stories (the Centre for the Children's Book). I have become a Trustee. They are looking for money to create a building in the centre of Oxford. They will have all sorts of events, as well as storytellings in schools, plus exhibitions and a number of collections. They have been offered a very substantial Lewis Carroll archive.

I am getting ready to go to Eastbourne for a magic convention! Two exciting days of constant magic from all over the world! Looking forward to it.

*The German production of TMG is going ahead quite soon, I believe. The play is to be translated by Angela Kingsford-Rohl, who has already translated several of my plays, including THE GINGERBREAD MAN. She is English, bi-lingual, married to a German. She is also the agent looking after the play. She reckons that if the first production goes well, the play will have quite a long life in Germany, which is nice!**

*In October, Jacqui and I go to Minneapolis for a few days, to see a production of THE BFG. Hopefully things will settle down a bit after that! I have the second act of a musical version of THE GO-BETWEEN**2 *to finish off. This is to be produced next year. It feels a bit grown-up to me! First time I have adapted an adult book, I think. Having said that, I am doing it very much from the little boy's point of view, so my children's theatre experience is coming in handy! Jacqui has started teaching again, and is enjoying her prison visits. Lots of prisoners wanting to do embroidery with her and her colleagues. She sends her love and very best wishes to you, as do I.*

Am hoping that I might be able to come and see you before the end of the year. Another lunch, perhaps?!

Best wishes to Sally and Ben, too.

All good wishes,

As ever,

David

---

* In fact, the first production in German took place in Vienna, Austria, sadly not before Philippa had passed away. I went to see it and was very impressed.

*2 This musical, based on LP Hartley's celebrated novel, had music by Richard Taylor, who had invited me to collaborate with him. It was my first adult show for about thirty-five years! An initial production played in Leeds, Derby and Northampton, and, after a wait of several years, opened in the West End at the Apollo Theatre, starring Michael Crawford. I loved working on this musical, using my regular device of seeing the story through the eyes of the child protagonist.

18.XI.06

Dear David,

It's always nice to be writing to you, but a bit sad on this occasion. Because, disappointingly, I can't manage any of the dates for lunch you suggest. Really: I never feel any use by lunch time on Tuesdays and Wednesdays, because I have gruelling exercise classes that run up to 1 o'clock. And on Thursday 13th a niece is paying me a pre-Christmas visit. (Thursdays are usually lovely free days – free of regular grandchild visits – altho' I wouldn't miss them for worlds, and normally of irregular visits by nieces, nephews etc.)

('Disappointed' – is one ever 'appointed'? Fatuous; but I'm reminded of Geoffrey Dearmer – son of Percy, the hymnologist – who would describe himself sometimes as 'gruntled'.)

Perhaps I'm not altogether disappointed even not to lunch with you just now. I don't drive after dark (or in the gloaming), which makes a long lunch-hour away from home rather anxious.

The answer, obviously, is to lunch here. Equally obviously not just before Christmas. But after Christmas? In the doldrums of January or – the nastiest month, except for Ben's birthday – February?

Think this over: lunch here.

I do want to hear so much more of your B'ham Pal. experience. I hope the wounds won't heal too quickly.

What a thrill to be working on The Go-Between! Your child-centred approach is absolutely justified by the text. Don't let anyone mess you up.

At Roehampton,* did you hear Morag,*2 over coffee, describing the wonderful iced adornment of 'my' birthday cake? I was longing to see it. On the Occasion, it was at one

* A week earlier, on November 11th 2006, Philippa and I had met at a conference in Roehampton University, organised by the International Board on Books for Young People (IBBY). During the day, Philippa was presented with a splendid celebratory cake.

*2 Professor Morag Styles, Emeritus Fellow of Homerton College, Cambridge, Professor of Children's Poetry and friend of Philippa Pearce.

end of a crowded room; I at the other. My experience of it was a rectangular piece of – admittedly delicious – chocolate cake; I never saw the many-splendoured thing itself.

Sorry to have gone on so long, so insubstantially.

As I said, 'always nice to be writing to you'.

Love to you all

Philippa

23rd November 2006

Dear Philippa,

Many thanks for your letter. No problem about moving our lunch – and, yes, I would be delighted to come to lunch there.

At the moment, the week beginning January 29th looks pretty clear. After that, I can offer February 5th or 6th, 12th or 13th, or another possibility might be to wait until March, when I could do either the 7th or the 9th. Let me know what you think!

I enjoyed your musings on "disappointed" and "appointed", "disgruntled" and "gruntled". By the same token, if we can be "disturbed", maybe we could also be "turbed". And, if you can be "disgusted", presumably you can be "gusted". Our language is a strange and wonderful jumble of anomalies.

You have shown interest in my Buckingham Palace experience, so please find enclosed a copy of my diary… Don't feel you have to wade all the way through it, but it does give an idea of the ups and downs we went through!

Last week I managed to finish the first draft of THE GO-BETWEEN. Now it is up to the composer to work his magic on it! I must say it is an extraordinary book. I think the opening section is somewhat over-written, to be honest. But the way Hartley manages to keep inside the child's head is masterly. Hopefully I have managed to do the same thing for the stage version…

Yes, it was tragic that you didn't see the cake. Nobody else did, as far as I could tell – except Morag! And presumably there was not a photo taken of it before the kitchen staff attacked it. It was very tasty, though!

Earlier this week I attended the funeral of Ronnie Stevens. He was a wonderful actor, extremely versatile – he could turn his hand to revue, Shakespeare, restoration comedy, television, pantomime etc. etc. Thirty years ago, when I wrote THE GINGERBREAD MAN, the director and I were discussing who should be approached to play Herr Von Cuckoo. My first choice was Ronnie, even though I had never met him! He accepted the offer, and was quite brilliant. He stayed with the show, on and off, for several years, playing Christmas seasons, directing the tour and even doing the choreography! His funeral was in Ruislip, not the easiest place to get to, but there were enough of us there to give him a good celebratory send-off.

Hopefully there will be news from Germany soon about the première of their version of TMG. I have also been in contact with my Japanese agent, to see if there is any movement there. I know that the book is still very popular in Japan.

All good wishes, as ever. Please send my best regards to Sally and Ben and the grandchildren.

Looking forward to seeing you soon.

Take care,

David

28.XI.06

Dear David,

This is very much an interim letter, because I am only a quarter way thro' the B'ham Palace narrative, must read it all, but have become a little dizzy in the head. '…to humanise the Queen… to include (or not) the World Cup… possibly to include the P.M. at risk of the whole show grinding to a halt in boos…'

I simply cannot imagine your working life – let alone having room for a private one.

And wouldn't you like this copy of your 'diary' back? I shan't want to keep it. (But, of course, someone authoritative ought to. What about Seven Stories in Newcastle? You must have thought of this…)

Now for the lunch here, which I'd like to be a foursome, with Sally and Ben. Of all the dates you suggest, the likeliest would be a Monday or Friday, one of which Ben usually adds to his weekend at home. (The holiday week beginning Jan 29th is really no good, mainly because of New Year celebrations.)

So these are the best possibilities:

Monday February 5th

Monday February 12th

Friday March 9th

I am just off to Durham and Newcastle (Seven Stories). I can't put dates to Sally and Ben until I get back. Then I'll write again.

Love to you all

Philippa

4th December 2006

Dear Philippa,

Many thanks for yours…

I have pencilled in all three dates – February 5th, February 12th and March 9th, in the hope that one of them will work.

Feel free to keep the copy of the diary as long as you like. Maybe I could collect it from you when I see you next year!

Love and best wishes,

David

Sadly, this proposed meeting wasn't able to take place. Two weeks later, on December 21st 2006, Philippa died during her visit to Seven Stories in Newcastle. It is perhaps appropriate that our correspondence now lives in the Seven Stories archive.

DAVID WOOD'S PHILIPPA PEARCE MEMORIAL LECTURE, SEPTEMBER 11TH 2008

Not long after the play was first produced, Philippa asked me what was the most difficult thing about adapting TOM'S MIDNIGHT GARDEN for the stage. I told her that it was finding logical reasons for Tom to stay in his pyjamas throughout most of the play. There are several scenes set in the 50s in daytime, when he certainly *wouldn't* be wearing pyjamas, but I wanted to avoid scene breaks or superfluous dialogue to cover costume changes. At one point Aunt Gwen finds him reading in his room. "Not dressed yet, Tom?" She frowns. "It's nearly lunchtime!"

I think Philippa enjoyed the fact that I had chosen an example of the nitty gritty, the craft of playwriting rather than some high-flown literary problem. A vital part of her artistry was the fact that she was a great craftswoman, affording great care to detail, choice of word or even punctuation mark.

Her practical approach made her sympathetic to the idea that children's theatre budgets might make it difficult to have a cast of more than eight, so doubling would be required. Two parts played by one actor. She could understand my pleasure in the fact that the two time zones meant that the doubling was relatively easy – Uncle Alan and Abel, Aunt Gwen and Susan, Mrs. Bartholomew and Aunt Grace – on paper it actually worked quite well, as long as time was allowed for their numerous costume changes.

Philippa enjoyed the fact that one of my first jobs was to 'find the interval'. Most theatre managers want to sell large quantities of ice cream, so insist on an interval. But, of course, the structure of a book is different from that of a play. You don't automatically find a good cliffhanging moment exactly half way through. Finding a strong end of Act One becomes essential – we want our young audience to want to come back into the auditorium for Act Two!

Philippa understood all this and was intrigued by the process of adaptation. She accepted that sometimes changes had to be made, the running order of events adjusted. She understood that the narrative voice telling the story in the book couldn't be exactly the same voice in the play. But I think she trusted me to be faithful to the story, which to me is a vital ingredient of adaptation.

And because we discussed things from day one, I like to think that she felt part of the process. There was a lovely moment when, as we watched a performance together, after one exchange of lines, she whispered to me, "Was that you or me? It was rather good! I hope it was me!"

But I'm jumping ahead. The idea – ten years ago – to adapt TOM'S MIDNIGHT GARDEN didn't, I'm sorry to say, come from me. It was Tony Graham, the Artistic Director at Unicorn Theatre, who suggested it. Rather arrogantly, I told him, no, I was certain it had been done already. Totally wrong. Yes, it had been done on radio, television, audio – and, we discovered, there was a film in preparation – but there had never been a stage version. From what we could find out, it seemed that previous requests to adapt the book for the stage had been refused. It made me wonder if Miss Pearce – who took on a rather stern image in my mind – simply wasn't interested in theatre.

Anyway, a meeting was arranged. I set off for Philippa's cottage in Great Shelford using a splendid hand-drawn map, plus detailed handwritten instructions. I was welcomed quite noisily by Clem, the dog, and not so noisily, by Worcester, the cat – I remember thinking this was a good omen, because Worcester was the name of my college at Oxford – and by Philippa. It turned out that 'stern' was one of the least appropriate adjectives to describe her. She cooked me a lovely lunch, ending up with cheese called 'stinky bishop' cheese. Sadly I've forgotten if she told me how it acquired this nickname – maybe Sally knows! Then we talked. And delicious talk it was.

I discovered that far from having no interest in theatre, Philippa loved it. She often travelled to London to see productions at the National or the RSC. We shared a love of the RSC's *Nicholas Nickleby*. This turned out to be rather helpful. I pinched David Edgar's use of narration by the character to whom things are happening – you may remember Roger Rees as Nicholas announcing, "And Nicholas went to London!" What's so great about this technique, particularly in children's theatre, is that it keeps the focus on the right character. Children don't have the same range of vision as adults. Their heads move as they watch the stage. So it doesn't help to have a narrator on the side of the stage telling you something when you are meant to be watching something centre stage. Human nature means that the eyes go to the moving mouth of the speaker. So, Tom became his own narrator, and Philippa approved.

I discovered that the reasons for saying 'no' to other requests to adapt the book were purely practical. Philippa found it difficult to see how it could be done satisfactorily, particularly with the two time zones, both as real and as important as one another. How would the settings be realised without cumbersome scene changes? She was also concerned about the ability of a child actor to sustain a major role not just for one performance, but for a whole season or tour. Again, she was very practical. She realised that Tom would need to be the motor running the play. His character is proactive rather than reactive. A child might be able to do it on camera, but live on stage? Little did she know then that the actor who was to create the role of Tom was well into his thirties – but totally accepted by audiences of all ages as a lonely 9 year old.

Philippa also put her finger on another possible hurdle. She said in one of the first of her many wonderful, treasured letters, '***there is always an element of dismissive snobbery about children's literature, which probably extends to children's theatre, I suspect***'. Philippa, I think, was worried that the play might not be taken seriously within the mainstream theatre industry.

But she did understand my belief that many of her ideas in the book are inherently theatrical – the voices of the house that talk to Tom, the clock striking thirteen, the two time zones, the theme of loneliness and longing for freedom, shared by both Tom and Hatty, the twist at the end – the wonderful Mrs Bartholomew revelation. I knew these ideas would translate well to the stage, and suggested it might be possible to encourage the audience to use their imaginations by not having a naturalistic set. I thought the costumes should faithfully reflect both the 1950s and the Edwardian periods, but that the locations, including the garden, could be created simply, using light and a few specific objects such as the grandfather clock or a door frame.

I think Philippa liked the idea of simplicity of staging. It would hopefully allow the story to breathe and flow.

Then Philippa explained how personal the inspiration for the book was. How traumatic it was for her when her family left the mill, and how she began to think about time passing, yet things staying the same – for example her dining room table. She wrote about this later in a programme note:

> ***'I was the youngest of four children. We lived in a big old house with a garden to match, with trees to climb and secret places. Long after I had left home, I remembered it all. There I had spent a happy childhood with my brothers and sister. There my father had been born, in that garden he had played with his seven siblings in the last years of Queen Victoria's reign, at the end of the 19th century.***
>
> ***I began to imagine two childhoods widely separated by Time, but taking place in the same garden. I imagined these childhoods superimposed upon each other, as ghostly and yet as real as two images coinciding from a wrongly working camera.***
>
> ***In my story a little Victorian girl would play with a boy from the 20th century. Eventually she would have to grow up, leave the garden: how would that happen?***
>
> ***My father told us about the Victorian garden. He also told us of the great frost of 1894–5, when he skated all the way from***

Cambridge (or Castleford) to Ely. Just what my story needed. Hatty would skate her way to a grown-up happy ending.'

And, of course, there we were sitting in her cottage, only yards away from the actual mill house and the real midnight garden! By the end of the meeting I understood how personal the book was. It really was Philippa's – if Sally will forgive me – other child. Quite naturally she feared that putting it on the stage could destroy something. No wonder she was reluctant to let me or anybody else get their grubby hands on it!

Philippa sensibly didn't say yes to the play straightaway. She read some of my work, and my book about children's theatre. She even came to see me perform in my magic and music show! Eventually she agreed to let me have a go and I did a synopsis. I always tend to do a very full synopsis, because with a children's play I feel the through line is very important.

From then on, Philippa was wonderfully hands-on – in a very constructive, supportive and sensitive way, reacting to the synopsis, the first draft and the second draft.

A couple of years before, I had adapted *The Sheep-Pig*, Dick King-Smith's lovely book. When I sent him the play for comment, he only had one – he complained that I had used the word rifle instead of shotgun! His lack of criticism was, I suppose, flattering, but a little unnerving. Philippa came back with pages of wonderfully detailed notes – I'll give you some examples.

I had given Uncle Alan a line in which he described Tom, confined to the flat in quarantine, as 'like a caged tiger...' Philippa wrote, '***this image seems wrong to me. I should have thought Tom might be restless in the daytime, but also subdued, even apathetic, longing for the night***'.

I had given Tom a torch, with which to read under the bedclothes. Wrong! The whole point is that Uncle Alan doesn't allow him to read after lights out. A torch would mean he <u>could</u>, and would give him a little victory over Uncle Alan, which would be wrong. Philippa wrote: '***Important that this (the torch) should be taken away for good? It shouldn't be an available alternative to moonlight later.***' She was rightly saying that if he had a torch, he would be able to see the grandfather clock, without having to open the garden door to let in the moonlight!

Still on the idea of light, Philippa wrote '***Is it going to be possible for Hatty to "hide in the shadows of the clock" if she's carrying an oil-lamp?***' She was so logical! I got away with this one by changing the stage direction to 'shielding the oil-lamp, she hides in the shadows of the clock'. Philippa accepted that.

Another question of logic – I had suggested that the Edwardian boys should enter with the terrier dog, Pincher, on a lead. The reason for this was that I had suggested the dog might be imagined rather than real or a puppet. If it was to be imagined, I rather liked the idea of a visible stiff lead with a collar on the end, to create a kind of illusion… Philippa wrote: '***Perhaps it doesn't matter, but one would not normally have a dog on a lead in one's own garden***.'

A bigger problem, and one we discussed a lot, was to do with language. Tom, in his role as narrator, often used some of Philippa's wonderfully descriptive phrases, particularly when seeing the garden for the first time. Philippa wrote: '***This is one example of many which raises quite a large issue. By using the wording of the original narrative in speeches (or letters) you have given these a non-realistic, literary tone (e.g. "thick beetle-browed yew trees"). You may have calculated that at certain times this heightened speech is justified by the whole atmosphere created. Something I can't properly judge. Even so there are some things which would seem outside Tom's experience of knowledge e.g. "a fan of peacock feathers" and "a housemaid".***'

This was a tricky one. I argued that Tom could have two voices – a narrative voice and a voice in role – his character voice. I thought, and still do, that the narrative voice could be more literary, almost as though an older Tom is looking back at what happened. Anyway, we managed to agree, and sometimes to agree to differ, until it was possible to see whether it worked in performance.

I used the word 'scrumping', in the mouth of one of the boys going off to find apples. Philippa pointed out: '***This usually means stealing fruit from <u>someone else's</u> orchard or garden.***' Quite right!

I wanted Tom to help Hatty get one up on her cousins. This would, I thought, help bond Tom and Hatty. So I had him interrupt a game of pig-in-the-middle, by catching the apple the cousins were throwing over Hatty's head, teasing her. Philippa pointed out that Tom couldn't catch the apple or hold it – it was not in his time zone. Similarly Tom couldn't fire a bow and arrow, only help Hatty to do it. Eventually we came up with a better apple idea. Hatty is told she can have the apple if she can guess which of the cousins is holding it behind his back. Tom, invisible to the cousins, goes round and points the answer to Hatty. This achieves the bonding, without the apple-holding!

This also led to an idea which became an important feature of the play. After this moment of triumph for Hatty against her cousins, I had her shake hands with Tom. Wrong! They cannot touch. So, with Philippa's approval, I introduced the notion of them TRYING to shake hands, but realising that they cannot. This becomes a gesture in which they hold up their hands, palm to palm but don't actually touch. They do it several times in the play, as a kind of greeting. It pays great dividends at the end, when Tom and Mrs Bartholomew – the grown up Hatty – do it, thus confirming to Tom that Mrs Bartholomew is actually Hatty. Then, right at the end, because they are now in the same time zone, the two palms actually do meet and touch, and fingers interlink, for the very first time. A lump in the throat moment I think Philippa enjoyed as much as I did!

You may remember that Hatty, in the book, writes a note to the fairies. I included this in the play. Philippa wrote: '***Since writing the book, I've come to feel uneasy about my invention of the King of the Fairies episode, simply because I once received an abusive letter from a group of (older?) girls playing on the double-entendre of "fairies". <u>Please think about this</u>.***'

The 'Time' theory that particularly interested Philippa was in a book by J.W. Dunne called NOTHING DIES published by Faber in

1940. She kindly sent me a photocopy of a chapter and also wrote '***re. page 78, I'd like it to be clearer that the minds of Tom and his uncle work in totally different ways. Tom is seduced by his imaginings; his uncle tries to stick to pure reason.***'

I think you can see how hands-on Philippa was, and always in a helpful way. She reminded me that what I had called the back door should be called the garden door. Occasionally she was, perhaps, a little pedantic. I wanted Tom and Hatty to throw goose feathers in the air – a nice theatrical effect. Philippa wrote '***I'm afraid you can't have these in the greenhouse. They belong only to the potting-shed, where Abel would pluck the goose and store the feathers in a sack for the making of pillows, feather beds etc.***' In the end I managed to persuade Philippa to let us have them in the greenhouse, and they do flutter very attractively!

What was for me reassuring was that we never disagreed on structure.

The Unicorn production went into rehearsal. A special performance was announced, to which VIPs were invited – Philippa herself, Laura Cecil, her agent, the Unicorn board etc. etc. My family came too. Before the performance the whole audience waited for what seemed an eternity in the cramped foyer. Eventually we were admitted to the auditorium and told that none of the stage lighting was working. This was incredibly frustrating, because lighting played a big part in the production, particularly when Tom finds the garden. But the brave actors had to do the show in the cold and dim working light state, plus all the house lights, which rather disturbingly stayed up throughout. Thanks to the actors, the performance went well. Philippa wrote:

> '***Dear David, I resolved not to write to you until I could tell you that I was seeing your (our?) TMG play again with the proper lighting. I've booked for the very last performance (November 4th).***
>
> ***But I was amazed and delighted last Saturday even at the lighting-less production we attended. One could see how good the play was in structure and coherence and performance.***'

As you can imagine, that meant an awful lot. And Philippa's generosity extended further. Right at the end of the play, when Tom returns to his mother, Aunt Gwen finds the skates – the one pair of skates that both Tom and Hatty magically and triumphantly use at one and the same time. Tom leaves them behind. I introduced the idea of 1950s Aunt Gwen looking bemused at these Edwardian skates as the final image of the play. Philippa very generously said after one performance – '***I wish I'd thought of that for the book.***'

There was also the problem of 'wow' and 'double wow'! Let me explain. The device I introduced, to help the narration, involved Tom writing letters to his brother Peter. Sometimes the voice of Tom writes them. Sometimes the voice of Peter reads them. Quite a lot of plot is usefully conveyed in the letters, which culminate in Peter being encouraged to magically arrive – in his pyjamas – at Ely Cathedral, where he meets Tom and points out to Tom that Hatty has grown up.

In the letter to Peter in which Tom describes seeing the tree crash down one night, but then the next night finding it magically upright again, I needed Peter to express awed surprise. Tempting fate, I used the word 'wow' and then, reacting to a second surprise, 'double wow!' Philippa wrote '***This is an anachronism for the 1950s, although to be appreciated by contemporary children. I leave you to decide.***' She did, but later on wrote '***"Wow! Double wow!" By now you know my aversion to this. It's American, and an anachronism for the 1950s. Worse, it will – like all slang – become dated – <u>with the wrong date</u>.***

However, I could not suggest an alternative that you – and young audiences – would like. So I had to trust to your ingenuity. In the meantime, if all else fails, OK.' I am ashamed to admit it is still in the script…

Well, over the next few years, the play managed to win two awards and go to New York in the original Unicorn production. Other productions followed, and I was delighted to accompany Philippa to some of them. We also shared the occasional joint question and answer session.

Philippa became not only a delightful correspondent, but a dear friend. We used to meet for lunch. Once Philippa took me to the Old

Fire Engine House in Ely – '***the very nicest restaurant I know. Only English cooking, and second helpings offered.***'

Once, when she couldn't manage a lunch date, she said she was disappointed – '***"disappointed"***' – she mused, '***is one ever "appointed"? Fatuous; but I'm reminded of Geoffrey Dearmer – son of Percy, the hymnologist – who would describe himself as sometimes "gruntled".***'

She wrote elegantly, delightfully and with great modesty. In early 2003 – '***since May last year I've been concentrating – as far as possible to the exclusion of outside attractions, however tempting – in order to work on a full length book for children. I was amazed – at my age – to find an idea gripping me – insisting on my dealing with it. I've been very slow – slower than usual, I think – but the end is in sight... and then I shall frisk.***'

When she sent me a proof of her new book, which was called THE LITTLE GENTLEMAN, I wrote back expressing my appreciation of the story.

'***What a lovely letter to have from you about THE LITTLE GENTLEMAN! (I <u>need</u> something to sustain me between finishing a book and holding it in my hand as a book. All the usual Best Butter from the publisher is no good, because <u>they</u> have a vested interest in the project anyway.)***'

When I was asked to write a play in celebration of the Queen's 80th birthday, Philippa wrote '***It has only just dawned on me that the D.W. of the Buckingham Palace Party must be you! You'll be run off your feet and at the same time take everything in your stride. <u>Don't let any royals try to boss you about</u>.***'

She was right about me being run off my feet – for seven months! I wrote a diary cataloguing some of the delights and more of the horrors of the job. Philippa enjoyed the gruesome stories. She invited me to lunch. '***I do want to hear so much more of your Buckingham Palace experience. I hope the wounds won't heal <u>too</u> quickly.***'

Philippa's last letter but one to me was dated November 28th, 2006. We were trying to find a date upon which she and Sally and Ben and

I could lunch. She suggests some dates, then says, '***I am just off to Durham and Newcastle (Seven Stories). I can't put dates to Sally and Ben until I get back. Then I'll write again.***'

Very, very sadly, she wasn't able to…

But Philippa is still very much a part of my life, because our play lives on – last Christmas Manchester Library Theatre revived their splendid production, and the Open University have just made a programme about it. I say 'our play', because I am proud and delighted that Philippa contributed to and approved of the adaptation. She ended one of her lovely letters with the words – '***I thanked you then and thank you again now – and congratulate us both! Philippa.***'

Philippa, thank you.

Philippa Pearce standing in the garden of Mill House, 1997 © Helen Craig

17.X.2000

Dear David,

I resolved <u>not</u> to write to you until I could tell you that I was <u>seeing</u> your (<u>our</u>?) <u>TMG</u> play again <u>with the proper lighting</u>. I've booked for the very last performance (Nov 4), to go either with Sally or with her partner, Ben Norland (also of Walker Books), who's very interested in this kind of project.

But I was amazed and delighted ~~at the~~ last Saturday even at the lighting-less ~~performance~~ production we ~~saw~~ attended. One could <u>see</u> how good the play was in structure and coherence and performance.

I thanked you then, and thank you again now — and congratulate us both! Philippa

Letter to DW from Philippa Pearce, 2000

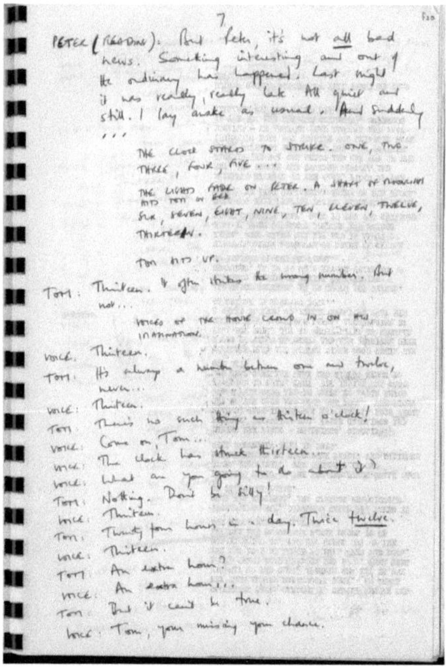

7

PETER (READING): But Peter, it's not all bad news. Something interesting and out of the ordinary has happened. Last night it was really, really late. All quiet and still. I lay awake as usual. And suddenly ...

THE CLOCK STARTS TO STRIKE. ONE, TWO, THREE, FOUR, FIVE ...

THE LIGHTS FADE ON PETER. A SHAFT OF MOONLIGHT ON TOM IN BED.

SIX, SEVEN, EIGHT, NINE, TEN, ELEVEN, TWELVE, THIRTEEN.

TOM SITS UP.

TOM: Thirteen. It often strikes the wrong number. But not...

VOICES OF THE HOUSE CREEP IN ON HIS IMAGINATION.

VOICE: Thirteen.

TOM: It's always a number between one and twelve, never...

VOICE: Thirteen.

TOM: There's no such thing as thirteen o'clock!

VOICE: Come on, Tom...

VOICE: The clock has struck thirteen...

VOICE: What are you going to do about it?

TOM: Nothing. Don't be silly!

VOICE: Thirteen.

TOM: Twenty four hours in a day. Twice twelve.

VOICE: Thirteen.

TOM: An extra hour?

VOICE: An extra hour...

TOM: But it can't be true.

VOICE: Tom, you're missing your chance.

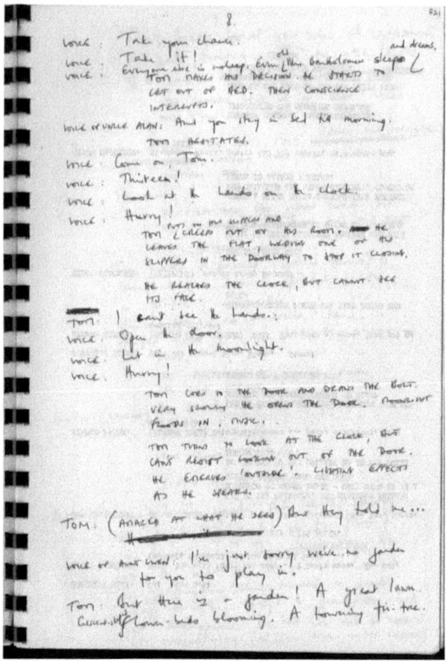

8

VOICE: Take your chance.

VOICE: Take it!

VOICE: Everyone else is asleep. Even old Mrs Bartholomew sleeps and dreams.

TOM MAKES HIS DECISION. HE STARTS TO GET OUT OF BED. THEN CONSCIENCE INTERRUPTS.

VOICE OF UNCLE ALAN: And you stay in bed till morning.

TOM HESITATES.

VOICE: Come on, Tom.

VOICE: Thirteen!

VOICE: Look at the hands on the clock.

VOICE: Hurry!

TOM PUTS ON HIS SLIPPERS AND CREEPS OUT OF HIS ROOM. HE LEAVES THE FLAT, WEDGING ONE OF HIS SLIPPERS IN THE DOORWAY TO STOP IT CLOSING.

HE REACHES THE CLOCK, BUT CANNOT SEE ITS FACE.

TOM: I can't see the hands.

VOICE: Open the door.

VOICE: Let in the moonlight.

VOICE: Hurry!

TOM GOES TO THE DOOR AND DRAWS THE BOLT. VERY SLOWLY HE OPENS THE DOOR. MOONLIGHT FLOODS IN, MUSIC.

TOM TRIES TO LOOK AT THE CLOCK, BUT CAN'T RESIST LOOKING OUT OF THE DOOR. HE ENTERS 'OUTSIDE'. LIGHTING EFFECTS AS HE SPEAKS.

TOM: (AMAZED AT WHAT HE SEES) But they told me...

VOICE OF AUNT GWEN: I'm just sorry we've no garden for you to play in.

TOM: But there is a garden! A great lawn. Crescent-shaped flower-beds blooming. A towering fir-tree.

Above:
Two pages from DW's original manuscript of his adaptation of *Tom's Midnight Garden*

Left:
Dale Superville (Tom) in *Tom's Midnight Garden*, Unicorn at the Pleasance Theatre, London, 2000 © Sarah Ainslie

DW and Philippa Pearce backstage at the Pleasance Theatre, London, 2000 (Photographer unknown)

L to R: Tony Graham (director), Philippa Pearce and DW backstage at the Pleasance Theatre, London, 2000 (Photographer unknown)

Childhood pleasures for the half-term

FOR A special half-term treat, parents should forget the recent film version of *Tom's Midnight Garden* and seek out Unicorn Theatre for Children's clear, evocative (and first ever) main-stage dramatisation of Philippa Pearce's Fifties classic about a boy's nightly voyage to a Victorian past. Adapted by David Wood, it shows, as much as anything else, that a company normally associated with experimental pieces is equally at home with more traditional, solid, BBC tea-time fare.

For those unfamiliar with the book, Tom (Dale Superville) is cooped up in quarantine at his aunt and uncle's house because his brother back home has measles. Weeks of dreary confinement stretch before him, but when the grandfather clock in the hall mysteriously strikes 13, he discovers an enchanting new world: the same house, with its present-day, tatty old concrete backyard, reassumes its Victorian past, with a beautiful garden and only one child who can see him – the orphaned Hatty.

Her unhappiness – she is tormented by her aunt and horrid cousins with such names as Hubert and Edgar – is classically Victorian, and familiar enough to the target eight-and-over audience. What might puzzle them is the disjunctive passage of time. Tom remains the 10-year-old boy we first meet, in neat grey school shorts, garters and polished shoes, but the slippage of years in the other world means Hatty matures, the girlishness so wonderfully conveyed in Debra

THEATRE

TOM'S MIDNIGHT GARDEN
PLEASANCE
LONDON

Penny's performance giving way to the concerns of a young woman being courted.

But, at its best, Jeanine Davies' lighting switches seamlessly between seasons, from dappled garden to icy river or ghostly candlelit interior with spooky nocturnal echoes. The story also offers gentle insight into growing up, the importance and limitations of friendship as well as, perhaps, sexual awakening.

It succeeds, above all else, by being modern without being anachronistic. Hatty's cousins may call her a "silly juggins" and Iain Stuart Robertson's gardener deliver zealous exhortations on Christian morality, but none of this seems alienating and the essentials of the story are never lost. Coupled with Tom's letters to his brother back home, all this heartily reassures the pint-sized audience. They share his excitable confusion, finding answers with him in a production sufficiently mature not to be patronising and lucid enough to tell a lovely story very capably.

BEN DOWELL

To 4 Nov (020-7609 1800/8753)

The Independent review of the first production of *Tom's Midnight Garden*, Unicorn Theatre, 2000 © Ben Dowell / Independent Digital News & Media Ltd

Flyer (front and back) for *Tom's Midnight Garden* in USA, Unicorn Theatre production at New Victory Theater (New York), 2001

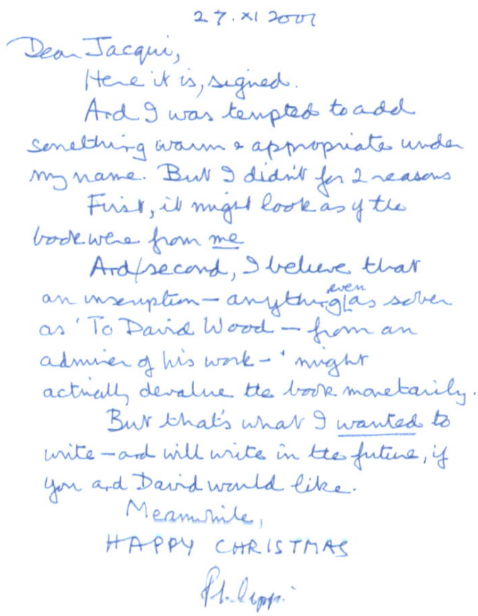

27.XI 2001

Dear Jacqui,

Here it is, signed.

And I was tempted to add something warm & appropriate under my name. But I didn't for 2 reasons

First, it might look as if the book were from me

And/second, I believe that an inscription – anything even as sober as 'To David Wood – from an admirer of his work –' might actually devalue the book monetarily.

But that's what I wanted to write – and will write in the future, if you and David would like.

Meanwhile,

HAPPY CHRISTMAS

Philippa

A. PHILIPPA PEARCE

TOM'S MIDNIGHT GARDEN

Illustrated by
Susan Einzig

Philippa Pearce
November 2001

London
OXFORD UNIVERSITY PRESS
1958

Philippa Pearce's thoughtful response to Jacqui Wood's request to sign a First Edition of *Tom's Midnight Garden* as a birthday present for DW

Left:
Tom's Midnight Garden – front cover of DW's First Edition

Below:
Arthur Wilson (Tom) and Claire Redcliffe (Hatty) in *Tom's Midnight Garden* at Manchester Library Theatre, 2007 © Gerry Murray

Theatre

Tom's Midnight Garden

Library, Manchester

★★★★★

THIS is the children's novel closest to my heart, and my relief and joy at how it has been shaped for the stage can hardly be exaggerated.

I wanted precision but dreaded the literal. If Philippa Pearce's Carnegie Medal-winning book had been adapted 20 or even 40 years ago (it was published in 1958) the chances are that elaborate sets would have tried to take us all around Cambridgeshire and the Fens. Into the wide Victorian garden that mysteriously replaces the tiny 1950s backyard when the grandfather clock strikes 13; up into the tree-house, along the high wall above the sundial, out skating on the Ouse, up Ely tower.

David Wood's adaptation transports us to all the above, and to rooms inside the house where Tom's uncle and aunt live in a small flat but which is also, for the orphan girl Tom meets in the garden, her unfriendly home in the previous century. But Roger Haines, the director, and his designer, Jamie Vartan, have set the play on a gigantic tilted clock-face, representing Time itself. And after old Mrs Bartholomew has given the grandfather its weekly wind, the sturdy hour and minute hands on the stage whirl around, and dark figures emerge from the wings to clamber over the face.

They too represent the remorseless forward tick of Time against which Tom later fights his despairing battle to rejoin Hatty, the girl he fears he has lost. And they are also the scene-changers used by Haines and Vartan in the most imaginative way to become hedge, tree, wall, cathedral steps, and the ribs of the greenhouse.

This gives a darker tone to a tale that could so easily have been rendered too sweet. For there is darkness and danger and fear in Pearce's original tale: Hatty badly treated by her chilling aunt, Tom exiled from his own home by his brother's measles and afraid he is losing his new friend too.

And of course there is happiness in it, comradeship, dangers surmounted and the intensely moving last scene that should bring tears of relief to anyone's eye.

Though Ben Elliot projects his voice more vigorously than is needed, his Tom is unsentimentally boyish; his face-pulling at adults too grown-up to see him left the Toms and Hattys in the audience well pleased.

Hatty herself, pretty and spirited in Kirsten Parker's performance, grows subtly older, lonely child transforming into happier young woman. Good performances surround them, notably from Romy Baskerville and Annie Fitzmaurice, and from Simon Markey as a fantasy-fearing uncle and the God-fearing gardener. Truly a show to watch with delight and remember in gratitude.

Jeremy Kingston

Box office: 0161 236 7110

The Times review of the Manchester Library Theatre production of *Tom's Midnight Garden*, Christmas 2002

Tom's Midnight Garden flyer for Rose Theatre, Kingston (Birmingham Stage Company), 2014. Part of a long tour!

If you want real theatre, though, try the Birmingham Stage Company's marvellous version of *Tom's Midnight Garden*. Philippa Pearce's classic story has a lonely boy creeping out as the clock strikes 13, haunted by a garden and a girl-child from the past. David Wood, the adaptor, had a tricky task, but beautifully renders its questing ideas of time and memory, and a boy's realisation that old people are just bygone children like him.

I sat amid 360 pupils from ages 7 to 11, bussed up from an enlightened Essex primary school, and breathed in their attentive wonder. They didn't need joshing, shouting or nudgey-funny-uncle jokes to be held by the story: the lighting and subtle projection transformed and made transparent a simple set of curves and arches by Jacqueline Trousdale. Neal Foster, the director, uses live musicians on cello, flute and guitar, and the movement is clever enough to convince the *CGI* generation that a boy walks through walls and hands go through a ghost. David Tute is a gruff boyish Tom, Caitlin Thorburn a touching childlike Hattie.

Libby Purves sees 'a marvellous retelling of a favourite story' in The Times review of Birmingham Stage Company's production of *Tom's Midnight Garden*, 2012

KATHLEEN HALE

ORLANDO THE MARMALADE CAT

The front cover of *Orlando and the Three Graces*, First Edition (1965)

KATHLEEN HALE

Kathleen Hale OBE was born on May 24th, 1898, in Lanarkshire, but was brought up in Manchester. Her father died when she was five years old, and her mother took over his job as a travelling salesman for Chappell's pianos. Kathleen attended Manchester High School for Girls, and in her last year went to life drawing classes at Manchester School of Art. She then won a scholarship to Reading University to study art. The college farm gave her many first-hand experiences of animals, which later influenced her work as an illustrator. Moving to London in 1917, Kathleen was introduced into Bohemian society and took various jobs to make ends meet. She won an open competition for poster design and, as a result, became secretary to the competition's judge, Augustus John. In 1926 she married Douglas McClean, a bacteriologist, encouraged to do so by his father, John, with whom she had fallen in love. She studied at the Central School of Arts and Crafts, and in 1938 the first two adventures of *Orlando the Marmalade Cat*, written originally for her two sons, were accepted for publication by Noel Carrington, the editor of *Country Life* publishers. Kathleen prepared the lithographic illustrations herself. Over the years, Orlando had eighteen adventures, the last one appearing in 1972. In 1976 Kathleen was awarded an OBE for her work as an illustrator. She published her autobiography, *A Slender Reputation*, in 1994, and died in Bristol in 2000, at the age of 101.

Key Players

Kathleen Hale	Author & Illustrator
David Wood	Adapter
Laurence Harbottle	Lawyer
Jill Brooks	Animation artist
Mike Stuart	Animation artist
Sally Floyer	Publisher – Puffin/Frederick Warne
Elizabeth (Liz) Attenborough	Publisher Puffin Books
Diana Syrat	Book Editor – Penguin/Frederick Warne
Michael Gabriel	Animation Art Director

How it all began...

In 1976 I received a message from Laurence Harbottle, the eminent showbiz lawyer, asking me to ring him. A few years earlier Laurence had been instrumental in setting up my touring children's theatre company, Whirligig, and had also negotiated contracts for my children's television series *Chips' Comic* and *Chish 'n' Fips*. I called him, and he asked me if I knew the *Orlando* books by Kathleen Hale. I replied that of course I knew of them, but had never owned any of the series as a child. However, my cousin Richard, a year older than me, had shown me the copies he had been given. I recalled their bright, idiosyncratic illustrations, in a very large format, which Kathleen later told me were inspired by the *Babar* books. Laurence told me that Kathleen, at that time eighty-eight years old, was keen to 'see Orlando move'. He wondered if I would like to discuss with her the possibility of an animated film version or series, and maybe help her get such a project off the ground. I expressed interest, and he offered to put me in touch with Kathleen, with the aim of setting up a meeting.

I quickly obtained copies of some of the books, and could certainly see the possibility of Orlando and his cat family adapting appealingly to the screen. The books were undoubtedly classics. However, they had fallen somewhat out of fashion, were no longer in print, and were, I felt, perhaps somewhat dated. But I was certainly more than willing to investigate further.

Before meeting Kathleen, I did some research and discovered her connections with the Bloomsbury Group. She had even acted as Augustus John's secretary. She was clearly a remarkable lady. When I arrived at her picturesque cottage near Oxford, I suppose I expected to be greeted by an elderly lady in a shawl. But no. Kathleen came to the door dressed in a smart denim trouser suit, wearing dangly earrings and holding a copy of Bob Geldof's autobiography. Here was a sparky, worldly, with-it octogenarian.

Her excitement about seeing her creations come alive on screen was palpable and infectious. I immediately decided to do my best to see her ambitions realised.

We agreed that the animations had to resemble faithfully her illustrations and replicate her use of colour. Kathleen suggested that the *Orlando and the Three Graces* story might be a good starting point. Set at Christmastime, full of magic and humour, it successfully introduces the enchanting world of Orlando the Marmalade Cat, his wife Grace, and their three kittens, tortoise-shell Pansy, snow-white Blanche and little coal-black Tinkle, who is the adventurous, often naughty one! Kathleen, with a mischievous grin, once told me that Tinkle was a version of her young, unconventional, sometimes rebellious, self. And as I got to know her better, her sparky, occasionally anarchic sense of fun and her zest for life echoed more and more the impish attitude of Tinkle. Kathleen *was* Tinkle!

Over the next fourteen years, as our correspondence shows, we made every effort to make things happen. Our hopes were sadly dashed, but not for want of trying. And our belief in the idea never faltered. I like to think that a warm friendship developed between us. Kathleen met and was enchanted by Jacqui, my wife, who in turn was enchanted by Kathleen. We visited often. Kathleen entertained us with stories from her past, many of which she was at the time noting down for her revealing and richly enticing autobiography, *A Slender Reputation*, which was published in 1994.

Towards the end of her long life, I visited her several times in the care home to which ill health had forced her to relocate. And, when she died aged 101, I was privileged to be asked to speak at her funeral. What an extraordinary lady she was. I was so lucky to be accepted as her friend. I so regret not having been able to help her fulfil her dream.

DW

'THAT DARNED CAT…'

Correspondence with Kathleen Hale

1987 – 1999

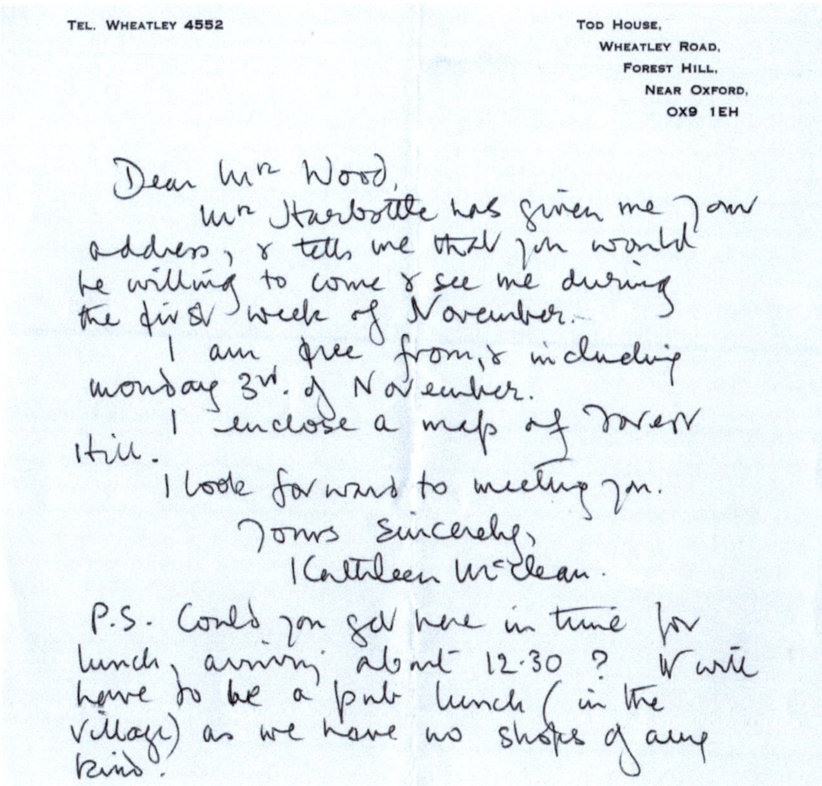

TEL. WHEATLEY 4552

TOD HOUSE,
WHEATLEY ROAD,
FOREST HILL,
NEAR OXFORD,
OX9 1EH

Dear Mr Wood,

Mr Harbottle has given me your address, & tells me that you would be willing to come & see me during the first week of November.

I am free from, & including Monday 3rd. of November.

I enclose a map of Forest Hill.

I look forward to meeting you.

Yours sincerely,

Kathleen McLean.

P.S. Could you get here in time for lunch, arriving about 12.30? It will have to be a pub lunch (in the village) as we have no shops of any kind.

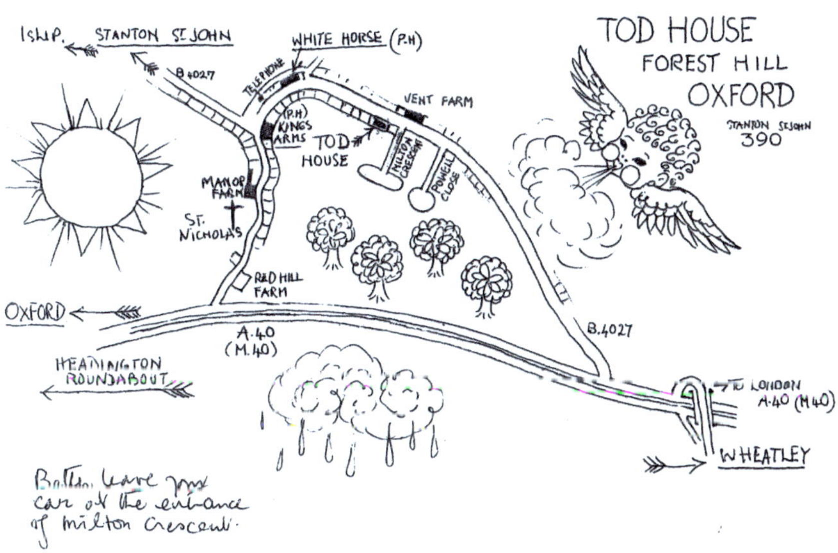

15 October 1986

Dear Mrs. McClean,

Many thanks for your letter.

My production of THE OLD MAN OF LOCHNAGAR visits Oxford Playhouse in December. Radio Oxford have expressed an interest to interview me, and it seemed a perfect opportunity to fix that up for the same day as my visit to you!*

We are waiting to hear from Radio Oxford and will come back to you straight away. We believe it will be 4th, 6th or 7th November.

Apologies for this delay in making our arrangements, but I look forward to seeing you anyway. Will be in touch shortly.

All good wishes,

Yours sincerely

David Wood

23 October 1986

Dear Miss Hale,

I can now confirm Tuesday, 4th November, and hope this is still convenient for you. Unfortunately, I may have to be slightly later than originally anticipated. Would 2.00pm be suitable? Please don't worry about food! A cup of coffee and a biscuit would be fine!

I have to do an interview with the Oxford Mail *before coming to you, but will endeavour to be bang on time.*

I look forward very much to meeting you.

All good wishes,

Yours sincerely

David Wood

* An adaptation of the children's book by HRH The Prince of Wales, with illustrations by Sir Hugh Casson.

5 November 1986

Dear Miss Hale,

Many thanks indeed for a most enjoyable meeting, and for taking the trouble to make lunch!

I will try to interest my partner into developing the ORLANDO television series idea further. We will approach the people who did THE SNOWMAN, in the hope of finding the young pair who were interested last time.

As I explained, I have not access to any magic doors, but will do my best to further the idea, and keep you in touch.

Thank you again. All good wishes,

Yours sincerely

David Wood

12/1/87

Dear David Wood,

Just to tell you that there was a fund-raising "do" at Aldeburgh over the w/end at the beginning of January & a production of "Orlando's Seaside Holiday" was read by Freda Dowie, illustrations to the book thrown onto a cine screen, & music specially written by Richard McLaughlin (composer of music for films on T.V.).

I thought the superb reading, & the music, might be of interest to anyone thinking of doing an "Orlando" Cartoon for Television.

Now this is only a humble suggestion, <u>& please don't bother to answer</u> – maybe these details could be kept in mind only, for the future – if any!

With best wishes,

Yours sincerely

Kathleen Hale.

<u>P.S</u>. The Sir Peter Pears' idea of the "do" to raise funds for the repairs to the Aldeburgh Moot Hall may be repeated in July or August. With all the concerts etc which comprised the whole programme.

Kathleen suggested Stuart Brooks Ltd as the animation company we might invite to work with us. Jill Brooks had worked on the much-loved animation film based on Raymond Briggs' *The Snowman* (1982). Mike Stuart was a director, best known for *Pink Floyd: The Wall* (1982) and *Yellow Submarine* (1968). I understood that Jill, as the main rendering artist on *The Snowman*, was considered by Kathleen a possible perfect match for her drawing style, and for Orlando's gentle, old-fashioned world.

19 January 1987

Dear Miss Hale,

Many thanks for your letter of 12th January.

I will indeed get in touch with Richard McLaughlin. I am delighted to hear the production at Aldeburgh went so well. If they do it again, could somebody kindly let me know?

I have been coming up against a series of brick walls! In particular, I cannot for the life of me trace the two animators who were interested originally – the two you mentioned to me. I have mentioned this to Laurence Harbottle, and I think he is as mystified as I am.

Meanwhile, I am due to talk to Channel Four about several projects, including this one, quite soon. And there is another man, who is a freelance, who works mainly for the BBC, who I think could also be very helpful.

I must admit that for the last few weeks I have been unable to do much because we have been doing a television production of my stage version of THE OLD MAN OF LOCHNAGAR. This will go out on Channel Four in about a year's time.

I will keep you informed of any developments.

Meanwhile, all good wishes, and thank you for letting me know about the Aldeburgh event.

Yours sincerely

David Wood

27/1/87

Dear Mr Wood,

Thank you for your letter of January 19th. I was whisked into hospital on the 21st and didn't get it before I went.

The name & address of the Animators are:-

Stuart Brooks Animation
1/3 Charlotte Street
London W.1

They did the Snowman & Pink Floyd's "The Wall" illustrated by Gerald Scarfe. They were keen to do "Orlando", both Mike Stuart & Jill Brooks having been brought up on my books.

I'm divorced from my Aldeburgh correspondence until Feb:14th when I can call in at home for the relevant letters, but I think if you wrote to Aldeburgh Fund Raising Festival for the Moot Hall at Aldeburgh, it would reach the people concerned, who could tell you of their plans for a repeat performance in July or August, and maybe give you information about how to hear R.L.'s music, & the extremely good reader of "Seaside Holiday". A woman who did all the different cat voices.

Please, if this idea materialises, & the "Orlando's Camping Holiday" is to be used, will you see that the small format is used – the original large one – the first of my books – was not lithographed by me – I am deeply ashamed of the result. The 2nd, small book is rather good, done by Self.

I do think you've pulled "The Old Man of Lochnagar" together marvellously! (the book.)

Forgive verbosity,
Yours sincerely,
Kathleen Hale

30 January 1987

Dear Miss Hale,

Thank you for your letter. I do hope you are progressing well. I will get in touch with Stuart Brooks Animation.

I have spoken to Richard McLaughlin, who in fact I have known for many years! I do not, however, feel that he can make any contribution at the moment. I have asked him to keep in touch, and to let me know if and when the Aldeburgh performance is to be repeated.

All good wishes,
Yours sincerely
David Wood

c.c. Laurence Harbottle
Mike Stuart & Jill Brooks
17 February 1987

Dear Miss Hale,

Yesterday I had lunch with Mike Stuart and Jill Brooks, who were the two people interested in ORLANDO.

They showed me samples of their animation work, which I enjoyed. They also showed me examples of their artwork, based on yours. I thought it was extremely good. I understand that a few years ago you saw this artwork and liked it.

I certainly feel that Stuart Brooks Animation Limited would make every effort to produce a series of films which would be faithful to the original, and which you would be pleased with.

I am contacting Laurence Harbottle to find out a little more about the rights situation, publishing situation, etc. Then we hope to cut together a package to present to you, and, if we gain your approval, subsequently to television companies and money people!

I do hope that you are well, and that your stay in hospital is over. I am sending this letter to your home and to the hospital, to make sure it reaches you!

All good wishes,
Yours sincerely
David Wood

26th March

Dear David Wood,
I have this morning just received your letter dated February 17th – it was forwarded from St Luke's Home to Nicholas* in Bristol & finally to me.

I am so sorry, for you must have thought me very remiss in not replying much sooner.

I'm so glad you approve of Stuart & Brooks.

I am also delighted to hear from Mr Harbottle that you have chosen "The Three Graces". I wrote it by the request of the defunct but once enterprising "Group Theatre" (Auden, Spender, Isherwood et al). Rupert Doone, the founder, asked me to write an Orlando Xmas play, & the 3 G's was the result. The G. Theatre used to put on, on a Sunday evening, plays that they selected, at a London theatre, & invited theatrical producers etc. to attend. The G.T. had no money & it was necessary to find sponsors. They asked the Arts Council for help. But the latter refused on the grounds that they were only interested in unknown & young playwrights & that I was already established. I had no money for such a project, so it fell through.

I look forward with pleasurable interest to the "package" you will be sending me. I have complete confidence in you, as well as in Stuart & Brooks.

Yours sincerely,
Kathleen Hale

* Nicholas McClean, Kathleen's younger son.

c.c. Stuart Brooks
30 March 1987

Dear Miss Hale,

Many thanks for your kind letter.

We are all away on holiday for a couple of weeks, but hope to get back to work in April. I hope you will receive something not long after!

I'm fascinated to hear that THE THREE GRACES was originally thought of as a possible play – maybe that's why it appealed to me as the first one to work on!

All good wishes,
Yours sincerely
David Wood

c.c. Stuart Brooks
7 July 1987

Dear Miss Hale,

ORLANDO

Things are progressing. I have adapted THE THREE GRACES, and Stuart Brooks are doing a storyboard.

Could we kindly pencil in a date on which we could bring you the treatment and talk about it? Or, if you would prefer, we could send you the material first.

A day in the beginning of September would suit us all best. Could you suggest a date?

Hoping you are keeping well.

All good wishes.
Yours sincerely
David Wood

/7/87 **(Kathleen left an unfilled space for the actual day's date)**

Dear Mr. Wood

Thank you for your letter of July 7th, with its most exciting news! I haven't dared to even think about this film.

I'm absolutely free all September – please choose a date that will suit you.

I would be very grateful if you would post the material before coming to see me, so that I can save your time by going through it before you come.

I suggest you both come to lunch – I'll take you for an "adequate" pub meal in the village.

It really is wonderful that you have already adapted the 3 Graces!

Oh, the local pub is impossible at w/ends – it fills up to bursting point with loud drinkers.

With very best wishes,

Yours sincerely,

Kathleen Hale.

16th October 1987

Dear Miss Hale,

Lovely to see you again. Thank you for your hospitality. Sorry you were sent the wrong text! We will now speak to Laurence Harbottle about the next stage. Fingers crossed!

All good wishes,

Yours

David

c.c. Stuart Brooks Animation

21/10/87

Dear David Wood,

Could you so kindly send me a copy of the script which you read aloud? There were one or two details which I forgot when you had finished.

I'm very allergic to "Mum" & "Dad" – Orlando only used pure English & brought up his family to do likewise.

I'm also doubtful about the ending (i.e. all a dream) which I thought a very good "dramatic" ending – but which, in fact, negates all the magic. Orlando, his family and Mrs Cattermole are all magic.

Children accept this as normal (young children) for instance:

When I was opening the Children's Library at Henley-on-Thames some time ago – when I'd finished my speech a small girl sidled up to me & whispered shyly –

"I saw Orlando & Grace yesterday."

"Oh," I replied equally seriously, "Where?"

"In his car in the High Street".

"What were they doing?" I asked.

"Shopping of course!!" & off she flounced.

Then a small boy advanced on me, his head thrust forward & shoulders hunched – very menacingly he pointed an accusatory finger at me & said:

"You didn't writ those books! Orlando writ them!" & he marched, military fashion, with a sense of indignation clearly expressed, back to his seat.

Again & again, children I have met have asked me questions about Orlando, obviously regarding him, "et al", as really existing.

I think touches like these, & Tinkle reiterating "I'm firsty" or "I'm hungry" – would give the characters their individual personalities. Otherwise the books could be about rabbits or any other animals.

But I'm writing without access to your story, which lays me open to being mistaken as to what you have written.

I liked it very much indeed, & I do hope you will be the Narrator?

Yours very sincerely

Kathleen Hale

P.S. Orlando is slightly pedantic, & a very authoritative father-figure, but so kind & wise.

Grace, extremely feminine & sometimes a trifle bewildered.

Pansy & Blanche are very maternal (like most girls) & patient & loving with Tinkle, distressed when he gets into scrapes.

Tinkle, a watered-down me, always getting into trouble, but "creative" (i.e. T's poems). He's macho, & superficially scornful of his sisters – "Poo! Girls!" (He calls Orlando "FARVER")

P.P.S. Your "See-saw" Tree* is marvellous. Thank you so much for giving me lunch. I did so enjoy seeing you all.

23/10/87

P.P.P.S!!

Everybody buys presents for others at Xmas, but (& it isn't clear in my book) in your script the Cats are buying presents for themselves.

Would it be a good idea if the first page be altered to:-

Orlando buys a Magic Carpet for Grace upon which she can go shopping & for foreign holidays (or "shopping" for she hates going by 'bus), & a Magic Box of Conjuring Tricks for Tinkle.

Grace chooses a Magnifying Glass for Orlando, for him to examine closely insects in which he is very interested.

Pansy selects a Compass for Blanche as she can't walk in a straight line (or often loses her way).

Blanche takes for Pansy a glass globe with a Castle in a forest inside; she shakes it & the globe is filled with a swirling snow-storm.

* I had sent Kathleen a copy of the script for my stage play *The See-Saw Tree*.

They decided to give Tinkle a Sailing Ship in a glass bottle. They had already made presents for Orlando & Grace – cotton-wool Tail muffs for winter wear. (or "wearing in cold weather".)

I don't think these alterations will upset the rest of the story, & the allotments of the presents will be more suitable.

Please forgive mistakes; it comes from my ancient mind which is prone to muddles.

Best of best wishes,

Kathleen

Three letters from Kathleen Hale to Jill Brooks, one of the animators on the 'Orlando' film.

In nightmare haste!
30/10/87

Dear Jill,

Herewith "Fire-side scene".

I think all your colours of the specimens you've sent me, are too strong. Do you think we'd better use paler colours? If SO, tell me, & I'll do "swatches" for you to follow.

Don't copy the technique of the enclosed drawing – it's a very hurried sketch in ink: – it's really only to indicate a romantic fire-light.

I think Grace should be putting a toy mouse or anything into Tinkle's sock which Orlando holds out for her. Head lowered to Grace.

Black sock.

I still have to do the Father X & Tinkle picture. Please copy the background from the book – I don't like the slanting of the arches etc. Will there be more details to this picture? Perhaps I ought to design some.

There's also the Shop with Mr. Cattermole behind the counter. This is a major piece of re-designing & will take me a few days.

Please tell me more about the Father X & Tinkle's background. Can the arches & caryatids all be in blue, not black – to suggest ice?

Kathleen

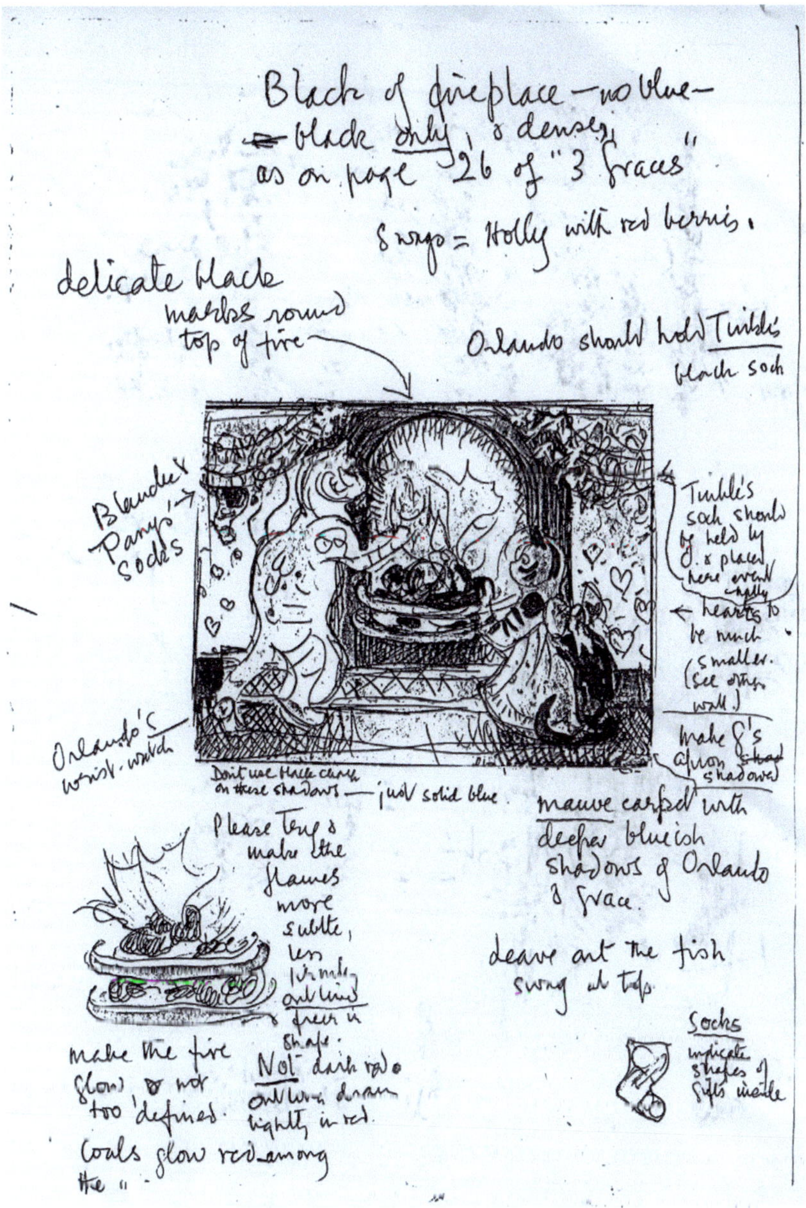

4/11/87

Dear Jill,

Herewith colour patterns. Especially for the red. Of course chalk can't give the brilliance of printer's ink, unfortunately.

I now remember there is to be a real fire burning in the grate (Fireside scene with Orlando & Grace & Kittens' socks).

Socks should be furry, & Pansy's with a blotch or two of orange & black. Blanche's white, of course, & Tinkle's black. All moons should be the face of a happy cat. Where it's possible to copy a page exactly, don't alter anything – (i.e. the caryatids should face forward, not sideways, & no perspective).

I've done a detailed drawing of the shop which I would be most grateful if you will follow it exactly (tho' my sketch is very small I'm afraid). I didn't have room to include the two girl kittens, but you will be able to fit them in on your larger picture.

I'll send you this as soon as I've made a copy for my<u>self</u> – in case yours gets lost in the post.

Yours with very best wishes!

Kathleen.

Soon after, Kathleen sent Jill her detailed drawing of Mr Cattermole's shop, with accompanying instructions.

9/11/87

Dear Jill,

Thank you very much for your letter. Your letter clarifies a great deal for me, & I now realise there are animation mysteries which are beyond my ken, & that I still see the pictures as if for static illustrations to a book.

I can help you I think, to find objects etc. in my various books for you to copy, so I send you a list:-

Page 8 of "Three Graces" for excellent toys, to be drawn on the Cattermole Shop. Add Teddy Bear to toys. Please put duck-headed umbrellas (owl, dog etc) near the door instead of rolls of paper (cut these out). I will send you drawings of Xmas tree decorations. i.e. little Father X, glass birds, glass fish, white clockwork mouse, glass ball etc. for you to copy. Also a re-designed, coloured sketch of the shop – I really (sorry) don't like the one you've suggested – too cluttered with meaningless objects – (forgive me). Too all-over hot colours. Please make the wall (entrance) thicker, should be a solid little building. Put your snow-laden tree (out of doors) to the left of the doorway – better design & not to be confused with Xmas tree inside shop. Brightly coloured counter – (red & blue & yellow over laid) with lighter top. Pale pink floor.

Could Mr. Cattermole be slotted into the picture (not animated) & slipped out when necessary leaving completed counter with goods, underneath. Could this also apply to carpet?

I think it'd be mysterious & magical if the shelves of toys be in Moorish alcoves, arched. Will send these for you to try out. Ship in Bottle; globe; copper jug; jars of "cat mints", witch's broom-stick prominent in front.

Page 19. "Keeps a Dog"

For Dressmakers' Dummy, gauntlets, fish-hand bag, white mouse tippet; add mouse muff to match, also hats, stockings (these are enclosed)

Page 17 "Keeps a Dog" (Garden.)

For picture of Pussy Willow tree & garden – but with snow patches. Very good to copy, part of the book. Enclose picture of Orlando looking out of window (indoors.) Could Orlando sit on Grace's sofa, when indoors? (drawing included.) Ask David Wood where O. is to be, in kitchen?

Page (Kathleen omitted the page number) "Keeps a Dog". For curtains.

I will design Father X's throne & send it to you. (A grandiose object based on G's sofa. Quilted blue velvet, & felt lion's head, claws & feet?)

An excellent idea for you to send me little sketches like the ones of O. & garden – then I can look up the books & pages can copy.

(I'll do some drawings of cat baskets, round, square) for shop.

Santa Claws's palace. Whew!! I'll have to think this out…

Could Father X be sitting on his throne at right of picture, leaning forward towards minute Tinkle? You needn't put all the caryatids in – simplify, I think.

About the fire-side scene, I forgot to ask you to keep your Christmas boxes etc. on the floor. And can you make the Kittens' stockings furry (drawing included) plus indicating the bulges made by contents. Also put mouse sticking out of one; a fish doll (drawing enclosed) out of other, & drum & trumpet? or motorcar, being put in Tinkle's stocking, by Grace & Orlando.

Back to Father X's palace – could the pillars on page 29 of "Three Graces" flank the ornate gilt throne, with steps leading up to the latter? Please suggest where you'd like the door of the palace & window & I'll design them. Icicles hanging outside the door maybe? Do you need a door as well as a window?? As to what's behind the caryatids – could infinite distance be suggested, without definite limits? Oh dear!

Instead of caryatids all round the palace room, would a screen at front with everything else happening beyond them?

I think you could plan this & copy the simple arches (in front) & the distant caryatids without me – I don't know how to deal with the perspective –

I much admire your drawing of the carpet beater (nearly gave me a stroke!!). The violin, pram, etc & the perspective of the shop.

I understand perfectly that the colour sketch I've done for shop, could not be possible for animation, but I send it nonetheless.

P.S.
All drawings will follow.

11/11/87

Dear David Wood,

Thank you very much for telling me of your "Shish & Fips"* – I have watched all three of the films, tho' a long-distance telephone call interrupted the last one. I am vastly interested in the ingenuity of the way you tackle "scale", having had this exciting experience over my Orlando Ballet, and I loved designing all the out-size props etc. (This comes in the way of abandoning oneself to the actual story content in my case.)

Shish & Fips is for town children (?) & I wonder if rural viewers will understand some of the settings – The "Island" & the Telephone booth?

I believe it is of great importance to make children aware of their environment, & therefore to be imaginative & observant of it. I'm sure, in this you are entirely successful, as also in engaging the whole attention of your audience.

I look forward to watching the ensuing series, & shall NOT answer the telephone.

"May Allah" continue, as always, "to give you Power"! How on earth, do you manage to write plays, films, & compose music? It took me ages to compose Tinkle's poem:-

"I have an I dea
My end is near."

Yours very sincerely,
Kathleen (Hale)

12/11/87

Dear David Wood,

I don't think I have told you how utterly delighted I am that you are doing the "Orlando" film – there is nobody else in whom I could have such great confidence.

* Kathleen is referring to *Chish 'n' Fips*, the children's television series I wrote for Holmes Associates/Central Television, based on my play *The Ideal Gnome Expedition*. The series follows the adventures of two garden gnomes exploring the big city.

It is an enormous pleasure for me to be associated with you, & the Stewart [sic] Animation company.

I have been in a depression for years, but now I awake every day with interest & stimulus – (a species of miracle). So I do thank you, most sincerely, for a great deal.

Kathleen.

13th November 1987

Dear Kathleen (if I may call you by your Christian name, and if you will reciprocate!),

Many thanks for your two letters.

Delighted you are enjoying CHISH 'N' FIPS. My fascination with scale goes back a long way. I wrote a play called THE PLOTTERS OF CABBAGE PATCH CORNER, set in a garden, in which the characters were insects. A giant cabbage took up half the stage – it was Slug's home! All of us, adults and children alike, are fascinated by oversize objects, as well as miniatures. And I find they help enormously. THE GINGERBREAD MAN, my best known play, is set on an antique Welsh dresser. I'm enclosing a copy of the paperback storybook version of the play, for your interest.

We all had a meeting with Laurence Harbottle the other day, and hope very much that we will be able to start looking for the all-important funding for the project. We hope very much to be able to make a 25 minute version of THE THREE GRACES, which would hopefully be the beginning of a series of films about Orlando. We are all very enthusiastic, but, of course, we have to be realistic about the financial side! If we can get the money, we will go ahead!

All good wishes,

Yours,

David

20/11/87

Dear David,

Thank you so much for the "Gingerbread Man" – I have heard so much about it, before I met you. I too was concerned about small children always having to strain upwards to see everything & people. I wonder if that's why the children love pets, being smaller than themselves.

I remember seeing a horse (from the top of a bus  years ago) & how like a carrot it looked.

I enjoyed "The Gingerbread Man" so much. Also the last two of the film series. I was too interested at the first ones, in the mechanics, to take in the story. Tho' Henrietta, the tortoise, delighted me from the beginning – her looks, & speaking like Edith Evans.

I had a (retired) Child Psychologist with me at the last but one, & she was enthralled & said she just couldn't wait to know what happened next. She reads a lot of children's books.

I wonder how the Gnome got out of the Pram & into the Launderette – there was a cut in the viewing at the beginning.

Please will you tell me if the alterations I asked Jill to make in the specimens she gave me, will be made <u>before</u> they are shown for acceptance? I have given her a list of pages in the various books, from which she can safely copy my drawings. That should help. She can't possibly "invent", only copy, at which she is so good.

I've written my Autobiography, which I will hold back from sending to an Agent until the Orlando film is sure to materialise, then the former might help, as a film would help it.

With the best of good wishes,

Kathleen.

11th April 1988

Dear Kathleen,

My apologies for not writing sooner.

Stuart Brooks have been very frantic doing nine animated commercials! And I have been on my travels – in Japan and France, as well as a look at Hong Kong! We had an exciting trip, culminating in seeing my play THE GINGERBREAD MAN in Japan.

I am hoping to meet everybody on the Orlando project again very soon. Meanwhile, my wife, Jacqui, and I hope to be coming to Oxford on April 25th. Might it be possible to pop in and see you at, say, 11.00am? I understand that Jill Brooks may also be able to come. She would also like to show you some new sketches.

Do hope you are well and that you are enjoying some of the beautiful weather currently gracing Wimbledon!

Yours sincerely,

David

17/4/88

Dear David,

It will be good to see you and your wife here at 11am.

What a wonderful life you have designed for yourself! Japan!

I went to the Lebanon before its troubles, & Peru.

I still have China & Turkey as my priority for future travel. But I can no longer go further than Oxford!

Yours sincerely

Kathleen

26.4.88.

Dear Kathleen,

It was very enjoyable to see you looking so well yesterday – and to hear about your balloonatics (if there is such a word!). Thank you from Jacqui and myself for your hospitality.*

*I don't know what to advise about the Methuen / Octopus situation. Laurence Harbottle is probably the best person for advice.**2

Meanwhile we hope we can soon strike up an agreement suitable to all parties, including Stuart Brooks, and raise some money for the films.

All good wishes.

Yours

David

22nd August 1988

Dear Kathleen,

Many thanks for your letter. Sorry to hear that you haven't been well. You didn't say whether you went up in the balloon! If you did, I hope you had a wonderful experience.

It seems to me that the republication of the books could be a bonus, and an added incentive for the money people to back a film or series.

However, I will speak to the Stuart Brooks people.

Meanwhile, we hope some sort of contract can be sorted out soon. We all had a good meeting with Central Television, and I understand there is a hope that they may put forward some development money. But these things do seem to take a ridiculous time to get started.

* For her 90th birthday, Kathleen's family gave her a trip in a hot air balloon.

*2 It was becoming apparent that attempts were being made by Kathleen's agent to chase which publishers held rights in which Orlando books.

I am at present on holiday in Cornwall. It is pouring with rain! But we have had a few good days.

Do hope you are feeling better.

Yours sincerely,

David

In November 1988, it became clear that her agent, having confirmed that all the book rights had reverted to Kathleen Hale, had struck a deal with a major publisher; as well as republishing two Orlando books, the package included all film, television, video and merchandising rights. This meant that Stuart Brooks and I no longer had the rights to develop our project, and had to abandon it.

22nd November 1988

Dear Kathleen,

ORLANDO

It is sad, but I fear we have come to a full stop.

The enclosed letter from Murray Pollinger means that, for now at least, there is nothing further I nor Stuart Brooks can do, because we have no legal right to pursue any production avenues.

Meanwhile, I wish you every success with the re-publishing of the books. We will have to see if the publishers are interested to talk about the possibility of a television version, and if so whether they will be able to help finance it. But it seems from Mr. Pollinger's letter that until the publishing deal is concluded, there are no further discussions we can have with him on your behalf.

All good wishes, as ever,

Yours sincerely,

David

Fortunately, the publisher who had acquired rights to all the Kathleen Hale Orlando titles proved to be Penguin/Frederick

Warne. Stuart Brooks and I were known to Sally Floyer, who now looked after Kathleen's list, and our project was revived, albeit in a new format.

30th January 1989

Dear Kathleen,

I thoroughly enjoyed your radio interview the other day. Nigel Forde, who interviewed you, was a contemporary of mine at Oxford – although I haven't actually met him for over 20 years!

I hope you will be pleased to know that Mike Stuart, Jill Brooks and I had a very pleasant meeting with Sally at Frederick Warne and Liz of Puffin the other day, discussing the possibility of 13 10-minute animated films.

We have submitted a budget to them, with which to work on a presentation, so that they can decide whether or not to go ahead and commission the series.

We are pleased that, in the new circumstances, our initial work appears not to have been in vain. I am sure ORLANDO is in good hands with Sally and Liz, and that the decision to go with them was the right one.

If Warne/Puffin give the go ahead, we will have two months to present outlines for all 13, plus script and storyboard for 1 episode, plus samples of artwork, etc. I'm hoping all will go ahead now.

I hope you are well and active as ever! And that we meet again before too long.

I am currently producing a tour of MEG AND MOG SHOW, based on the books by Helen Nicoll and Jan Pieńkowski. This has played very successfully at Unicorn for 10 weeks, and now tours for 20 weeks. Am also planning a tour of the stage play about the garden gnomes!

All good wishes, as ever.

Yours sincerely,

David

Six months passed, in which no progress was made. Quite why this delay occurred is unclear. We know that in 1992, three years later, the animation series *The World of Peter Rabbit and Friends* began being broadcast. The series was produced by the publisher Frederick Warne Ltd. It is reasonable to suppose that preparations for the series started in or around 1989, thus delaying preparations for a possible Orlando series.

28/6/89

Dear David,

I have always felt sure that the Orlando films will materialize…

About the music – I would very much love it to be entirely wood-wind – with a Peruvian flute et al. It would be quite unlike any other children's film music, & could be so haunting & joyous & simple.

I do urgently hope you agree?

Otherwise I feel the films could be amorphous – sound-wise, among such a lot of uninspired tunes – except for the appealing "Postman Pat"!

Wouldn't it be wonderful if James Galway was the flautist!!!!

Wouldn't it also be economical to employ just 3 or 4 musicians? rather than an orchestra?

But <u>you</u> know all about these matters. I only have my deep preference for wood-wind.

With very best wishes to you,

Sincerely

Kathleen.

29.6.89.

Dear Kathleen,

Lovely to hear from you.

At the moment we are all waiting for Penguin and a company called Vision Ventures to come up with a small sum of money to enable work to go ahead on the 'development' of the series.

We are all hoping that work can begin soon.

I love the sound of woodwind too. We will certainly make it known to everybody that you would like Mr. Galway to lead a small ensemble of players on the signature tune and incidental music!

I am hoping to put forward a signature tune/title song of my own for consideration, and will bear your thoughts in mind.

Meanwhile, I hope you are keeping well and enjoying the Wimbledon tennis. It's ironic that it seems to rain the moment Wimbledon starts! We live ten minutes' walk away from the courts, and went down on Monday evening. We managed to stand for an uncomfortable quarter of an hour on the Centre Court and watch the brilliant young Michael Chang in action.

I may well be in your area in a couple of months' time. I will let you know, in the hope that I can pop in and say hello. Meanwhile, with the family, I go away for a couple of weeks in France on 13th July. Later in the summer we have our usual three weeks in Cornwall, when I aim to do some work!

All good wishes,
Sincerely,
David

The lack of progress continued for nearly a year. By this time the two Orlando books were about to be republished. One was *Orlando – A Camping Holiday*, which was the first book in the Orlando series, first published in 1938. It was round about this time that Kathleen started working on her autobiography, which was commissioned by Sally Floyer for Frederick Warne Ltd. Diana Syrat, a sympathetic editor, was assigned to work with Kathleen. She visited her regularly, collecting anecdotes and memories, sometimes scribbled by Kathleen on the back of utility bills! The splendid result, *A Slender Reputation*, was published in 1994.

Perhaps Sally Floyer thought that sales would be enhanced by the republication of the two Orlando titles. And maybe she also hoped that the proposed animation series would also lead to an Orlando revival, to be appreciated by a new generation as well as offer a nostalgic trip down memory lane for the older generation.

16.4.90.

Dear Kathleen,

I see the 'run-up' to the exciting re-publication day has started! Many congratulations on your thoroughly-deserved revival!!

Sally Floyer should by now have sent you a copy of my first draft of a possible new Orlando story for the film series. I do hope you like it. I have tried to be faithful to the characters – but please point out any obvious howlers!

My new play, SAVE THE HUMAN, opened well at Cambridge in February, then toured. In the autumn, Whirligig, my own company, will tour it for three months. We hope to come to the Apollo Theatre, Oxford (ex-New Theatre), so maybe I can take you to see it. Am frantically correcting the proofs of the Samuel French edition so that the play can be published in June, ready for hopeful school sales before & during the tour!

Finally, if you can bear it, I'm acting in a children's series called TRICKY BUSINESS, every Thursday at 4.30pm on BBC 1. Very light – fun in a magic shop – I play the owner – I do a few magic tricks, which is fun!!

I do hope you are well. Very good luck with the new Orlando launch. Here's to great success in the nineties (the 1990s and your nineties!) – and I'm very optimistic that the t.v. series will be with us soon!

With love & best wishes –

Yours

David

23/4/90

Dear David,

It is real good to hear from you, and I thank you very much for your congratulations on the Lazarus behaviour of Orlando.

Sally Floyer is still in Australia, so I haven't yet received a copy of your first draft for the film story of the cats.

It is you who really deserves congratulations – on your many achievements – "Save the Human"'s success & also touring so widely. Thank you for offering to take me to see the play at the Apollo Theatre – I shall enjoy that.

I look forward to watching "Tricky Business" on Thursdays on BBC1 (4.30). It will be nice to see you then, for I've only met you once – or I think twice.

I only hope the Orlando animated film will be on a T.V. Series; I know projects like this one take a hell of a long time, & I doubt I'll be able to see it through! However, if Michael Gabriel will do the background pictures, he'll be of great help to Jill,* as he is an old friend of mine & likes my work.

I am immersed in my autobog, with a really excellent secretary – she sent the first third of the mss we've done, to Penguin who said over the phone "We <u>love</u> it!" But it's a tiring job, & I have to keep 3 consecutive mornings for it – & an afternoon nap.

I've just completed signing 500 Orlandos for Hatchards, & advertising posters to do. The flattering reviews are beginning to drop through my letter-box – I like especially an announcement on the cover of one, which says "Ole Green-Eyes is Back!"

I've marked Thursday BBC-s in my Diary, beginning this week. It's good to have things to look forward to.

May Allah give you Power!

With love to you and your enchanting wife.

Kathleen.

---

* Jill Brooks was still very much on board.

25th April 1990

Dear Kathleen,

I'm being very lazy and dictating this onto a little machine for typing later on! Have you discovered the little tape recorder which you can carry round with you and spout all your thoughts and sudden inspirations into?

Thank you very much for your newsy letter. Delighted to hear you are so busy, and hope that you are getting enough afternoon naps!

This is really just to explain a little more about the proposed television series. It is a series rather than a one-off programme that is being planned. 13 ten minute films. In consultation with Sally Floyer, it was decided, just to see how it would work out, that I would submit, as part of the development, two script/storylines, one of which was an adaptation of an original Kathleen Hale Orlando story (we chose The Three Graces) and secondly a new storyline by me, using your characters, and written to the best of my ability in your style. This was to see whether it was felt that we could do, in the end, more stories than your books might first yield.

So, the story I hope Sally will be sending you soon is my first attempt at a new Orlando story. I hope you will approve!

In the meantime, the various companies involved have been to an international television jamboree event in Cannes, with the hope of getting interest from abroad in the series. We are all crossing fingers that work can begin before too long.

I hope you enjoy watching TRICKY BUSINESS. It has been fun to do.

All good wishes, as ever, from Jacqui, my wife, who thanks you for your nice comments (!) and myself,

Yours,

David

1/5/90

Dear David,
Thank you very much for your letter & "Orlando's Grand Sale".

This is a new project to me, & I was not consulted, so I'm rather mystified by it. I haven't had a moment in which to read your story – considerable pressures all the time to do things for Warne & publicity for Orlando – & then the last two w/ends spent with my two families, & I just <u>had</u> to relax with them, & be just happy.

Then a monstrous interruption prevented me from seeing "Tricky Business" – in the form of a sudden descent on me by dear kind ex-neighbours, who had once been kind to me, in weeks of stress some time ago – they came from Bristol & I couldn't shut the door on them, could I? and as it was a rare & flying visit I hadn't the guts to turn on the television. But I understand "T. Business" is a serial? Heavens, I hope so.

I've written to Warne about the "new story about... Orlando" & will of course write to you immediately I know more of the project.

With very best wishes,

from the bottom of a deep pile of beastly commitments, for Warne.

Kathleen.

9/5/90

Dear David,
I only received your first draft for a new Orlando story for the film series – about a week ago – after Sally Floyer had returned from Australia.

Without reading it, I'm afraid I was disturbed at the idea of anyone <u>other</u> than myself – filling out my original text in the books, to fit the illustrations.

However, Sally has written & explained the difficulties of adapting books to film. Jill had already explained this problem which applies to adapting the book-illustrations to animation – i.e. that the characters must be able to come in & out of the scenery etc. But I hadn't realized this, in its way, was also applicable to text.

And I have therefore, calmed down somewhat! And I hope I can cope, without undue interference from me.

I am now, at last, fairly free from newspaper interviewers et al, & can read your script, which Sally thinks you have "done quite well for a first stab".

So there's no difficulty there. Encouraging. And of course, having done quite a lot of work (before Penguin – Warne materialized) with Jill Brooks, I am confident of the excellence of her work for Orlando.

Please forgive my initial anxiety, & looking forward to reading your story,

Yours very sincerely,

Kathleen.

P.S. I shall enjoy working with you, of that I am certain, & I hope I shall behave myself!

Can you possibly have this letter photo-copied for me? It takes a whole morning to get on the scarce busses (I will NOT spell them as "Buses") to the nearest copyists, & home again. Or do you have a similar obstacle to overcome?

28/5/90

Dear Jacqui & David,

How lovely to receive your beautiful Bouquet. And how the messenger beamed in anticipation of my surprised delight. Apart from some of my favourite flowers, such as Sweet William, carnations et al, there are several others which I have never seen anywhere else & nobody can tell me their names.

Each species has a different scent which they puff out in the evenings, taking turns, I do believe – spicy, nostalgic and alluring.

I would like to paint them, but alas, I have no time now for such "creative lethargy" to quote from Eileen Agar's autobiography.

Thank you again, & with best wishes to you both,

Love from Kathleen

Another year passed, in which no progress was apparently made, with little indication of whether or not the Orlando animation series was still in the pipeline, or whether it had been put on the back burner. By now, I had forged a special friendship with Kathleen. My wife, Jacqui, had accompanied me on visits to have lunch with Kathleen in a local pub. We sent her birthday flowers each year, and tried to perpetuate a belief that the Orlando animation wheels were turning, when in fact there was no evidence to support such positivity.

27/5/91

Dear David,

I really cannot describe my delight at the unusual beauty of the flowers you sent me – especially the many lilies (my favourite ones) – "Rubrum Speciosium". The scent of the Freesias send me quite dotty & coupled with that of the stocks are enough to make me walk 2 inches off the ground.

One of the "perks" of living in a Village is that we all know our bus-driver by his Christian name – also the owner of the shop at Stanton St. John, and of course our Postman. The latter brings me what he knows by instinct are gifts – & hands them & the lovely bouquet as though he himself was the giver; his face & gestures are one great beam of delight. Thank you both, you & Jacqui for the flowers & you for your letter & card.

Congratulations for the "American Emmy"* reward – you certainly deserve it & many others, which surely will come to you.

When you are in Oxford in September, do indeed come & see me, if you have time. I can't read the title of the "MAN" you are to open, at the Playhouse – is it for children? Would I, I wonder, be able to hear it – I've been too deaf to go to theatres for at least 18 years. But maybe the Playhouse has that thing, which attached from stage to members of the audience – enables the latter to hear?

Nobody tells me what is happening – if anything – to Orlando's film, & I don't receive any of the Animators drawings for me to help by correcting some of them – & providing new drawings for them to work from. Time, for me, is short.

I look forward to seeing you in September – Weds, Thurs & Fridays are dedicated to my Secretary. From 3–6.30pm.

Again I bless you for my birthday card, letter & Bouquet.

Kathleen

10.6.91.

Dear Kathleen,

Many thanks for your letter – apologies for my illegible writing – the play at Oxford Playhouse during the week beginning September 9th is THE GINGERBREAD MAN (I think I gave you a copy of the Puffin story-book version!).

I will be in touch again in the hope that you might be able to come – the performances are daytime – I will enquire about the special 'loop' system for the hard of hearing!

All good wishes,

David

* This was only a nomination, not a win! My television screenplay based on Michelle Magorian's novel, *Back Home*, produced by the Disney Channel, TVS and Verronmead Limited, the small company I ran with Maureen Harter, was nominated for a Daytime Emmy. The film, starring Hayley Mills and Hayley Carr, was particularly well received in the United States. Its UK peak-time evening screening on ITV was somewhat patronisingly reviewed by critics who unfairly saw it as a children's film.

I decided to contact Nick Comley, Administrator of Stuart Brooks Animation, in the hope of discovering what the true situation was. I mentioned Tim Woolford, who had already produced the TV movies *The Tailor of Gloucester* and *The Tale of Pig Robinson* for a company called Dreamscape. These were not animation films. Quite why production of these films should have affected Orlando plans, I don't know.

3rd July 1991
Nick Comley
Stuart Brooks Animation
1–3 Charlotte Street
London W.1.

Dear Nick,

ORLANDO

I assume you've had no news since we last spoke (Barbara has since confirmed this to me), and presumably you have not been paid second stage development money. I do think Tim Woolford, if it is he causing the delay, should be chivvied.*

I spoke to Liz Attenborough of Puffin last week. She assumed all was going along nicely, but I put her in the picture. She said she would try to speak to Sally Floyer.

Meanwhile, I had a nice letter from Kathleen Hale, thanking me for her birthday card. In it she expresses impatience for action! She says she can't keep waiting much longer!

All good wishes,

Yours,

David

* Barbara Scott, my assistant.

29th August 1991

Dear Kathleen,

I'm still hoping all is going ahead on the ORLANDO series. But I must admit I haven't heard anything from anyone for some time. I have written again to Sally Floyer and Stuart Brooks to see when they next want me to do something. But the decisions are very much in their hands.

Meanwhile, I'm directing THE GINGERBREAD MAN, which will be opening, as I think I told you, at the Oxford Playhouse the week after next.

I would be delighted to take you to see the show on Wednesday, 11th September, or Saturday 14th September. The times of the show are as follows – Wednesday 2.30pm and 5.30pm, and Saturday 10.30am and 2.30pm.

I would pick you up and take you home, of course.

Failing that, perhaps I could pop in and see you.

Do hope you are well and enjoying the weather.

With all good wishes,

Yours,

David

2/9/91

Dear David,

How very kind of you to invite me to the "Gingerbread Man" – especially as you will be much in demand…

Saturday, 14th Sept will suit me perfectly. Will you be my guest at the Randolph for their Special Bar-Snacks – before the 2.30 performance? I can easily go to Oxford, it's difficult to get back to Forest Hill as there are no busses & the taxis at St. Giles are rare & eccentric.

So please will you tell me what time to meet you at the Randolph?

I confess to you that I am rather deaf, but as I enjoyed

seeing The "Ginger B" man on television, I shall know what happens, & will re-enjoy your ingenious scenery & props. I am quite fond of your Dustbin!

Maybe the Playhouse has one of those devices, which, if connected with the audience who wear hearing-aids, I'll benefit.

I too, know nothing of what is going on about the Orlando film – they tell me there are "wheels within wheels" which have to be sorted out. I think each wheel is equipped with a Brake, & a strong one.

I harry Sally F. from time to time, & say it would be disastrous if we lost you & Gabriel (Michael).

I'm promised other publications of my other (non-O) books – but I think those wheels have rusted up.

It will be so good to see you again.

Yours very sincerely,

Kathleen.

4th September 1991

Dear Kathleen,

Many thanks for your letter.

Saturday, 14th September it is!

I'd be delighted to meet you at the Randolph, if that is convenient for you. Shall we say 1.00pm?

I will see you safely home, either in my car or in a hire car. It will be a great pleasure to see you again.

I ought to point out that although the dustbin does feature in THE GINGERBREAD MAN, you never see it on stage. You may be confusing it with CHISH 'N' FIPS, the series about the garden gnomes! For some reason a lot of my plays have dustbins in!

THE GINGERBREAD MAN is set on a Welsh dresser. I think I gave you the Puffin storybook version of the play. If not, and if you would like one in advance, let me know and I'll send one!

Meanwhile, I will enquire whether the theatre has one of those special loop systems you mention.

Looking forward so much to seeing you.

With all good wishes,

Yours,

David

6th September 1991

Dear Kathleen,

When I was booking the tickets for THE GINGERBREAD MAN, the theatre expressed a great interest in the fact that you were coming.

As a result Radio Oxford have asked if they could do an interview with you, live from their studio at approximately 12.30pm. They would be delighted to pick you up from home and take you to the studio and then, after the interview, deliver you to the Randolph.

Would this appeal? Or do you hate the idea?

If you want to let me know by letter or by ringing my home number and speaking to either Jacqui, my wife, or Barbara Scott, my assistant, I can then inform the Playhouse and Radio Oxford.

I could be with you during the interview should you wish it!

All good wishes,

Yours sincerely,

David

9th September 1991

Dear Kathleen,

The arrangements now are as follows, and I hope you will be happy with them.

Tei Williams, publicity person at the Oxford Playhouse, and

I will arrive at your home at approximately 11.45am, and we will all drive to the Radio Oxford studio. I will accompany you.

Then we will be driven to the Randolph, see the performance at 2.30pm, and then I will drive you back home.

Looking forward very much to seeing you.

With all good wishes,

Yours,

David

Kathleen enjoyed seeing *The Gingerbread Man* and showed considerable stamina throughout the day, which had included the BBC Radio Oxford interview. She mentions that Penguin/Warne, presumably Sally Floyer, have told her that the BBC are interested. I wasn't sure whether this encouraging news was serious or was a tactic intended to keep Kathleen happy and engaged, bearing in mind she was now ninety-three years old and impatient for progress to be made.

16/9/91

Dear David,

Thank you so very much for taking me to see the "Gingerbread Man". As I warned you beforehand, I wouldn't be able to hear – but there's a great deal to see. I liked the scenery, the costumes & the wonderfully timed dramatic lighting. I wish I had read the book before, but I can now relate the plot to the visual side, having the book with me. I do admire the indefatigable acting! The spontaneous energy is astonishing. Though some of the juvenile audience were too young to understand the exciting play itself, they weren't bored – no squirming in their seats and fidgeting etc!

I don't see Orlando as a musical, or given to many lyrics – he's too serious a fella, tho' not a bore! Some rough & tumble among the kittens is very desirable, don't you think? Children adore scrummages & high spirits. Grace is a little frivolous but influenced by O's level-headedness. But the feminineness, & a touch of flibberty-gibbeting pops out from time to time, which endears her. Anyway you know all about children.

I understand from Penguin-Warne on Friday last week, that the film project rumbles on & that the BBC are very interested, & want it. Though they don't pay awfully well, which I think is one of the hurdles to be negotiated.

You must forgive me for any remissness – such as quite forgetting to suggest a cheese course after the prawns. You must have become very hungry. Without my husband to fill in the gaps I leave, friends are not awfully well looked-after by me.

I think the interior of the Playhouse is as glum as a village-hall. Not a hint of theatrical mystery & glamour.

And there is so much talent – especially among art students, whom I believe would have jumped at the opportunity to give mystery, lustre & thrills to the proscenium – for free! It'd only be for the management to provide the expenses of materials & paint. What a lost opportunity.

The Playhouse should be ashamed of such misplaced economy.

About my Ballet, I was allowed some of the leading dancers (Sally Gilmour, Harold Turner et al) to do the dancing to the choreography by Andrée Howard, but that was long ago (for the Festival of Britain in 1957(?)). A hugely tall man was found for the Katnapper, who doubled for Mr Cattermole, to get the relative sizes of cats to humans. It was difficult to find one.

Maybe some of my scenery designs/or the Ballet could be used by Jill Stewart?

Yours with best wishes, & sincerely,

Kathleen

19.9.91.

a palindrome date today!

Dear Kathleen,

Many thanks for your letter, and for my delicious lunch on Saturday – no cheese was required, I assure you! Prawns, wine (and more wine) and coffee was quite sufficient! I'm glad you enjoyed the day. It was a great pleasure to be 'your escort'! I agree with you about the Playhouse's bald, stark, dull interior. Too functional by half.

THE GINGERBREAD MAN is in Bristol this week, Canterbury next. Meanwhile I'm directing the next one – my adaptation of Roald Dahl's THE BFG. I'm sending you a copy of the book, which has become a huge favourite among children – I'll be interested to see if you like it.

'Orlando on stage' is a thought, but I fancy you are right about him not singing! The other challenge would be to find a 'through' story line suitable for a full-length play – 1½ hours or so.

Incidentally, I'll pass on the information about the ballet designs to Jill Brooks.

I have heard from Stuart Brooks and Warne/Puffin too. Movement on the t.v. series is expected soon – I should think so!

Recently read A.A. Milne biography by Ann Thwaites – very interesting – what a sad man! What do you think of his writing? I fancy adults enjoy WINNIE-THE-POOH in nostalgic retrospect much more than when they read it as children...

All good wishes, as ever –

Yours

David

BFG book to follow under separate cover

19/9/91

Dear David,

I was full of enthusiasm when I got home, for you & the play – but I got gummed up & bogged down by a plethora of "career"-based demands etc (you know what it's like) & I was nearly strangled by the telephone.

I send you the 1st (2) of my 2 Puffins – just out I think. And letter will follow, expressing some guilt-ridden apologies. (Oh dear!)

With very best wishes,
Yours sincerely
Kathleen.

26/9/91

Dear David,

Thank you so very much for the two books… I imagine The BFG is an early one? But alas, I never keep up with children's books – what I have dipped into of R. Dahl (ie The Choc. Factory & others) I think he really developed his full personality in the latter titles? But he was a great feller, & a real classic.

I salute you for your intrepid courage on tackling the very Hot Potato in "Save the Human". I was on tenterhooks (whatever they may be) from the first word – my husband being a Bacteriologist & engrossed by research into Small Pox vaccine, & another project at which he made a real discovery – he needed Rats & tired old horses who were blissfully contented in the Elstree rural retirement with only a small vaccination which they didn't feel. All the animals were gently put down after only one trial. But of course there are horrible cases of cruelty among unscrupulous scientists. But once your book moved from the harrowing beginning & gave the Humans their point of view, I relaxed! But alas, there seems to be no lovely desert island in real life. The young audience must have been really galvanized into participation with each moment of the play – I wish I had seen them. It's a splendid book.

I never meant "Orlando" to be put on the stage – I misled you – I was referring to the animated film.

Thank you again so much,

Kathleen.

Another eight months passed, with little further development. But there were still hopeful signs.

11th May 1992

Dear Kathleen,

I heard from Sally Floyer a few weeks ago, saying that they were still planning the ORLANDO television series, and that I would be asked to write something soon, but I'm afraid I have heard nothing since then. I'm sure one day it will happen, however.

Meanwhile, the television series based on THE GINGERBREAD MAN is currently on ITV every Friday afternoon at 3.55pm. The reaction so far seems to have been good.

I have just come back from South Africa, seeing if it is possible to set up a production in Cape Town. It was quite an eye-opener. I hope, however, it will be possible to put on a show with a multi-racial cast and multi-racial audiences.

Am also working on an adaptation of Roald Dahl's THE WITCHES, which will start a theatre tour in October.

Hoping you are well and that the new editions of the ORLANDO books are selling well!

With all good wishes,

Yours,

David

Meanwhile, Stuart Brooks were, though I didn't realise it, working on a short 'taster', to show how Orlando and his world might appear

when animated. It had become clear, too, that funding had come through for the Beatrix Potter animation series, which was still taking priority over Orlando. Maybe, in addition, Frederick Warne were sensing that Orlando might not have enough commercial appeal. However, I never discovered how well the two republished Orlando titles were selling.

14/5/92

Dear David,

David, I'm SO glad to hear from you – I'm always fearing Penguin-Warne will lose you for my Orlando Animation film & also the Brooks animators – I can find out nothing about the film except they've done the little 2-minute introduction and it's very good.* I'm told that P. Warne are working all out on their Beatrix Potter film, having got the money, & that they're concentrating on the film for all their worth. Then I believe they've somehow got to get cash for Orlando – the latter was much approved of at Cannes. Did they accept your plan for your story-board for O.?

How interesting that you will do an adaptation of Roald Dahl's "The Witches". Will it come to Oxford in October? That man fascinates me – by his stories.

I'd like to know more about your plans for Cape Town – why it's "an eye opener" or rather in what way. I can imagine the circumstances.

With love from

Kathleen.

18th May 1992

Dear Kathleen,

Many thanks indeed for your letter of 14th May. I very much

* The Orlando taster was indeed delightful, although Kathleen hadn't yet seen it. She gives her response to it in a later letter.

hope that Jacqui, my wife, and I can come and take you out to lunch in late June or early August. Any preference?!

I think you are right when you say that all the time and effort and money at the disposal of Penguin/Frederick Warne is being lavished on the Beatrix Potter film. And until that is completed, I fear they will not concentrate on ORLANDO. *Having said that, I know they are very pleased with the two minute introduction and want to stay with the same team. So hopefully Stuart Brooks and I will still be on board!*

As you may remember, the original plan was to do a series of shortish films, say 10 minutes each. I understand now that the most likely thing they will aim for is a 'special', lasting half an hour or so, which would become a 'pilot' for a series, should it prove popular enough. Funnily enough, this goes right back to our very first idea some years ago, when I did some work on ORLANDO AND THE THREE GRACES. *Indeed, I think this book might be a very good one to start the ball rolling, mainly because of its fantasy content and its suitability for a Christmas showing.*

My adaptation of Roald Dahl's THE BFG *returned to the Apollo Theatre, Oxford, last week. The production has, I'm glad to say, been very successful and will tour until July. The West End season went particularly well.*

My adaptation of THE WITCHES *will hopefully visit Oxford, although there is no date yet. It would come to the Apollo and I hope I might be able to accompany you, particularly if we can get the special 'hearing loop' working for you!*

The television series I wrote based on my play/book THE GINGERBREAD MAN, *still going out every Friday afternoon on* ITV *at 3.55pm, seems to be going down well. It is frustrating, however, trying to get publishers interested in doing a series of books based on some of the television episode stories, many of which are new stories developed from the original. Maybe in time, if the programmes are popular enough, something will happen.*

Yes, Roald Dahl is a fascinating children's writer, whose popularity seems to know no bounds. THE BFG celebrated its 10th birthday only last week, yet is already, I believe, a classic. Children are quite devoted to it! THE WITCHES has been quite a challenge to adapt, and is going to require a lot of theatrical trickery, which I hope will be exciting.

It seems to me that Dahl's skill is to take traditional children's favourite areas in folk lore, myth and legend – such as giants, witches, a good queen to save the day, very basic good versus evil struggles, magic, dreams, rags to riches, etc., etc. – and very cleverly couch them in contemporary terms. Structurally his stories are classical, but the treatment of his themes is modern. I think this is why they affect children so deeply. Quite apart from that, of course, he's a very good storyteller! There is no doubt that the reader wants to know what happens next and keeps on turning the page! Interestingly, too, many of his books feature a central relationship between two contrasting characters. In THE BFG, the two extremes are represented by two misfits – a vegetarian giant living in a world of flesh-eating giants, and a maltreated orphan. The core of the story is really an asexual love story. In THE WITCHES, the central relationship is between a grandmother in her 80s and a little boy. Again, it is almost a love story, in that their relationship survives all the extraordinary things that happen to them.

When we see you, I will fill you in on Cape Town! The idea is that I will direct THE BFG at the Baxter Theatre, Cape Town, next year. Quite apart from the extraordinary political situation over there, I found the most tiring part of the trip was trying to wear so many hats. You were looked at not simply as a theatre director or even an adaptor of the book, rather as an educationalist, a social worker, a guru and (most important of all) a diplomat. After three of four days, I realised that to satisfy everybody, I would have to cast the play with a mixture comprising a couple of English speaking white actors, a couple of Afrikaaner speaking white actors, a Black actor, a Coloured actor, a couple of actors who had been through the University of Cape Town Drama Department, similarly at least one from the University of Stellenbosch nearby, and also a member of the local children's theatre company! I also became aware of the huge problem in trying to play to multi-racial audiences, even though they are 'allowed' to come. They can't afford to pay the price of a ticket, let alone be bussed from the Townships. Not only that, the book itself is not translated into their first language, Xhosa, so it is difficult for teachers to read them the story before coming. Even then, one wonders if the Dahl story would have much relevance for them. Having said that, all the fairy tale elements I mentioned above would apply as much to their culture as ours, I suspect. So, all in all, an interesting and – as I said in my last letter – an eye-opening trip. I came home with a very guilty conscience, having seen the extreme differences between the haves and the have nots: but at the same time, you only have to look at the Los Angeles riots and even at the homeless in cardboard boxes near Waterloo Station, to realise that the whole world is a pretty unpleasant place, and that, as an individual, one can only do a little bit to help.

A very happy 94th birthday!

With love and best wishes,

David

14/5/92

(nb this date is wrong – it should be a date after 18.5.92.)

Dear David,

Thank you so very much for your letter, & for inviting me to lunch with you & Jacqui in late June or early August. I haven't made any dates so far ahead, so please state what will suit you! I so look forward to this!

I can't remember whether it was Sally Floyer of Penguin or Diana Syrat*

– but one of them told me that the Orlando (BBC are keen) film series, will be in 26 parts as "the Americans want this" – so I don't know how long each event will last –

They & I agreed at the beginning of this project to make a "mish-mash" of all the books into one sequence. I doubt if they really know what to do!

I suggested to them at the onset, that "Orlando & The Three Graces" would be a good Xmas choice, but I don't think "The 3 Graces" could be stretched over 26 chapters, do you?

I have insisted that Stuart Brooks do the animation and that Michael Gabriel does the background drawings. But none of them or you can wait for ever – or start work at the drop of a hat. Anyway I doubt if I shall still be around (at 94–95) to help Brooks with the main drawings. The story is for you entirely! That is beyond me though I'd like just to read it through when absolutely finished. Otherwise it's in your province, & thereby hangs the tail.

The two-minute introduction (animated) I was shown was excellent, tho' one bad mistake – Grace's hat was dead straight making her severe & ridiculous.

About "The Witches" at the Apollo – I was taken to the Festival Theatre to see George (the ?th) by Alan Bennett – & used the special "hearing loop" for the deaf – Hardly any use to me, alas; I could only guess what was happening having read the synopsis printed in the programme.

* Diana Syrat, working for Frederick Warne/Penguin, was the editor of Kathleen's autobiography, *A Slender Reputation*, which was in preparation at this time.

I think almost the most attraction of Roald Dahl's stories is that he is so deliciously subversive about Parents, general "naughtiness".

Love from Kathleen.

15/6/92

Dear David,

Firstly, thank you for your little celebratory "Doggrel" on my birthday!

I'm afraid both Forest Hill pubs are going down the drain – all Brewers are trying to sell off their country & unlucrative inns, & ours are now only staffed by temporary tenants who don't care about cooking. At one we get "Whiskers" warmed up, & at the other – "Pal". (tepid)

There's a good & lovely pub at Beckley but they won't book tables. They are well known for their quisine, but become full of local gentry who go for their morning drinks, & they just stay on & on, occupying the tables. This happens even on Mondays. But I'll see what to do. The best & only hope of getting a table is to be there at 12.15 midday. Can you manage to get here by 12.00??

Otherwise there's a French restaurant in Headington, but I must find out if they close on Mondays as they do in France.

Please don't bother about the "hearing loop" at <u>any</u> theatre – they all say theirs works perfectly.

Looking forward to seeing you both,
with love from
Kathleen

17th June 1992

Dear Kathleen,

Many thanks for your letter of 15th June.

We were delighted to hear that you can come out to lunch with us on June 29th.

We will aim to arrive between 11.45am and 12.00 noon, so

that we can get straight off to Beckley, where I'm sure we will be able to bag a table. That sounds a splendid choice.

We are very much looking forward to seeing you.

With love and best wishes,

David

June 30th '92

Dear David & Jacqui,

I forgot to thank you (as all well-brought-up children are taught to do) for taking me out; for the lunch; the special bottle of sherry (muddle-headed as I am prone to be – I failed to realize until now, that it is indeed special, & far above my usual tipple!). Above all for the pleasure & relief from anxieties that your company provided. I really did so much enjoy everything.

I do love Jacqui's saga about the Tortoise! I wish I had one to "cowdle in my bosom" (from "Cold Comfort Farm").

And now I must sink into my Treacle Well, emerging stickily, in time to work with Diana Syrat.

Love to you both,

Kathleen.

8th July 1992

Dear Kathleen,

Many thanks for your lovely letter of June 30th.

We did enjoy seeing you last week, and thank you so much for choosing that excellent location for lunch.

Do hope your latest meeting with Diana Syrat went well. And that you can see some light at the end of your autobiographical tunnel.

Since we saw you, I have been trying to get some bits and pieces out of the way before we go on holiday to Cornwall – to

Jacqui's parents, as usual. They have a house in a remarkable location on Gillan Creek. When the tide comes in, the house is surrounded by water on three sides. I've always found it a good place to write, and every summer for fifteen years or so I have come back with something to show for it – a play or a book. This year it looks as though it will have to be a dramatic saga of the colourless RUPERT BEAR! In fact, if he's on the stage, maybe we can inject some colour into him! In honesty, some of the Alfred Bestall Rupert stories – he wrote them for years and years – are rather well thought out and have a genuinely magical quality. But Rupert's friends, character-wise, blend into one, and it is quite difficult to make them into stage characters. However...

I'm also trying to cast THE WITCHES (Roald Dahl), which is proving tricky! That one starts rehearsal in September.

We will hope to see you before too long – maybe we should repeat the luncheon in Beckley before summer is out!

With lots of love and best wishes from us both,

Yours,

David

Another five months passed, with no progress. Kathleen, however, was busy, occupied with writing and checking through the manuscript of her autobiography.

Undated

Dear David,

Thank you very much for your letter – you certainly know how to live as well as work!! I am envious.

I am DESPERATELY trying to finish my book by the new dead deadline for September.

I have to live away from all social happenings till then – which is not a cheering existence! I miss my friends.

Diana Syrat comes every Tuesday to go through the MS – finally – & she helps me a lot – 'cos I'm getting a bit feeble.

Good luck with your Witches and love to you both.

Kathleen.

18/11/92

Dear David,

It seems a generation ago since I saw you both! How time flies – driving all before it.

Michael Gabriel who is working on the B. Potter film, says that Jill Stuart **(she means Jill Brooks)** et al have their studio walls plastered with drawings for our "Orlando" film – & that it will go ahead once Penguin are quit of B. Potter (who should be on television this Xmas).

But have you any news of our project? It was rumoured that there are to be 26 sequences, as "the Americans always do their children's films in 26-es."

But perhaps you have more concrete news? I think a short, perhaps genuine Argentino tango would be the perfect theme-song for O. It would certainly be "catchy" for both adults as well as children.

I've also gathered a rumour that Penguin have now to find the money for the film – do you know anything about that obstacle? Michael Gabriel is very qualified to do any Orlando drawings for Jill, as he can copy my style most perfectly!*

I do hope you are both well – "alert & free from pain" as used to be the advertisement on some medicine bottle or other.

Will you be coming this way any time? I am beleaguered in this isolated village full of ancient widows & no shops!

Best wishes,

Love,

Kathleen

*Should I be twanging a harp in Heaven – not unlikely at 94+

The plan now seemed to have changed somewhat. A half-hour 'special' was envisaged, to be followed up by a series of twenty-six ten-minute episodes.

23rd November 1992

Dear Kathleen,

It was lovely to hear from you. Indeed it does seem a long time ago since we saw you. We would love to come down to take you out to lunch again, if you would like that. How about Tuesday, 15th December?

I will try to answer some of your questions, although I'm in much the same boat as you!

I understand that the idea, once they have got all the Beatrix Potter filming over, and once it has established itself as, hopefully, a success, they will concentrate on Orlando.

The intention I think is to first of all produce a half hour 'special', which could well be ORLANDO AND THE THREE GRACES. This was the one, if you remember, which I originally did a bit of work on, and came to read to you. You were very complimentary at the time!

Then, I think the idea of the 26 x 10 minute long films would be considered and hopefully embarked upon. You are quite right that they like to do things in batches of 13 or 26, mainly because it is easier to sell abroad.

As I understand, the 26 programmes would be individual stories in the life of Orlando. Most of them would be adaptations of your books, obviously. But there is also the possibility that I might come up with some new storylines for Orlando, as faithful as possible to your originals. These would make up the 26.

However, I don't think anybody intends to run before they can walk! The main thing would be to get the first film done, and indeed that is what I'm hoping will happen. But nobody has contacted me since I last saw you.

I will let you know anything I hear as soon as I hear it.

We are all well, I'm glad to say. Jacqui sends her very best wishes to you. Katherine (16) and Rebecca (13) are busy at school. I have just recently opened my new adaptation of Roald Dahl's book THE WITCHES. It is on tour and will be coming into the Duke of York's Theatre in the West End for Christmas. It seems to be going well.

An illustrator, with whom I work regularly, and I have just had two little novelty books accepted by a publisher – they are called BABY BEAR'S BUGGY RIDE. I remember being pushed around in what was called a pushchair as a child. Now they all have 'buggies'. I rather like the word and thought it might make a nice little book. Fingers crossed!

Let me know if that date in December might suit.

All good wishes, as ever,

Love from us all,

David

Undated reply to DW letter of 23.11.92.

Dear David,

Thank you so much for your letter. It would be real good to see you on Tuesday 15th December.

I understand Orlando's "3 Graces" is to be re-issued by Penguin this spring – (I have my spies who are in contact with the animators…)

Will your adaptation of "Witches" become a television programme? R. Dahl is to my mind – one of the best writers for children in his original field of "Subversity" and Sendac (k?) the illustrator of the same ilk. I wish Orlando was in the same genre.

It cheers me to know that you belong to the "Buggy Club"! I always thank my friends who take me out for an airing in their cars "Ta for the Buggy Ride". (Let me know please when Baby Bear's Buggy Ride is published.)

I do so look forward to seeing you both – I will book a table at the "Star" or the Abingdon Arms if you like.

With best wishes, and love from

Kathleen

30th November 1992

Dear Kathleen,

Thank you for your letter.

We look forward very much to seeing you on Tuesday, 15th December. Last time we took you out to lunch, we went to The Abingdon Arms which was excellent. But if you would rather book a table at The Star, we would be very happy with either.

My adaptation of THE WITCHES is not destined to become a television programme as far as I know! It opens tomorrow night at the Duke of York's Theatre (the theatre where PETER PAN had its first performance in 1904!).

All good wishes, as ever,

With love from Jacqui and myself,

Yours,

David

Yet again, progress was slow. Another six months went by, with no apparent developments, until another Kathleen birthday was celebrated.

30/5/93

Dear David and Family,

It is wonderful to receive the perfect Bouquet of flowers on my birthday – they are/it is delighting me now & are obviously going to continue to do so for some time – the colours chosen, exactly conform to those I grow in my garden – like the famous Lady-gardener (contemporary) Beth Chatterway – her & my colour-scheme is palest lemon-yellow daisy-like flowers – creamy pink ones, pure white & with a touch here & there of muted rose & near-orange. Wonderfully soothing & easy on the eye.

The reason I haven't written before to thank you all for the touch of joy – is because I had two whopping falls, one which landed me in the casualty hospital ward where I was kept over night, & the other has been making it difficult to use my "write" hand (but it's getting better).

I was about to write to you just before my accidents, to tell you that Diana Syrat told me suddenly, that things are beginning to hum re. Orlando film, & that it will materialise for sure, though not in my life time, she thinks! Maybe you've heard something also… I'm about to re-iterate in a letter to Sally Floyer, stating that unless you (& Jill the Animator) & Michael Gabriel are to work on the film, it mustn't be done at all, unless substitutes are found who can carry on your work, & precisely. I think I should write this as though it is my legal Will, 'cos as Michael says, changes may have to be made in the future but if only because one or all of you are contracted to other commitments.

With love,
Kathleen.

04/06/93

Dear Kathleen,
Many thanks for your letter of 30th. We are pleased that the flower arrangement arrived and you approved of it!

Very sorry to hear that you have suffered two falls. Do hope you are feeling stronger.

Thank you for your interesting news about the ORLANDO animation film via Diana Syrat. I haven't heard anything from them for some time, but will drop them a line, I think!

I've been very busy on various projects, including a trip

to Japan about a musical play they want me to adapt. All about an elephant! In the end, I didn't go to South Africa to direct, for various reasons, but the play went ahead and was a success, apparently.

Meanwhile, RUPERT AND THE GREEN DRAGON, my latest play, all about Rupert Bear (who is 20 years younger than you, by the way!), is still touring the country. Business is not very good, I'm afraid. It's coming to Oxford in a couple of weeks' time.

Love and best wishes,

David

Penguin/Frederick Warne still insisted that Orlando was a live project, but details were vague, and another seven months went by with no real news. Kathleen was now ninety-six years old, still actively engaged with the Orlando project, but, perhaps understandably, beginning to lose faith that any programmes would be produced in her lifetime.

20th January 1994

Dear Kathleen,

We were delighted to receive your Christmas card, and hope that 1994 will prove an exciting one!

I'm sure it will, because I met Sally Floyer yesterday and she told me that the autobiography is finished! Congratulations! I hear it is due to come out in May, and much look forward to it.

I hope you don't miss Diana's weekly visits too much! And I hope you were happy with the results of all that hard labour.

Sally told me that there are still positive plans for the ORLANDO series, although it might not be for a little while…

I have been fairly busy with theatre work. Before Christmas I adapted and directed a version of one of the works of your *friend, the Pied Blighter…* I was asked to adapt NODDY for the stage and resisted for a while, but then read the very first book, which actually had some rather nice Pinocchio-like things in it, and agreed to go ahead.*

The show has been on tour for some time and was at the Lyric, Hammersmith, for Christmas. It has been very well received and will be touring through till August.

Then I had to revive my adaptation of Roald Dahl's THE BFG, which opened in the West End at the Albery Theatre. It has just finished its run and now goes on tour, again till August.

Just before Christmas, I revived THE WITCHES, my other Roald Dahl adaptation, this time at the Olympia Theatre, Dublin.

My colleague, Richard Fowler, and I, have just finished a rather splendid pop-up theatre for Kingfisher Books. It is a toy theatre which is inside the covers of a book. With it you can do a play version of CINDERELLA. To be published in October.

Jacqui and our daughters are all well and send you every good wish.

Last time we tried to entice you to lunch at the pub, you were not feeling well enough. How do you feel about a visit in the near future?

With love and best wishes,

Yours,

David

The happy news that Kathleen's autobiography was now completed, and was being prepared for publication, was tempered somewhat by the ominous news, received first by Kathleen, that the animation company Stuart Brooks had ceased operations.

---

* I was ironically referring to Enid Blyton, whose writing for children Kathleen famously disliked. She always called her 'the Pied Blighter'. I never knew whether she had coined the name, but felt this was very likely!

23/1/94

Dear David,

I do so enjoy your letters; and how very perceptive of you to sense that I might be missing Diana's visits now that the "Slender Reputation" is finished. Factually, Penguin-Warne let her come quite often, "to keep in touch" as she says, & I say "just for fun" (i.e. coffee, & pink gin & laughs).

Before I forget – can you give me the October date of the publishing of the Toy Theatre (Kingfisher books)? I have a great-grand son who will be the right age for it.

When you say you "revived" the "Witches" what does this entail? Makes me think of Red Cross war-time classes.

I saw a brief – I think trailer – of the Pied Blighter's "Noddy" which I thought seemed free of the "Twee-ness" & insensitive "morality" & was quite invigorated.

Sally's "positive plans" for the Orlando film I'm afraid are Pie in the sky – in need of money-bags to weigh them down to earth. And Jill Stuart, et al, went bankrupt,* but I hear they are still at work. Somewhere.

I would like to know if Roald Dahl's "BFG" & other books for children are published, & which titles – for my g-g son. I'm doubtful about the P. Blighter, 'cos if the new version is good, then my sons (both retired!) will never forgive me for banning the Noddy books to enter the portals of their Noisery. They denounced me, when they were about 10 & 13, for not having them christened – "Do you realise Ma, that we shall never be allowed to have White Weddings?" And indeed they both chose registry offices thank heavens.

Thank you for your invitation for lunch – I'd love to accept. Providing you realise that I am now really old – & have to walk with a stick & someone's arm, & am back-bent as well. I feel SO ashamed…

---

* Kathleen means Stuart Brooks, the animation company.

With love to you & your family, & the best of best wishes,
Kathleen

26th January 1994

Dear Kathleen,

Thank you for your lovely letter of 23rd. Jacqui and I were pleased to hear your news. And we're much looking forward to reading your 'Slender Reputation' (what a modest title!).

From your description of Diana's visits (coffee, pink gin and laughs), she will be missing them as much as you!

Now, to answer some of your questions – the Kingfisher pop-up theatre – am not sure of the actual date of publishing, except that they have told me October. However, I will probably have some copies before then and can let you have one!

I'm delighted with the work Kingfisher have done on it so far – Richard Fowler, with whom I collaborate, has designed a splendidly engineered toy theatre, which literally pops up before your eyes as you open the covers! And there's no glueing, cutting out or assembly necessary. In many ways this is rather sad, because I think part of the fun of these things is 'making-it-yourself' – but in these days of instant gratification, children, it seems, don't have time or inclination to do the work before getting the fun! Having said that, I personally would rather the children ended up doing performances of the play, using the theatre, rather than got halfway through building it before giving up!

I love the thought of you 'reviving' as part of your Red Cross war-time classes! I'm afraid my 'reviving' wasn't quite so practical… What I meant was that the production of THE WITCHES, based on the Roald Dahl book, which I had adapted and directed last year, was re-produced (revived!) in Dublin for Christmas, which meant starting again with an Irish cast, which was an enjoyable experience.

NODDY – yes, the television series (which I had nothing to do with, I hasten to say) has been very successful and, to a certain extent, has taken a lot of the tweeness out of the stories.

I must say I enjoyed working on NODDY, and managed to carve a good story out, I think. I'm sending you a programme to look at. Hope memories of the Pied Blighter don't come rushing back with such a vengeance that you have to have too many pink gins to recover!

THE BFG play is coming to the Oxford Apollo – February 15th – 19th. Every day at 2.00pm and 7.00pm. If you like, Jacqui and I could come down and take you to see a performance (though I know your hearing gives you problems in the theatre!). Certainly, during that week of February 14th, we are free to come down and take you out to lunch, which we would love to do. So maybe you would like to let me know which day would be best for you, and also if you fancy going to the theatre or simply going to lunch (or both!).

Sorry to hear that Stuart Brooks have gone bankrupt – I didn't realise… Nobody had let me know that. But, as you say, I'm sure they are still working in some sort of freelance capacity, and hopefully will be available as and when Sally pulls her proverbial finger out…

You ask about the Roald Dahl books. Am wondering how old your great-grandson is, but certainly THE BFG, THE WITCHES and all his other books are published by Puffin and very readily available. I suppose the ideal age for reading them is 7 or 8 upwards.

I'm sending you a copy of my adaptation of THE BFG – I don't think I have shown you this before.

We much enjoyed reading of how you banned the Noddy books in your household! I don't think your sons suffered too much from this act of principle!

Have just come back from Blackpool, having seen THE BFG into the Grand Theatre. It is a wonderful theatre, designed by the greatest theatre architect of them all, Frank Matcham. It celebrates its hundredth birthday this year. The sea was wonderfully rough along the prom, but there were no illuminations and hardly anybody around! I rather like seaside resorts out of season.

Have recently been entertaining a lot of Japanese theatre folk. Two of my plays have been successful in Japan, and I think I told you I went to Tokyo last year to discuss adapting a Japanese musical for British audiences. Now, whenever members of the Japanese theatre community come over here, they seem to have been given my phone number! Jacqui has even got a special meal which she always prepares for them, and they seem to like! They are all delightful, I must admit, but it is very tiring trying to converse and communicate. Not that our Japanese extends beyond one word (the word for 'thank you'!), and some of them speak English remarkably well; but trying to discuss something, while making sure everybody understands what everybody else means, is virtually impossible!

All for now – let me know what you feel about our proposed visit during the week of February 14th.

With love and best wishes,

Yours,

David

6/2/94

Dear David,

Thank you very much for your good, newsy letter, with so many "Interestingies" –

Also for your so inviting invitation. I would love to have lunch with you & Jacqui on the 15th Feb… 19th whichever date suits you; & to go to the BFG matinée. What a treat for me. Or have I left it too long before replying to your letter? I seem to tread along overgrown lanes, trying to make dates with my older friends who can no longer drive their cars –

this means O.Fs has to contact & fix a date with one of O.F's friends who have cars. I send out tentacles to try & grub up submerged "friend of friend & Car" before the meeting actually materialises.

No, I can't take Noddy – nor can I forgive the smugly vulgar pictures – or vulgarly smug.

Thank you for telling me where to get Roald Dahl's books. I can give my g.g. son sets of them, for his 7th birthday. Thank you also for your adaptation of the BFG – it's wonderful! I love it.

I sympathise with Jacqui cooking for the Japanese visitors – I had to try & adapt my cooking to Douglas's* Thais, Chinese – as well as Europeans – but I gave up & decided they'd be critical of my rice et al, & made them do with IRISH STEW or some such British food.

I wonder if your Kingfisher Theatre is like the "Castles" – & other subjects that are done nowadays – & Snow scenes & oh, other themes? I wish some publisher would "revive" my nice "Puss in Boots" Peep Show book. (Chatto & Windus, long ago.)

You know one of my reasons for being so dilatory in answering your letters is because they make me garrulous in my replies – & it takes time!

With love to you both,

Kathleen.

*Bacteriological overseas visitors to D's Labs, & spent the nights with us at home. A Danish Scientist slowly turned blue & finally passed out – he was allergic to pepper & should have warned me.

8.2.94

Dear Kathleen,

Many thanks for your letter!

Now – FRIDAY 18th would be good for Jacqui & me – we

could go to the 10.30 AM perf. of THE BFG and then to the RANDOLPH for lunch. We would aim to arrive between 9.30 and 9.45 and take you to the theatre!

Are these arrangements all right? If not, we will rethink!!

Love & best wishes

David

Kathleen's autobiography, *A Slender Reputation*, was published. Kathleen signed a bookplate for me to stick in my copy of the book. However, the signed bookplate remains with her archived letters, because a few weeks later Kathleen sent me a personally signed copy of the actual book.

21/2/94

Dear David,

Herewith another Book-plate properly signed, so you could destroy the stupid one I gave you –

When you wanted to know what I felt about the BFG, I made a dreadful mistake, for instead of saying (as I did) "I couldn't hear a word!" I ought to have prefaced this with "in spite of not being able to hear" & then launching forth into the eulogy I was about to try & adequately express; which was how enchanting & enthralling it was, with incredible ingenuity re. the props; the brilliantly thought-out scenery designs; the ever constant magical surprises & sustained drama. And of course the dedicated cast – being in fact, the characters they represented – each one providing a polished performance even when they moved out of the lime-light. I tried to watch them even when they had left their scene (the maid who dropped the Queen's breakfast tray – moved away out of sight, & still kept her personality – ending up in a charming pose, at the foot of the stairs). There are so very many heavenly surprises like the huge face of the BFG at the window, (I gasped!) and when he did his "walking" part, I felt I was walking also – just as one taps one's foot to a catchy tune.

I think that the audience – mothers as well as their children must have felt like I did – identified with each actor.

The whole wonderful creation, of course, created by you, & written by you for the BFG.

It was delicious to hear the mothers chuckling naughtily at the Belches etc! They Really – Really enjoyed them.

Brilliant & enchanting.

You are an important "Achiever" in your brief life & should never forget what you are doing for, & influencing, children, for their valuable development.

Though I shan't see my Orlando film in my life, you must do it, with Michael Gabriel (he works for Penguin Warne) as artistic adviser & background painter to the films – he can uncannily copy my drawing to the life.

Thank you for a delicious lunch. I'm now a devotee of many-flavoured Crème Broulet (spelling?).

With love to you both, & to the Big Giant & all the cast,

Kathleen (Hale)

And now Orlando reared his head yet again! In spite of the demise of Stuart Brooks Ltd., Sally Floyer still seemed to want to go ahead, still using Jill Brooks. Once again, Kathleen excitedly reiterated her creative suggestions.

22/2/94

P.S.

Dear David,

Please will you cross out (re Michael Gabriel) "artistic advisor". He was this to my book – selecting the best of my paintings for illustrations – but he mustn't have anything to do with your choice of scene designers – costumes etc. etc. etc. His only job is to draw Orlando cats where needed as links between the movements, of the animation – & to draw the backgrounds & he must consult you on everything he does. You are the Director & creator.

Michael has worked with Jill (animator) & others – (all of the best) – & this would be an advantage. He worked on B. grounds for Pink Floyd's "The Wall" for 18 months in Paris. Also for "The Snow Man" & now for the Penguin B. Potter "Peter Rabbit" series.

If you'd like to meet, we could fix a meeting here when convenient.

I have quite a lot of drawings I did for Jill, which relate to the beginning of the film, which I can show you…

With love from

Kathleen.

24th February 1994

Dear Kathleen,

First of all, it was lovely to see you last week. Jacqui and I were delighted that you enjoyed THE BFG and the many-flavoured crème brûlée!

I know the cast of the play were delighted to see you, and I will pass on my best wishes from you to them!

Thank you for all your splendid comments about THE BFG. These are much appreciated.

As far as ORLANDO is concerned, I understand all you say. And I agree with you that Michael Gabriel and Jill Brooks are the best people to be in charge of the visual side.

I would certainly like to meet Michael Gabriel at some point, because I have never met him. Maybe we should all go to that nice place for lunch (not your local pub, but the one a couple of miles away).

I would certainly be able to make a meeting some time after Easter. In the meantime, I am, once again, directing my play THE GINGERBREAD MAN, which will open at Unicorn Theatre on March 31st.

Meanwhile, don't worry too much about the film series. I fancy nothing can happen until Sally Floyer decides to spend a bit of time away from Peter Rabbit! Last time I saw her she said she hoped it wouldn't be too long before we could start things going again. I'm very sorry, for all of us, and particularly for you, that it has taken so long. But I promise that I will be as involved as possible in adapting your stories, as and when it becomes possible. I will do my best to be faithful to your intentions.

All good wishes, as ever, and thank you again for your lovely letters.

With love,
David

5/3/94

Dear David,
Thank you so much for your letter & that you'd like to meet Michael Gabriel.

I've had to delay this letter until I could see Diana (& a Publicity Lady) yesterday, to hear their plans for the publicity drive with the media (re my autobog). I shall have to be prepared to give interviews at the drop of my hat, & for a few weeks my life won't be my own. But I'm going to limit them.

BUT I'll contact Michael & we'll choose a date for you both to come at "Cocktail" time one morning (sounds like Noel Coward) but I <u>must</u> flop onto my bed by about 1.30, for I get rather tired. The BFG & the Randolph kept my adrenalin working on till the afternoon…

With love, & looking forward to seeing you & Jacqui again,
Kathleen.

23rd May 1994

Dear Kathleen,

Birthday greetings!

And my delighted thanks for the copy of A SLENDER REPUTATION, which arrived a couple of days ago. Your generous inscription is much appreciated!

I so enjoyed the book I could hardly put it down. I had to go to Bristol to see a performance of THE BFG (the one you saw in Oxford), but was late for curtain up, because I had started another chapter in the hotel room!

It really is a smashing read. What is so delightful is that your wit and delightfully idiosyncratic sense of humour (!) shines through on every page. And, of course, the period of your first 'heyday', as it were – those years after the First World War, make such riveting reading – all these wonderful artists, to my generation, famous people who left a great legacy – you knew them all! You were there!

I was delighted they had included such a wide and delightful selection of your paintings and drawings.

And all the background information to Orlando, some of which you had already told me, was fascinating to read about.

It's such an honest book, and so friendly to read! And as a document of historical interest, I'm sure it will be widely admired.

Jacqui and I were delighted to see the splendid review in The Observer over the weekend, and hope there will be many more!

When all the excitement of publication has simmered down somewhat, we would love to see you again, and have another nice lunch!

Meanwhile, enjoy your special day and all the attention I hope you are deservedly receiving at this time of renewed recognition and acclamation.

We are delighted for you, and congratulate you on a wonderful book. All those pink gins with Diana were worth it!

With love, admiration and all good wishes,
Yours,
David

June 3rd 1994

Dear Jacqui & David,
Your splendid Bouquet awaited my return last week from Bristol – (spending my beastly birthday very happily with my son et al.). The former was sitting patiently & well cared for by the rain. It is weathering its solitary awaiting – miraculously, & was such a joy for me. I ought to have written to thank you before, but I fell ankle-deep into correspondence requiring immediate replies to several demands etc. connected with Slender Rep & an interview for Kaleidoscope last Wednesday.

I really only want to sit quietly snoozing in my Ingle Nook, wearing a mob cap, & with a warm old cat on my lap & clay pipe. I've got an Ingle Nook, & a lap, but no cat. Or cap. Or clay pipe.

Your wonderful letter is a true reward for all my labours & work on & because of that darned Cat Orlando.

I do thank you very much.
With love from
Kathleen

The lack of activity on the Orlando animation front almost went unnoticed over the next five months, during which Kathleen was receiving considerable attention following the publication of her autobiography. She had fan mail to answer, and was interviewed on BBC Radio 4's *Desert Island Discs*. I visited her, took her out to lunch, and showed her a proof copy of *Pop-Up Theatre: Cinderella*, a toy theatre I had co-created with Richard Fowler, which was soon to be published.

2/9/94

Dear David,

Thank you for taking me out to lunch & for my favourite "Elegante" dry sherry. In fact, I had my last bottle & was about to ask Peregrine to bring me some this week. How perspicacious of you to know just what I like!

When you opened up the miraculous toy theatre on the pub table, I felt suddenly afraid for its safety & how vulnerable it is to spilt coffee or rough treatment or accidents.

But I really would love to possess one, over which I could exert supervision.

I think knowing my Great Grandson, that fairy stories won't appeal to him – he's v. macho & loves Dinosaurs & motors, Rockets, Submarines et al. Even "Nature" doesn't interest him. He is intelligent & adventurous & full of curiosity in inventions & such like.

I think you could write an action-packed play, of Dinosaurs & their weapons & means of attack & defence Versus – machinery et al & huge wars between them! Bat Man & a Giant could be adversaries!

I could write one but I'm too old, too busy & I don't want to make the effort.

The theatre could be advertised as ONLY FOR BOYS! – what a "wow", & would get the girls on their mettle!

Forgive, & thank you!

Kathleen.

September 8th, 1994

Dear Kathleen,

Thoroughly enjoyed our lunch. Thank you for your thank-you letter!

I'm glad I got the right sort of sherry. I'm not a great sherry drinker, but it has always struck me how many different kinds and tastes there are. I wonder if they still have sherry parties at the Oxford colleges. I remember it was fashionable in the sixties!

Thank you for your kind comments about the POP-UP THEATRE: CINDERELLA. You will definitely be sent one when copies become available. Then you can examine it at your leisure!

The Sunday Times has a Theatre Club, which people can join and have special events at various theatres. They have taken a fancy to the toy theatre and are presenting a kind of performance (with me demonstrating, children helping) at the Theatre Museum in Covent Garden on October 15. During the week before (Children's Book Week) I will be touring round demonstrating it in various cities. I'm delighted with the reaction to it so far.

I think you are absolutely right about aiming another toy theatre more firmly towards macho boys! I think it is very true that boys can be put off the theatre by what they think of as a soppy story. Having said that, CINDERELLA does seem to work for everyone. But an epic adventure with dinosaurs would undoubtedly whet the appetite of little males more than, perhaps, a fairytale. Although, I think it would appeal to lots of girls too!

This whole thing of what appeals to girls and boys is very interesting. Somebody rang me the other day who is doing some sort of thesis on why it is that so few children's cartoon/puppet animation series feature a female as the main character. POSTMAN PAT, PADDINGTON BEAR, NODDY, SPOT THE DOG, even my GINGERBREAD MAN and your ORLANDO are all male.

The theory is that both boys and girls are very happy to watch male characters. But female characters only appeal to girls. In other words, girls like, or certainly don't object to, male characters, but boys object to female characters…

I wonder why that should be. Are girls more passive and therefore happy to accept things as they come? It is certainly true that when a play toured based on the book THE WORST WITCH, which is set in a girls' school (an academy for young witches actually), audiences were severely affected by the lack of boys who wanted to go.

If Kingfisher, who publish the POP-UP THEATRE, want another one, I will certainly bear your thoughts in mind. I would hate to be excluding masses of boys from an interest in theatre-going!

Jacqui sends her love. She starts teaching embroidery to adults again next week. Katherine, our eldest, sets off for Homerton College, Cambridge, on September 19 and Rebecca, who is fifteen, has just started back at school doing eleven GCSE subjects! She's even doing Greek, which is something I never did!

Love and best wishes, and hoping you're keeping well.

Yours,

David

10/10/94

Dear David,

"Cinderella" is ENCHANTING – & now that I can see & enjoy it in the safe surroundings (unlike the pub premises) of my sitting room, I really appreciate the ingenuity and surprises popping up in odd places – like the clock.

It's so well-thought out in details, & truly designed for real children. (The inclusion of the little story book, among the envelope of actors & actresses.)

You really think deeply about the children themselves – that you create for them.

What gratifying news of Katherine! Such encouragement on the threshold of her adult life, & augurs well for her future.

Again thanking you so very much,

Love to you & Jacqui,

From

Kathleen.

October 12, 1994

Dear Kathleen,

Thank you for your lovely letter. Delighted you enjoyed playing with the POP-UP THEATRE!

Last week I went to Halifax to a wonderful children's 'hands-on' museum called EUREKA! Am enclosing a leaflet for your interest. I went up to do a presentation of the POP-UP THEATRE to prizewinners in a Sunday Times competition. It seemed to go very well. I do it again at The Theatre Museum in Covent Garden on Saturday.

We had a meeting the other week to discuss doing a follow-up, and I mentioned your thoughts about a second one being a bit more 'macho' to appeal particularly to the boys. Everybody thought that was excellent thinking! Various ideas are being pushed about at the moment.

I was glad to hear that the POP-UP THEATRE had been selected as one of two hundred books in the 'BOOKS FOR GIVING' catalogue which is distributed free from masses of bookshops. It is a promotion by the Booksellers Association. Apparently it's quite a prestigious thing to be selected! Not many children's books get in.

I'm coming to Oxford to do my show – The David Wood Magic & Music Show – on the 27, 28, 29 October. Will give you a ring beforehand, to try to fix up a time to meet or a time for you to come to the show, if you would like to.

Meanwhile, love and best wishes from us all,

Yours,

David

30/10/94

Dear David,

It was good to see you bearing gifts! The dear little Rose sits prettily in what was a blank space in my sitting-room, & is an instant focus for my visitors.

I do wish I could have gone to see your show – it really would have done me good & dispersed the "In-looking" condition of my caged existence!

But I truly can't go anywhere now, 'cos of increasing arthritis pain & tendency to fall. My sons come & stuff me into their cars, unstuff me on arriving at their homes – & do the reverse. Only they. I shall never forget your enchanting & ingenious "BFG" at the Apollo. The pleasure & stimulation of all you do in theatre & film etc is enduring.

I, alas, am too immobile to enjoy your & Jacqui's invitations to lunches. You speak very clearly, but amongst other people's talk, their voices & noises-off bombard my hearing.

My life is increasingly interesting – socially – but I have to retreat into my "retirement", to avoid being dumb in public & a bore.

I have every intention, once I've cleared my decks of answering fan-mail, both personal & "public" – to begin to draw again. I've ascertained that I haven't lost my touch – & it will be a blissful occupation.

With love,
From
Kathleen.

By now our correspondence related more to general matters than to the Orlando situation. On October 30th, Kathleen's *Desert Island Discs* was broadcast, and was remarkable for its humour and honesty.

October 31, 1994

Dear Kathleen,

It was lovely to see you on Friday, even though it was rather a short visit! Thank you for the tea and biscuits. I hope you enjoyed the Hobnobs I brought you. I find the trouble is that if I have one I have to have another one and so on. Very more-ish.

It was interesting to hear you talk about the Desert Islands Discs experience. Having heard the programme on Sunday, I can assure you that you came over very well. It is true you could have said much more, but I don't think much more could have been broadcast in the time available! And what you said was always entertaining and interesting.

I was also fascinated to see how well they had constructed the programme. By that I mean that whatever memories you were sharing always led neatly into your next choice of music. For example, you seemed to be talking very naturally about ORLANDO'S MAGIC CARPET and straightaway we heard the fascinating song from Beirut.

I thought the balance of the conversation was just about right, starting off with your childhood, University, coming to London, the Epstein/John days, your family life leading to the birth of Orlando, plus many fascinating details about publishing difficulties and subsequent successes.

All in all a very enjoyable programme! Congratulations!

*Your choice of music made a good change from the rather heavy classical choices many people make. Your selection actually reflected the times through which you have lived. I loved the Gertrude Lawrence song, which I hadn't heard before. Scott Joplin is a favourite of mine and I enjoyed the zither music and the rumba, and the Spanish piece was quite extraordinary!**

You obviously like slightly unusual sounds. I heard an advertisement on the radio the other day for a record made on the pan pipes. It sounded lovely, but I wondered whether hearing it on twenty six different recordings all lumped together might not be a little too much!

---

* Kathleen's music choices were 'Experiment' by Cole Porter (sung by Gertrude Lawrence), 'Rumba Azul' by the Lecuona Cuban Boys, 'Maple Leaf Rag' by Scott Joplin, 'La Sardana De Les Monges' by La Principal De Perelada, 'The Café Mozart Waltz' by Anton Karas, 'Khitay!' by Chiraz, 'Annie's Song' played by James Galway and Fugue in C Major by JS Bach played by Glenn Gould.

All for now. Hope to see you soon.
All good wishes from Jacqui and myself.
Take care,
With love,
David

Five months went by with no Orlando news to share.

31/03/95

Dear Kathleen,

Jacqui and I hope you are well, and hope very much to see you soon.

The POP-UP THEATRE: CINDERELLA you were kind enough to admire has sold quite well. But the publisher does not want another one yet, I'm afraid!

Am doing various things, although the children's theatre side has dried up a little in recent months!

Last month I went to Minneapolis for three days to observe a splendid children's theatre there. It was a very good trip, but extremely cold! What they call the 'windchill factor' was -35°!

The other day I travelled on the new Eurostar train to Paris for the day, which was fun! The train didn't stop once between Waterloo and Paris! Going through the Channel Tunnel was rather like – well, going through any tunnel, to be honest! But when the train gets up to speed – 186 miles per hour we were proudly told by the 'train manager', it is pretty impressive!

We both send our love and very best wishes.
David

17/4/95

Dear David,

I'm very remiss in answering your letter of March 31st but I'm being badgered beyond belief – by fan mail – requests for my autographs: photos: & the Lord knows what else – very many long & interesting correspondence that must be answered. People wishing to visit me, & bring their children also… this is not possible. Am too old, & increasingly incapacitated – wheel-chair &/or walking frame.

I really believe publishers are daft – WHAT an opportunity to design & produce a melodramatic Dinosaur theatre – it's exactly the climate for it, right now. Publishers have charming manners but sometimes awfully cold feet.

With love to you both,
Kathleen

June 14, 1995

Dear Kathleen,
I'm enclosing a copy of my new book, which I hope you may enjoy playing with – as long as you can get the wretched cellophane stuff off. They decided it had to be shrink-wrapped, because of the 'moving part'. The book seems to have been well received. Last week, Richard, my collaborator, and I went to a couple of bookshops to demonstrate it to classes of schoolchildren. They all responded splendidly.

I have managed to finish the first draft of another NODDY play. I hope you will forgive me for contributing to the Pied Blighter's Estate again! The play goes into rehearsal in September, before going on a long tour.

Did I tell you about the ice-ballet for which I have contributed the story line? The Russian All Stars, a troupe of twenty six ex-Olympic skaters are to perform it in theatres up and down the country, and possibly abroad. It was a new and interesting experience, writing something without words, if you see what I mean! But it was quite fun conceiving something on a larger scale than my usual plays for children. There are well over 150 costumes in this one!

All for now. Our love and best wishes to you,
Yours,
David

Jacqui and I were invited to a preview of an exhibition of Kathleen's artwork at the Gekoski Gallery, arranged in association with Frederick Warne. It took place on November 27th, and was a very happy occasion, at which we met up with Diana Syrat, Sally Floyer and Jill Brooks, as well as Gina Pollinger, the children's book agent. We also met, for the first time, Kathleen's son Nicholas. He was accompanied by his wife Andy, whom we remembered from eating several times at the restaurant she co-ran. Kathleen, by now ninety-seven years old, was in a wheelchair, as was her great friend the poet and author Naomi Mitchison. It was a delight to see them chatting away like two excited schoolgirls. A few days later, in the *Independent* newspaper, Madeleine Marsh wrote an excellent article about Kathleen's exhibition, which included the following:

'Most of the paintings and illustrations on display have never been seen by the public before. At the age of 97, the artist has decided to sell the entire contents of her studio.

"At my age," she says unsentimentally, "I have to think of what I'm leaving to my sons for them to cope with. There are far too many paintings for them to house. I might have to leave my home and go into care, and there would be no room for all these paintings there." '

November 28, 1995

Dear Kathleen,
Jacqui and I were thrilled to be invited to your exhibition preview, and we were delighted to see you so clearly enjoying the event! The exhibition has been beautifully laid out and the framing is excellent. And I have never seen so many little red dots at an exhibition preview before! Many congratulations!

It was a great pleasure meeting up with Nicholas for the first time, and Andy (Andie?), whom we hadn't seen for many years – since she ran the splendid SPOT THREE restaurant. It was good to see Diana again, as well as Sally Floyer, Jill Brooks and Gina Pollinger.

All in all, a wonderful evening. And how appropriate that it should take place in Bloomsbury, your former stomping-ground! I wonder if the driver gave you a quick guided tour down Fitzroy Street!

Yours, with admiration and affection,
David

The saga continued. Five months later, the Orlando animation was still in development, and Kathleen was still showing concern about the technical details of the process. By now, quite frankly, I was sceptical about the possibility of anything actually happening. But, perhaps like Sally Floyer and others, I tried to keep the project alive for Kathleen's sake.

April 30, 1996

Dear Kathleen,

Thank you so much for such excellent tea and company yesterday afternoon. It was lovely to see you and chat about 'things'!

It is always fun to share depressing stories about royalties and to laugh about the Americans!

I am making notes of your concerns re. colour reproduction. I will make every effort to ensure that colour guides come from the best examples of the original editions of the books, rather than from the recently re-printed versions. I hope there will be a meeting soon at which Sally and the film company will discuss their thoughts. I will always keep you informed of the latest developments.

Thank you so much for signing my two Orlando books. And thank you for your nice comments about THE MAGIC SHOW and BEDTIME STORY. Am enclosing copies of these for you as requested (and already paid for!).

I have taken the liberty of signing the books, in the rather pompous hope that your great grandchildren will be pleased!

Thanks again for a lovely afternoon. It was a real treat.

Jacqui joins me in sending you lots of love, and all good wishes,

Yours,

David

Encs.

On Kathleen's 98th birthday, Jacqui and I, as usual, sent her flowers. I had posted Kathleen a copy of the novelty book *The Magic Show*, which I co-created with Richard Fowler and had been published a few months earlier. I had already given her a copy of *Bedtime Story*, another Wood/Fowler novelty book that was later republished as *Mole's Bedtime Story*.

3/6/96

Dear David & Jacqui,

Thank you so very much for the charming Bouquet in its elegant basket, and for your kind wishes on my (regrettably) 98th burst-day – giving me a new lease of life by the pleasure it has given me.

My Great Grandson aged 8, is completely enthralled with "The Magic Show". He manipulates it again & again, with great care – treasuring it, & with enduring interest.

The younger G-G-Son aged about 2–3 is not allowed to touch or handle "The Magic Show", & it has to be kept out of his sight & reach. But his (He loves watching it being unfolded) "Bedtime Story", he is allowed to play with – & now he knows every detail & procedure by heart – he insists on reading it (telling) to his parents & brothers, using it delicately & with great care.

Both these books are of endless interest to the boys…

I do wish the paper-card (?) pages could be infused with some permanency – giving, strengthening – substance. They should be strong & long-living enough to keep, & hand down to the next generation – so good are they. Could a species of varnish be sprayed on them? – colourless like that which is used on oil-paintings.

Immortality should be yours!

With love from Kathleen

The animation company now working with Frederick Warne was Clive Juster's King Rollo Films, originally set up by David McKee to produce the animation series based on his books featuring King Rollo and Mr Benn. Things looked promising again.

June 10, 1996

Dear Kathleen,

Many thanks indeed for your lovely letter of June 3. We are pleased you liked your birthday bouquet, and hope very much you had an enjoyable 98th celebration!

I'm delighted that THE MAGIC SHOW and BEDTIME STORY seem to have gone down so well with the great grandsons. With this type of 'interactive' book, it is always a pleasure to watch children 'using' it, becoming more dextrous the more times they turn the pages. In these days of learning by computers, it is reassuring to see children actually enjoying books. Hopefully reading will not become a dying pleasure!

I agree with you that in these technologically advanced days it ought to be possible to develop an extremely tough, child-proof, paper. I think there are a number of processes that can effect this, but they are expensive, and might make it impossible for the various paper engineering feats to be accomplished!

I'm hoping to have a meeting with the ORLANDO animated film people very soon. They said it would be before the summer really starts and people go away on holiday. I will obviously let you know what happens.

Meanwhile, the same animated film company, King Rollo Films, is making a video of bedtime stories, including my own BEDTIME STORY. I'm pleased to say that Richard Fowler, who did the book illustrations, is delighted with the way they are translating his work to the animated screen. Some new artwork for the backgrounds arrived the other day and he couldn't tell he hadn't done them himself! This hopefully bodes well.

The other day I went to a memorial service for Kaye Webb, who did so much for Puffin books. Presumably you knew her, although she must have started after Puffin had published some of the ORLANDO books. The event took place at St. Martin's in the Fields, and a number of notables said their bit about her. Christopher Fry (did you ever know him? He is only ten years your junior!) spoke of 'Kaye's chuckles', and Michael (PADDINGTON BEAR) Bond recalled her energy and how she would outrageously use people! Once he was to pick her up in his car to go to lunch. She asked if he could come a little early as she had an errand to make. He asked what time. She replied 8.30a.m.! He ended up driving her sixty miles, then waiting in the car for an hour and a half before returning to London for the lunch!

Robin Bailey, the actor, read from Plato's Republic – the passage which says how children's minds are like blotting paper (he didn't actually use that analogy!) – a lovely thing about how whatever goes into a child's young mind is likely to remain there indelibly forever. And this means that those of us who write for them have a tremendous responsibility that what goes in and will never come out is of quality. It made me think there is no new thought under the sun!

Kaye was an extraordinary woman, married for a time to Ronald Searle. When she retired from Puffin she took on a part time job with Curtis Brown as a children's authors' agent. She asked me to let her represent me, which I willingly did. Her first job for me was to negotiate the deal on the book version of THE GINGERBREAD MAN, which Pavilion Books wanted to publish. The book was the very one which she, on behalf of Puffin, had turned down a few years before, when Viking (the Puffin hardback imprint) had suggested it for publication! I don't know whether she ever realized she was negotiating for a book she hadn't liked very much! She never said, even if she did!

I have finished (I hope) casting my next production, which is a revival of my adaptation of Roald Dahl's THE WITCHES. It goes into rehearsal in September. So I'm looking forward to that. Next excitement, however, is the family holiday. We are going to Turkey, to a place by the sea called Kusadasi, which is near the famous ruins of Ephesus. Rebecca, our sixteen year old, is very keen on the classics, so she will enjoy it I know – as I'm sure we all will. She is mid-way through her GCSE exams! Katherine, the one at Cambridge, comes home in a couple of weeks' time, which will be nice.

Jacqui joins me in wishing you all the very best. We hope to see you soon

With love and best wishes,
Yours,
David

After another year, there appeared to be no development. Kathleen and I had now been friends – and the Orlando animation had been blowing hot and cold – for ten years. In May 1997, Kathleen, aged ninety-nine, moved into a care home in Bristol. She had no wish to leave her cottage, but her health made it impossible to live there alone. I paid her a visit in July. She greeted me with her usual bright-eyed enthusiasm, but it was clear that the routine of her new life, in a semi-basement room overlooking the car park, was limiting, to say the least. She really disliked it. She was by now unable to hold a pen strongly enough to write letters, but I believed she still enjoyed receiving correspondence, so continued to send her my news. Following my visit, I jotted down some notes…

Kathleen – visit 10th July '97 – <u>Stoke Leigh</u> notes by DW

- *other residents – the bursting plum (large, round lady with slobbery bottom lip)*

- *'I'm 90', says one resident, proudly –*
- *'I'm 99', says K (unable to resist) – & isn't talked to for the rest of the meal –*
- *cabbage the colour of army uniform –*
- *religious lady – always praying for an 'easy end'*
- *music at parties – a painter who played the guitar & his wife who danced gypsy dances.*
- *Ford Madox Ford biog – by <u>JUDD</u> (she has it in proof form) – she knew Ford.*
- *Supper early – 5.45 – K didn't want it, because I (her visitor) was giving her food of the <u>brain</u> –*
- *taken to lunch with Nicholas, Andrew – + guest – she felt she had nothing to contribute to conversation. Determined to keep mind alive, but difficult – easy to just sleep –*
- *looking for someone to talk to – woman who had her own pictures with her – but found out to be photo of her father (so he is the first person I see every day) and a photo of Buckingham Palace.*

Five months after my visit to the care home, I wrote to Kathleen, and felt obliged to tell her that I had no news about our Orlando project.

16th December 97

Dear Kathleen,

The time seems to have flown by since I spent that happy afternoon with you, seeing your semi-subterranean room and enjoying the light, airy spaces of the conservatory.

Apologies for not writing sooner. I can only plead pressure of work, which seems to have increased as the year has gone on…

I do hope you are well and have made some more friends, and that you will be spending a happy Christmas with members of your family.

I have just returned from Newcastle where I was supervising a revival of my adaptation/production of Roald Dahl's THE BFG. This is the one you saw at the Apollo Theatre, Oxford, a few years ago. I'm glad to say that the production is still in good shape. There is a brand new cast, of course, but they all fitted in splendidly. A member of the original cast directed the actors on my behalf, but I had to keep an eye on it! It seems to have opened well.

Just before then, I directed my brand new adaptation of a book called THE SHEEP-PIG, by Dick King-Smith. This is a delightful book about a pig who wants to become a sheepdog! It was made into a successful film a year or two ago. The film was called BABE. I decided to call the stage play BABE, THE SHEEP-PIG in order to attract fans of both the book and the film. We managed to get some money from the Arts Council and from Barclays Bank to put on a long tour of the play. It is currently in Manchester for a Christmas season. I'm glad to say it went well, although there were a few teething troubles!

No more children's books out this year. The main thing for me over the last few months has been the publication of my book about children's theatre, a copy of which I enclose. You don't have to wade all the way through it! But I thought you might like to see it. It has had one or two very nice reviews, and I'm told there is no other book in existence quite like it, which will hopefully mean it will sell a few copies!

I'm afraid there has been no news re the Orlando film or series. I have several times tried to speak to Sally, but have never got through. I'm very sorry about this, because I feel I have let you down somewhat. I really thought that Penguin were going to cough up the money and that we would have got going a year or two ago. Alas, no. If I hear any more news, I will be in touch.

Meanwhile, I'm hoping to come to Bristol in the New Year, in which case I hope I will be able to visit you, if you would like that.

Lots of love and every good wish for Christmas and 1998, which will be a momentous year in your remarkable life!

Yours, as ever,

David

Another four months passed by. My next letter omitted any reference to the Orlando animation.

20th April, 1998

Dear Kathleen,

You must forgive me for not having been in touch for some time. I can only plead busyness, in that things have really been busy, busy – so I mustn't complain! Jacqui and I hope very much that you are well and happy at Stokeleigh. We both very much hope it will be possible to visit you again, if you would like that. And, of course, we are very aware of the approaching celebrations on 24th May, and will be thinking of you then with all our respect and admiration.

The other day I was looking at the bookshops in Cecil Court, off Charing Cross Road. There are several now who specialise in first edition children's books. In fact I have bought two of your first editions there! One of them you kindly signed for me a couple of years ago.

On this visit, I found a delightful ORLANDO novelty book, a clever pop-up book depicting several rural scenes with Orlando and family at work and play. I very much wanted to buy it – until I saw the price! It was, I think, £350!! You must forgive me, but I decided I didn't have enough money, not on that day anyway! But I was delighted that the worth of your work is so rightly recognised.

You may remember I sent you my book, published by Faber, called THEATRE FOR CHILDREN. I am glad to say that this has been selling quite well, even though it is obviously a limited market. And my recent adaptation of Dick King-Smith's book THE SHEEP-PIG has been successfully touring the country since last October. I don't know whether you have come across Dick King-Smith's work. He writes splendid stories, mainly about animals. He is never condescending or twee. Amazingly, he didn't start writing until he was 56 years old. He is now 77 and lives not far from you, in Keynsham. His book THE SHEEP-PIG is a delightful read about a pig who is brought up with puppy sheep-dogs, and ends up winning The Grand Challenge Sheep-Dog Trials! It was turned into a hugely successful film called BABE. My stage version continues touring until the beginning of June. It has been great fun to do, particularly staging the sheep-dog trials! We use seven local girls of about 13 years to play the sheep! And also we find three local boys of about 8 years to play puppies. They join up with our professional cast of 10 actors, and the result has been very pleasing. I'm enclosing a programme, which I hope you will enjoy looking at, particularly the photos of the costumes which are really splendid.

The actor playing the Farmer is the same actor who played the BFG, when you came to see it with me at the Apollo Theatre, Oxford.

I have been working on a children's opera! Not the music, which is being left to a very clever composer. But I have written the first draft of the libretto of THE FOREST CHILD, based on a book by Richard Edwards. It is about a child raised by animals in the forest (shades of Kipling!). She is caught by a hunter and brought back to civilisation to be educated. Naturally this doesn't work out at all, and in the end, she is rescued by the animals who take her back to the forest. The idea is that the opera will be performed by three professional singers and three professional musicians, working alongside lots of children, who will be singing, acting and playing musical instruments. Welsh National Opera will produce the opera in several schools later this year. I think it could be rather exciting. Hope so!

I have also just finished giving some performances of my MAGIC AND MUSIC SHOW at the Lyric Theatre,

Hammersmith, which has been exhausting but fun! I enjoy occasional performing, because I feel it keeps me in touch with children. Similarly, I enjoy going into schools and talking to children, plus doing storytellings.

With love and all good wishes,

Yours,

David

During the next seven-month period, Kathleen had her 100th birthday. I hoped very much that she might be happy to receive a visit from Jacqui and me. Knowing I wouldn't receive a written reply, I contacted the care home and a meeting was set up.

17th November, 1998

Dear Kathleen,

My apologies for not writing to you since your birthday – the big one! – in May. It is no real excuse to say I have been busy (although I have!), but I was hoping that Jacqui and I would be able to visit you, and, until now, this has proved impossible.

However, we are now going to be staying in Bath from Friday evening through to Sunday lunchtime, November 27th – 29th. We are hoping that we could come and see you on Saturday 28th or Sunday 29th. We could come for coffee or tea, or we could take you out for coffee, lunch or tea!

Things have indeed been quite busy. My adaptation of Dick King-Smith's THE SHEEP PIG, entitled for the theatre BABE, THE SHEEP-PIG, toured with considerable success up until June of this year. Then it was announced that the Dallas Children's Theater in Texas wanted to mount the American première. I managed to get an invitation to go, mainly paid for by fees from schools in Dallas where I went and talked or told stories (as I do in this country). So I had a lovely week – in temperatures of over 90° most of the time! Everybody was very kind and enthusiastic and hopefully they will do another one of my plays soon!

Earlier in the year I had been to Chicago, where the Chicago Children's Theatre were presenting the American première of my adaptation of THE BFG, by Roald Dahl. This was the play you came to see in Oxford! The Chicago production was enjoyable, although they resolutely refused to venture into the darker areas of the story! It was as though the whole performance was above sea level! The murkier waters were not explored at all, which was rather a shame, because that is where much of the strength of the story lies! However, everyone was very kind and I was invited to talk to some students at Northwestern University. The amazing thing was that they had a professor there, whose official title was Professor of Children's Theatre and Storytelling! I wish we had something like that over here! I'm glad to say that they seemed to like what I said and did and have invited me back next year as a Visiting Professor, to work with the students for a short time. I'm looking forward to it.

Well, I will finish now, in the hope that we can see you in a couple of weeks' time. I will ring you soon, or you ring me if you would rather!

With love and best wishes, as ever.

Yours,

David

8 December, 1998

Dear Kathleen,

Jacqui and I were delighted to be able to visit you on Sunday. Thank you for spending so much time with us. I hope we didn't exhaust you! You were great fun, as ever, and we enjoyed our conversation.

We managed to find a copy of the new Raymond Briggs book for you, and hope you enjoy it. It has had very good reviews, although we haven't yet read it.*

* The book was *Ethel & Ernest.*

I am still trying to find out for you when Michael's successor to THE SNOWMAN is coming up on television, and also what the title is! When I find out, I will let you know.

I have just received a catalogue from Marchpane, a specialist children's second-hand bookshop. They are advertising a first edition of ORLANDO AND THE WATER CATS for £40! It was good to see how prized your work is. I'm sure nothing I have written will be around in 50 years' time!

Jacqui and I send you lots of love and all good wishes. We will hope to see you again before too long. Meanwhile, thanks again for your warm welcome on Sunday.

Yours,

David

14 January, 1999

Dear Kathleen,

I do hope you are keeping well and warm!

Things seem to be quite busy here. I have just adapted Roald Dahl's THE TWITS for a production at the Belgrade Theatre, Coventry, opening in March. THE TWITS is a rather unpleasant story about two nasty people, a husband and wife, who take great pleasure in playing nasty tricks on one another! They eventually get their come-uppance from a flock of birds, a family of monkeys and an exotic Roly-Poly bird from Africa! I won't go into detail as to how Dahl weaves these threads together, but suffice it to say that the book is incredibly popular. Hopefully the play will work well.

I have also been beavering away on two volumes of Collected Editions of my plays, which Methuen will be publishing later in the year. I was flattered to be asked to join their distinguished list of playwrights. All my plays are published, in acting editions, by Samuel French, but having them in Collected Editions will give them a new market, hopefully. Having said that, it always surprises me to find that people actually buy plays to read!

On January 25th I have to give a lecture to the Magic Circle, all about children's magic. I have been a member for some time, but have never been asked to talk about my magical ideas before. Fingers crossed for that one.

Later this year I have been invited to Northwestern University, Chicago, to run a course in children's theatre. That could be very exciting.

I have to come to Bristol on Friday March 12th. In the afternoon I will be attending a performance by Welsh National Opera of a short children's opera I wrote for them called THE FOREST CHILD. They visit primary schools with three professional singers and three professional musicians, work with the children for a week or so, and then put on a performance for parents and other children. Hopefully I will be able to visit you in the morning for coffee. But I will get in touch nearer the date to check that you would like me to come.

All good wishes, as ever.

Lots of love

David

Encs.

Before my proposed March 12th visit, Kathleen had a fall and was taken to hospital, where she stayed for a while.

16 February, 1999

Dear Kathleen,

There is a beautiful blue sky today, although it is still quite cold – but spring is certainly on the way. Jacqui and I hope you are well and that some bright sunshine is creeping into your semi-subterranean room.

I am still hoping to be in Bristol on Friday, March 12th. I could pop in for a cup of coffee at 11.00am, if that would be convenient?

Richard Fowler and I have been working on some more children's books. Another pop-through-the-slot book has just been bought by Transworld. Called SCARY MARY, it features a family of hippopotamuses (or is it hippopotami?!) with a daughter who enjoys going round scaring everybody!

We are also working on THE TOY CUPBOARD for Pavilion Books. This was an idea we had several years ago. The book is designed like a cupboard, with several spreads featuring shelves on which sit various toys, many of which are interactive, with pop-up parts, wheels that turn, a miniature book that is removable and readable, a magic trick, a musical box that plays, etc. etc. In all there are nineteen features. I think it will end up being rather expensive, so I hope the publishers don't have cold feet at the last moment!

The most immediate excitement is that we have been invited to take my production of THE GINGERBREAD MAN to Dubai for a week – Easter week. This involves shipping out the set and costumes weeks before we even start rehearsals! I have never been to that part of the world before, so hopefully it will be interesting and enjoyable.

We all send you our very best wishes, as ever, and I hope very much to see you on March 12th.

With love,

David

30 March, 1999

Dear Kathleen,

I was very sorry to hear that you had had a fall and had broken a bone – I'm not sure which one it was. I hope you are comfortably on the mend. I popped in to Stoke Leigh when I was in Bristol, but you were still in hospital. I hope you got the flowers and the silly pencil!

The performance of my children's opera, THE FOREST

CHILD, went well in the Bristol primary school. What the children's voices lacked in tunefulness they more than made up for in enthusiasm!

I am now busily directing rehearsals of my play THE GINGERBREAD MAN, which we take to Dubai for eight performances over Easter. This will be a bit of an adventure! Apparently we are the first children's play to travel to Dubai. Most families who live out there, apparently, speak English, so hopefully we won't have any language barrier.

I recently finished adapting SWALLOWS AND AMAZONS for the radio. Many years ago I did the screen play for the film, so it was quite interesting to revisit it. The book is apparently still incredibly popular. I never met Arthur Ransome, I wonder if you did – but I did get to know his widow, Evgenia. She, as you may remember, was Trotsky's secretary, whom he met while reporting the beginnings of the Russian Revolution. They eloped in a boat and lived sort of happily ever after! She was a tough lady, though I certainly admired her. She worked hard to preserve her husband's reputation after his death, even though it was clear that she didn't respect his talent very much! In his autobiography, which she refused to allow to be published until after her death, he often said how rude she was about his latest effort, over which he had sweated blood!

All good wishes, as ever, from Jacqui and myself. We hope very much that you are feeling better.

Yours,

David

I still feel guilty that nine months passed before I wrote again to Kathleen. Sadly, this turned out to be my last letter to her. But I suppose it was appropriate that my final paragraph should be about our unachieved hopes for an Orlando animation. Kathleen's wish 'to see Orlando move' was fulfilled, albeit only in a two-minute 'taster'. For me, Orlando is one of the 'ones that got away'. But what

a privilege and joy it was to get to know and spend time with this remarkable lady.

07 December, 1999

Dear Kathleen,

This is to wish you a very happy Christmas and millennium New Year!

I'm so sorry I haven't been in touch for some time. This is mainly because I have been abroad rather a lot. I spent some time teaching in Chicago at Northwestern University, doing a course in children's theatre. I have also been speaking at theatre Conferences in America, promoting my book about children's theatre. It has been a busy time.

Hopefully you are well and comfortable at Stoke Leigh. Jacqui and I hope very much to be able to visit you again before too long.

Over the past year I adapted SWALLOWS AND AMAZONS for Radio 4. I found it quite a challenge writing scenes for six children, trying to make sure it was clear who was talking! On radio, six children's voices all sound rather similar! To help the process, I introduced a narrator. In fact she was the character Titty, telling the story from today's perspective, as an elderly lady. To play the part we engaged Jean Anderson, one of my favourite ladies, having worked with her as an actor years ago. She is ninety-one years old now, not quite into three figures like you!

At the moment I am working on a play for pre-school children, based on the books about SPOT, the puppy. The books, by Eric Hill, are looked after by Sally Floyer, and the same team that look after Orlando. This play is due to open at the Oxford Playhouse in the spring.

You may have heard about the creation of a Children's Laureate, which was a nice way of promoting children's books and their importance. Quentin Blake, the illustrator, is the first Laureate, who has already attended many events and made some important speeches. Do you know his work? He illustrates the Roald Dahl books and also does his own stories. His illustrations are a very clever and what appears to be a free use of squiggles and hurried sketching. Rather like a quirky Ardizzone. However, I think Blake is very disciplined and the casual look is deceptive.

From time to time I ask the Penguin people about the animated Orlando series we tried to get off the ground some years ago. But I'm afraid I don't get a very positive response. Such a shame, because I really thought we would achieve a film or a series of films. Maybe we will one day!

Meanwhile, all good wishes as ever, from Jacqui and me.

Lots of love,

Yours

David

OBITUARY

Kathleen Hale died on January 26th, 2000, in Bristol, aged 101. I was proud to salute her in a eulogy at her funeral on February 4th, 2000. She was a remarkable woman, who became a dear friend; it was to my great regret that the Orlando film or series never happened.

DAVID WOOD'S SPEECH AT KATHLEEN HALE'S FUNERAL, 4TH FEBRUARY 2000

'Go down to Oxfordshire', said Laurence Harbottle. 'Kathleen Hale wants to see Orlando move. Maybe you can help.' This was in 1986. Kathleen was 88. I remembered Orlando from childhood, but knew nothing of her. I suppose I was expecting a granny in shawl and slippers in a picturesque cottage. I was right about the cottage... but Kathleen was wearing denim and dangly earrings, and was reading the autobiography of Bob Geldof... Later, rereading her books, I realised she wasn't an elderly version of motherly Grace, she was Tinkle alive, alert, witty, gleeful – with an undiminished rebellious streak. Like all classic children's books hers can be read on many levels, appealing to the child in all of us, at any age. In real life she displayed the same humour, observation, wordplay – she told me about 'Big Mick, the mowing postman', who did her lawn, and the rotund lady with drooping lip she secretly called 'the burst plum'. She complained about 'cabbage the colour of army uniform.'

Working on the proposed Orlando film script, I was somewhat daunted, wanting to create a faithful adaptation. My best moment came when she laughed at a line, looked up and said 'I like that – is that you or me? If it was you, I wish I'd thought of it!' In fact I think it was her not me, but from then on I think she trusted me.

Kathleen taught me about the importance of <u>quality</u> in children's writing – 'they have no <u>taste</u>', she said, 'they'll accept anything because they know no better – why should they? It's our responsibility to give them the very best we can.'

She rather disapproved when I adapted NODDY for the stage. Enid Blyton – or 'the PIED BLIGHTER' as she called her – once in public to her face I believe – was twee and sentimental – she preferred Roald Dahl – she wrote to me, 'he is so deliciously subversive about parents etc.' – I took her to see my adaptation of THE BFG at the Oxford Apollo, and afterwards she entranced the Company backstage, going up the line like a royal visitor.

On that day, Jacqui and I took her to lunch at the Randolph – she wrote, 'I'm now a devotee of many-coloured crème brulée.'

Once, when I visited her at Stoke Leigh – she was nearly 100 – her rebellious streak came delightfully to the fore – I had arrived later than intended. Suddenly Kathleen was summoned to supper – she refused to go.

'But, Mrs. McClean, it's the magician tonight!'

'I have my own <u>personal</u> magician.'

'But Mrs. McClean, you must <u>eat</u>.'

'My friend is giving me food of the <u>brain</u>!'

Her mind stayed ever young, and when – in her nineties – she wrote her autobiography (surely a record!) she did get tired – but she referred to it with humour. This is from one of her letters, all of which I treasure –

'I ought to have written to thank you before, but I fell ankle-deep into correspondence requiring immediate replies to several demands etc. connected with SLENDER REP and an interview for Kaleidoscope last Wednesday. I really only want to sit quietly snoozing in my Ingle Nook wearing a mob cap and with a warm old cat on my lap, and clay pipe. I've got the Ingle Nook and a lap, but no cat or cap or clay pipe…'

She did see Orlando move, alas only in a two minute animation trial – but she loved it. It was a privilege to know Kathleen. And Tinkle! Kathleen enjoyed the flowers and dry Elegante sherry I took her – but for Tinkle, the best present I <u>ever</u> took was – a pair of socks with giraffes on.

Above:
Kathleen
Hale painting
an *Orlando*
illustration, 1949
© Kurt Hutton /
Picture Post via
Getty Images

Left:
The front cover
of *Orlando The
Marmalade Cat : A
Camping Holiday*,
First Edition (1938)

Above: Kathleen Hale with Orlando in the late 1930s / early 1940s © Country Life

Below: Letter to DW from Kathleen Hale, 1987

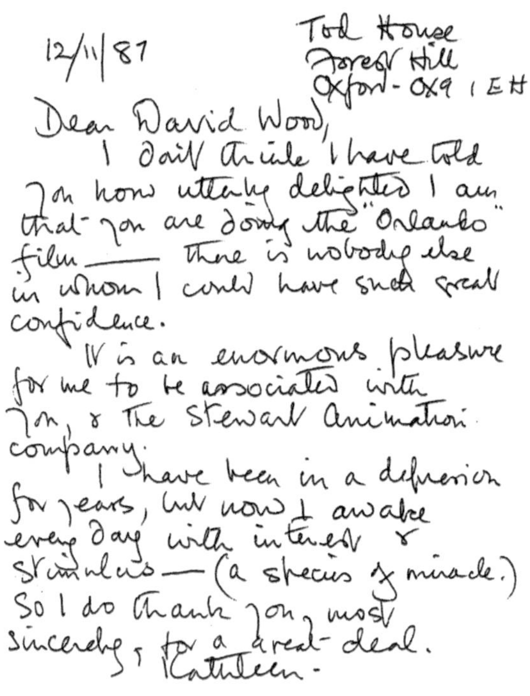

12/11/87

Tod House
Forest Hill
Oxford - OX9 1EH

Dear David Wood,

I don't think I have told you how utterly delighted I am that you are doing the "Orlando" film — there is nobody else in whom I could have such great confidence.

It is an enormous pleasure for me to be associated with you, & The Stewart Animation company.

I have been in a depression for years, but now I awake every day with interest & stimulus — (a species of miracle.)

So I do thank you, most sincerely, for a great deal.

Kathleen.

Kathleen Hale at home in Oxfordshire, 1988 © PA Images / Alamy Stock Photo

Synopsis

NARRATION	Comments and suggestions for visuals where they are not immediately apparent in the Narration.
Orlando, his wife Grace, and their three kittens, are buying Christmas presents at Mr. Cattermole's Magic Shop.	
Grace chooses a magnificent magic flying carpet.	
Orlando chooses a magic magnifying glass.	
Pansy buys a sailing ship in a glass bottle.	
Blanche finds a small glass globe with a castle, surrounded by a forest inside it. Shaking it makes a swirling snowstorm.	
Tinkle stays outside and makes snow-balls - real ones. 'Stop playing, Tinkle,' says Orlando. 'Time to go home.'	TINKLE THROWS A SNOWBALL, HITTING ORLANDO AS HE EMERGES FROM THE SHOP.
'Take care with your presents,' warns Mr. Cattermole. 'They're magic.'	CATTERMOLE WAVES GOODBYE AS THE CATS AND KITTENS SET OFF HOME.
On Christmas Eve, Orlando and Grace fill the kittens' stockings with presents.	
Next morning, before it is light, the kittens open their presents. 'Hey, look at this!' cries Tinkle. 'A magic set!'	
Because he's forgotten to buy any presents, Tinkle has to think of some. He gives Blanche and Pansy his pet spider called Ida.	HORRIFIED REACTION FROM BLANCHE AND PANSY

2

'What about Mum?' thinks Tinkle. In his magic set are two bottles. 'This looks like pongy perfume. Perfect!'	
'Merry Christmas, Mum,' says Tinkle.	
'Thank you, dear,' says Grace. 'I'll try some right now.'	GRACE SPRAYS 'PERFUME' ON HERSELF. MAGIC TRANSFORMATION INTO THREE GRACES.
(THREE VOICES SUPERIMPOSED, OVERLAPPING)	
'Lovely, Tinkle, thank you!'	TINKLE BLINKS, ASTONISHED BY THE SIGHT OF THREE GRACES.
(THREE VOICES) 'Merry Christmas. Thank you, all you kittens.'	ALL THREE KITTENS BLINK, REACTING TERRIFIED AND HIDE.
'Dad, Dad! Help!'	
'Quiet!' cries Orlando. 'I know it's Christmas, but ...' He sees Grace. He sees three Graces.	WIDE-EYED ORLANDO.
(THREE VOICES) 'Why are they frightened of me?'	GRACE ADVANCES ON ORLANDO - ALL THREE GRACES!
'Stay there, Grace, er Grace, and ... er you, Grace,' warns Orlando. 'Which Grace is the real Grace?' he asks himself. 'Which Grace is my wife?'	
(THREE VOICES OVERLAPPING) 'Merry Christmas, Orlando! Merry Christmas, Orlando! Merry Christmas, Orlando!' say the three Graces.	THE THREE GRACES ADVANCE TO HUG ORLANDO. HE RECOILS.
'Help!' cries Orlando.	
He decides to ask Santa Claws for help. That means a long journey, so the whole family, including all three Graces, climb on the new flying carpet. Orlando waves a carpet beater like a magic wand and chants a spell.	
'Magic carpet, through the sky Alicaz - I command you fly!'	

3

Two pages of DW's synopsis for *The Three Graces* animation film, 1987

Mike Stuart's storyboard for *Orlando's Grand Sale*, c1990
(pages 1-3) © Mike Stuart

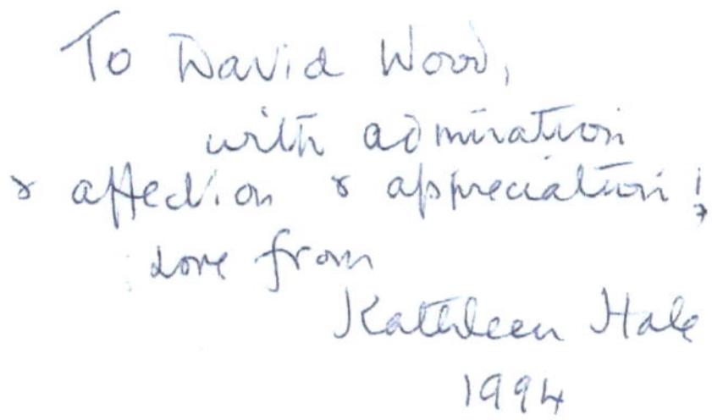

Book dedications to DW from Kathleen Hale – on the bookplate for *A Slender Reputation*, and on the inside of the book

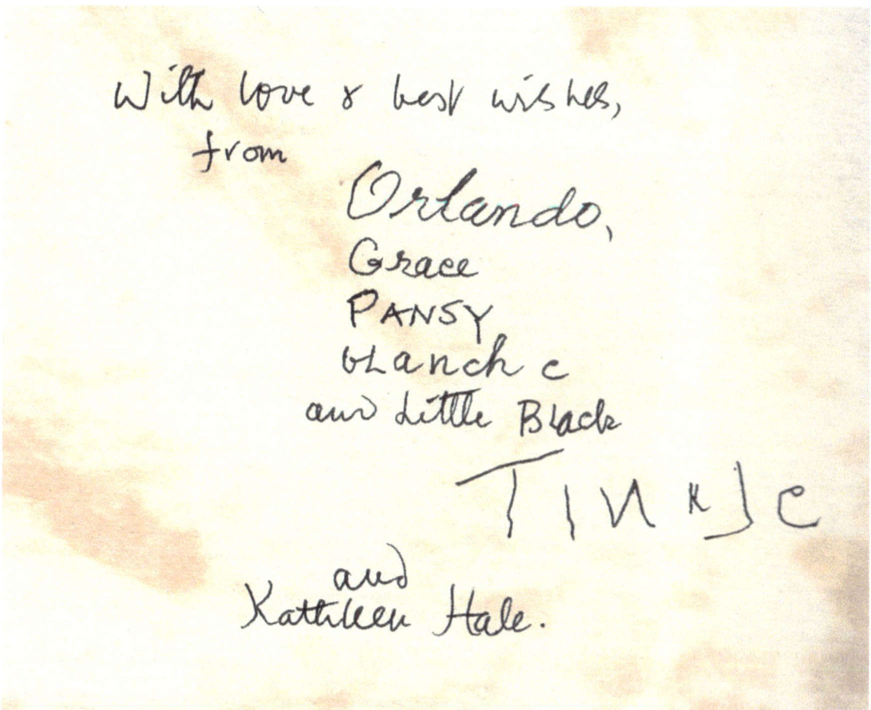

Book dedication to DW from Kathleen Hale, with the cats' signatures, including Tinkle

Afterword

Revisiting these correspondences has made me appreciate anew how fortunate I was to form genuine and lasting friendships with this trio of iconic children's writers. Collaborating with each one of these 'grandes dames' was a great privilege, giving me a rare insight into their individual working practices. I thank them all for their great generosity and for many special memories. And I hope that sharing these records of our working relationships will shed some light on the craft of adaptation from page to stage or screen, especially when the creator of the original material is still very much alive and involved in the process.

DW

Acknowledgements

My thanks to the families and Estates of my three brilliant collaborators; Judith Kerr's daughter and son, Tacy and Matthew Kneale, Philippa Pearce's daughter, Sally Christie, her husband Ben Norland, and his mother Helen Craig, and Kathleen Hale's granddaughter Nancy McClean have been both encouraging and helpful, allowing me to publish letters, emails and photographs.

Thank you, too, to Jane Devonald for carefully transcribing the original handwritten letters and typing up the manuscript, and to my daughter Katherine Wood, for her assiduous research, proof-reading and computer skills.

Last but by no means least, thanks to my friend and editor, Tamsin Collison, for wisely guiding me through the process of assembling the various ingredients for the book and for diligently checking, abridging where appropriate and suggesting a workable format. We visited my archive at the splendid Seven Stories in Newcastle to find missing links and check details, and were warmly welcomed and assisted by Michael Geary and his team. Thanks to them, too.

DW

Appendix

Philippa Pearce based the scene in *Tom's Midnight Garden* where Tom and his Uncle Alan discuss the nature of Time in this chapter from J.W. Dunne's *Nothing Dies* (1940).

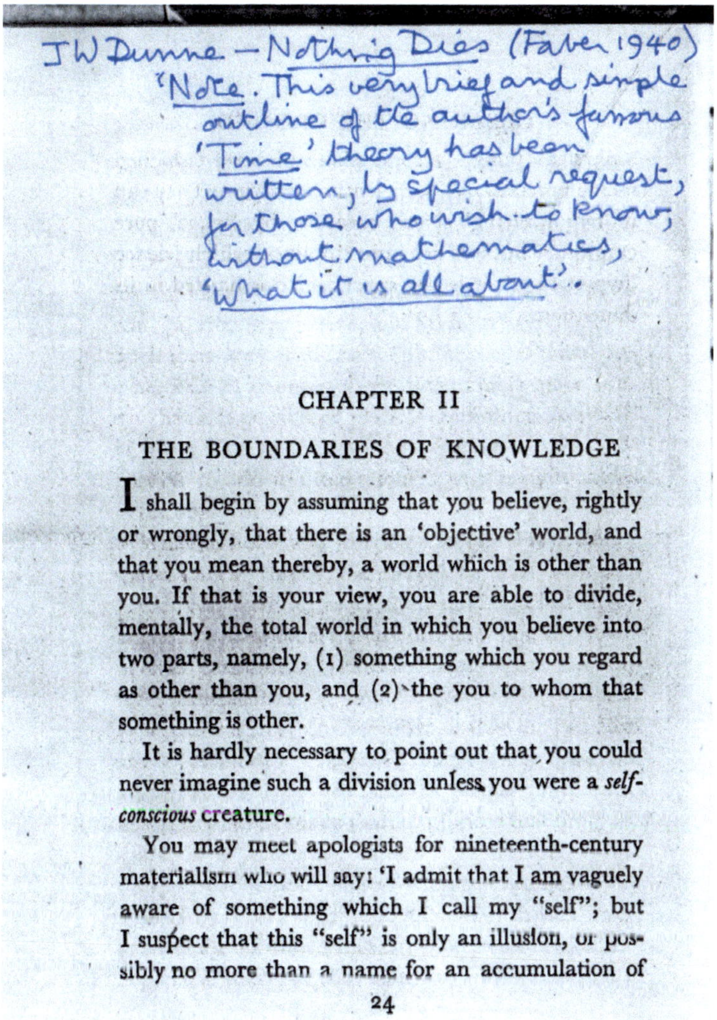

J W Dunne – Nothing Dies (Faber 1940)
'Note. This very brief and simple outline of the author's famous 'Time' theory has been written, by special request, for those who wish to know, without mathematics, 'what it is all about'.

CHAPTER II

THE BOUNDARIES OF KNOWLEDGE

I shall begin by assuming that you believe, rightly or wrongly, that there is an 'objective' world, and that you mean thereby, a world which is other than you. If that is your view, you are able to divide, mentally, the total world in which you believe into two parts, namely, (1) something which you regard as other than you, and (2) the you to whom that something is other.

It is hardly necessary to point out that you could never imagine such a division unless you were a *self-conscious* creature.

You may meet apologists for nineteenth-century materialism who will say: 'I admit that I am vaguely aware of something which I call my "self"; but I suspect that this "self" is only an illusion, or possibly no more than a name for an accumulation of

24

personal memories.' We shall see later that these apologists are wrong. Apparently, however, the great leaders of materialism were men of keener vision. Unlike their propagandist followers, they were scientifically chary of making vague claims which they might not be able to substantiate later; and they seemed quite prepared to find that self-consciousness was a fundamental fact outside their science.

Now, in this chapter we shall accept the universally admitted fact that each of us is aware of someting which he calls, 'himself': but we shall not trouble our heads as to what this supposed self may be or how a man can become aware of it. You may favour the uncritical guesses of the smaller materialistic fry, or you may incline towards the sterner attitude of the leaders—it will make no difference to the argument which follows in this chapter. What we are going to ascertain is merely: *what relation would you have to bear to a world which you* could divide into yourself and not-yourself?

You will have to begin by forming from observation some opinion of the world which you regard as other than yourself. You may, conveniently, symbolize this opinion by a picture supposed to be drawn by you. The nature of the picture will not affect the argument that follows in this chapter, and the sketch below will serve our purpose. I have labelled it A_1.

FIG. 1.

This gives you a starting point for your picture of yourself. For you, being self-conscious, know, of course, that you are the man who is capable of forming that particular opinion and of doing so from observation. The relation which a person with *those* limited characteristics bears to the world other than himself, which world he is portraying, can be represented symbolically by an artist, B_1, standing in a countryside, A_2, and making the A_1 picture thereof. This gives us Fig. 2.

FIG. 2.

Again it does not matter, for the purposes of the argument in this chapter, whether the picture of your B_1 'self' and of the A_2 countryside in which that 'self' is standing are or are not accurate. What matters is that you should realize that Fig. 2 symbolizes the relation which someone with *limited characteristics* bears to the world which is other than that *limited* him. The limited characteristics in question are those faculties and that amount of knowledge which were employed by you when you drew A_1 as representing your opinion of A_2 *only*. These you symbolized as the artist B_1. What you asserted thereby was: *I myself am something which is aware of a world.*

Now, in drawing Fig. 2 you are symbolizing, as we have noted, a limited self and a world other than that self. The question we have set ourselves to answer is: What relation would you have to bear to a world which you could divide into yourself and not-yourself? This does not mean, of course: What relation do you bear to any picture that you draw? (Obviously, you have just drawn that picture.) It means, in our symbol: What relation do you bear to the world, which, ultimately, you *portray* as consisting of yourself and not-yourself? Your next step, then, is to ask yourself: What relation do I bear to the world which I portray (in Fig. 2) as consisting of my B_1 self and its A_2 environment? That relation you can symbolize in Fig. 3.

It is to be noted here that C_1 symbolizes yourself as equipped with more knowledge than is granted to B_1. C_1 is aware of a self, B_1; but B_1 is not credited with any knowledge of B_1. C_1, moreover, knows that B_1 is *his* (limited) self. For he represents the you who knew that B_1 was *your* limited self when you drew Fig. 2. C_1 and A_3 constitute, therefore, a more adequate representation of the yourself and not-yourself into which you divide the total world you know—more adequate than do the un-self-conscious B_1 and the A_2 countryside. You say, in effect: *I myself*

FIG. 3.

am something which is aware of both a world and a limited self.

The question, therefore, of how you are related to the world which you divide into yourself and not-yourself has become the question of how you are related to the world which you *portray* as C_1 standing in A_3.

But, if you proceed to draw a further picture showing yourself as D_1 standing in a countryside A_4 and drawing Fig. 3, then D_1 and A_4 will become a much improved picture of the world which you are able to divide into yourself and not-yourself. For D_1 will be a picture of someone possessed of the knowledge which enables him to draw Fig. 3, which is the knowledge that you utilized when you drew Fig. 3: while C_1 will be a picture of someone possessed of only so much knowledge as will enable him to draw Fig. 2. Note that C_1's knowledge may be acquired by any method you choose to consider—by consultation with others, if you like. You, in drawing Fig. 3, have given evidence of a degree of mental clarity which is not possessed by the individual represented by C_1. But that higher degree of mental clarity depends upon the initial fact that you are self-conscious.

We have it, then, that D_1 will be aware of C_1 (as you were aware of C_1); and he knows that C_1 is self-conscious. But C_1 is not aware of C_1. He describes himself as B_1, an un-self-conscious creature. D_1 will be, therefore, a picture of what you recognize as yourself which is more adequate than was the picture C_1.

And so it must go on. For no description of yourself that you can contrive will describe a you possessed of the degree of knowledge which you, in effecting that description, give evidence that you possess.

We can translate that last paragraph into simpler language, thus: *The description of mind made by any science of yours must be, always, an inadequate description of the mind which can make that science.* Thus, no description of mind as something evolved mechanically from dead matter can be a true description of the facts. Whatever may be thought of the remainder of this book, that question seems to be settled at last. It would appear, then, that any biologist who ignores that solution and endeavours to continue to base his work upon a contrary hypothesis, will be simply wasting his own and, what matters more, his pupils' time.

Psychologists, moreover, might note this: *We have always more knowledge than we suspect ourselves of possessing.*